The London Custom House
Top left: the Elizabethan Custom House, built in 1559, and destroyed in the Great Fire of 1666
Bottom left: the Custom House built by Christopher Wren in 1668–71, and destroyed by fire in 1715
Top right: Thomas Ripley's Custom House, erected in 1718–21 and destroyed by fire in 1814
Bottom right: built by David Laing in 1814–17 and partly rebuilt by Sir Robert Smirke in 1825–26, this is substantially the present Custom House *HMSO*

Something to declare

Something to declare

1000 years of Customs and Excise

GRAHAM SMITH

Librarian and Archivist
H.M. Customs and Excise

Harrap London

To Val

First published in Great Britain 1980
by GEORGE G. HARRAP & CO. LTD
182 High Holborn, London WC1V 7AX

© *Graham Smith* 1980

ISBN 0 245 53472 5

Designed by Robert Wheeler

Filmset by Woolaston Parker Ltd, Leicester
Printed and bound in Great Britain by
Redwood Burn Ltd, Trowbridge and Esher

CONTENTS

Illustrations

Acknowledgments

I would like to thank Her Majesty's Commissioners of Customs and Excise for their permission to consult the Departmental records. However, I must point out that this is not an official publication and the Commissioners of Customs and Excise do not accept any responsibility for the contents. The transcripts of Crown-copyright records in the Public Record Office and in the Department appear by permission of the Controller of Her Majesty's Stationery Office. I would like to express my thanks to the various members of the Department for reading through the manuscript and making useful suggestions, and to the photographic section of the Investigation Division for their help.
Finally I owe a deep debt of gratitude to my wife Val for her enthusiasm, patience and typing, without which this book would not have been possible.

CHAPTER ONE

The Formative Years

For the majority of people 'The Customs and Excise' recalls either the dilemma of whether to pass through the red or green channel at the end of their overseas holiday or of late value-added tax, and all that it entails. Few indeed are familiar with the wide range of duties performed by the department today, let alone during its long history, when for centuries its activities touched many aspects of the economic and social life of the country.

Her Majesty's Customs and Excise as a department is relatively young in years, being formed in 1909 by the amalgamation of the two separate services. However, both can trace their emergence as government departments to the reign of Charles II. Even then the Customs was already old, its lineage dating back to Anglo-Saxon times; whereas the Excise was of more recent origin, being introduced at the time of the Civil War.

In order to understand the department's more recent development it is essential to look at these early beginnings of both services, because from them emerged the basic structure of administration, which has remained largely unchanged up to the present day. The department, quite rightly, takes a great pride in its long history, and the fine traditions evolved over a period of 1,200 years.

Customs duties are, in all probability, as old as civilization itself. There is abundant evidence that import and export duties and tolls (*portoria*) formed an essential part of the well-organized system of taxation of the Roman Empire. However, despite the importance of Roman Britain as a trading country and the prominence of London as a centre of commerce, no direct evidence of *portoria* and their collection in this country has been discovered. The recent excavations in Lower Thames Street uncovered the remains of a Roman quay, but did not disclose any evidence as to the possible site of a Roman *portoria*, or Custom House.

The earliest written reference to Customs dues is to be found in a charter dated 743, granted by Aethelbald, King of Mercia, to the Abbey of Worcester. This allowed the Abbey the dues of two ships 'Which shall be demanded by the collectors in the hithe of London town'. Two years later a further charter of the same King granted to the Bishop of London 'the toll and tribute of one ship which formerly accrued to me of right'.

In 979 there is evidence of import duties being collected at Belinsgate (Billingsgate)—'½d. on a little ship, 1d. on a larger ship with sails, a ship full of wood, one piece of wood as tax, Men of Rouen who shall come with wine or large fish shall give a due of six shillings, Men from Flanders, Normandy and France shall be free of tax.' There were other duties on cloth, cheese, butter and eggs. Even in these early days, with the various exemptions, the duties were already complicated. Whether there was some form of Custom House to collect the duties is not known, but it seems more than a coincidence that from the early thirteenth century there has been a Custom House within very close proximity to Billingsgate.

These early references demonstrate the long and ancient connections the department has had with the City of London, and throughout the succeeding centuries its headquarters has firmly remained in the City, forming a chronicle that provides a colourful backcloth to the changing City scene.

After the Norman Conquest there was a considerable increase in the import of wine, especially from Gascony; this new trade led to the imposition of a wine 'prise', a duty which was collected in kind. The new levy was called 'prisage', and was used mainly to supply the King and his Court with wine. The King's Butler was entrusted with the selection of wines: not more than one tun in twenty, one from before the mast and one from behind. He was also allowed to taste the wine, and thus chose not only the best wine but also the fullest tuns. As the King's Butler or his agent could not go to every port, it was required that wine should be imported only into certain places. Subsequently prisage was commuted, with the agreement of the merchants, into a money payment of two shillings per tun; this duty became known as 'butlerage', and as such survived until the early nineteenth century.

The advent of a nationally organized Customs service—as opposed to separate grants at individual ports—may be traced to the reign of the much maligned King John. Among the major administrative reforms of the reign (such as the establishment of the Exchequer, the reorganization of the Navy, and the foundations of formal Archives) is to be found the first attempt to place the collection of Customs on a national footing.

At the Winchester Assize of 1203 a duty of one-fifteenth was placed on all imports and exports. This was called the 'quindecima', and detailed records have survived of the amount of duty collected at the various ports. Some of these places have long since disappeared (some physically), but many are still in existence—e.g., Hull, Dover, Southampton, Shoreham, Immingham, Grimsby, Fowey and of course London. It was decreed that henceforth 'all the customary dues at the port' should be accounted direct to the Treasury and not through the local lords and sheriffs. The ports were thus placed outside local control and into a central system administered by the Exchequer.

The Exchequer control was achieved by the duties in the port being paid to a collector, who was compelled to secure the monies under lock and key and submit the duty collected to the head collector, with an account, which had been recorded on a roll. The head collector submitted his accounts to the Exchequer. Another official was appointed at the ports to keep a counter-roll of all duties received, although he received no monies himself. This official was known as the contrarotulator (from the Latin *rotulus* = roll), which name duly became corrupted to comptroller and later controller. This official was required to pass his independent account directly to the Exchequer, and thus acted as a check on the collector. The present head of the department's accounting division still has the old word in his title—Accountant and Comptroller General.

Magna Carta makes reference to 'the ancient and rightful Customs', which would appear to be the wine prisage, various local dues and the export duties on wool. Later, in 1275, Edward I introduced a further export duty on wool, woolfells and hides, which became known as the 'new Customs'. The duties were charged at half a mark ($33\frac{1}{3}$p, or 6s. 8d.) on each sack of wool, a mark for every 300 woolfells and each last (240) of hides exported.

The introduction of the new duty was an opportune moment to make some improvements in the nascent Customs administration. A new post of 'customer' was established; the main function of these officials was to safeguard the duty collected and to make such payments as they were directed by the Exchequer. They were invariably local landowners, who had a staff of retainers to transport the money safely to London. There was no salary for the work, but the customer was entitled to take a small fee from the merchants. In some of the smaller ports the posts of customer and collector were combined.

There were also appointed 'searchers', whose original duties were to arrest persons bringing in false money, but who later became largely concerned with the examination of imported and exported goods, the making up of accounts, and generally ensuring that all the goods imported and exported had paid duty. A few years later the post of tronour was set up. The tronour's original duty was to weigh wool on the scales known as the tron. These were the 'official' scales, in the form of a beam, and they became known as the King's Beam. There was normally a King's Beam outside every Custom House.

Thus was established the basic system of Customs control and account at the ports which with very little variation has survived to the present day. The important feature of the control was that the officials responsible for the receipt and accounting of the duty took no active part in the examination and assessment of the goods and duty, while the officials assessing the goods did not receive any duty. Both officials were checked by an independent third party, the comptroller. All three officials submitted their accounts to the Exchequer, thus giving a system of triangular control.

The actual collection of the 'new custom' was entrusted to the Italian bankers of Lucca. The lease of Customs duties to merchants or financiers was known as 'farming' (possibly from the Old English word *feorm*). A contract price was agreed for the annual rental of the lease of the duties, this sum being paid outright or in regular instalments to the King. In return the 'farmer' gained the right to collect the Customs duties, and appointed his own officials to arrange the collection. The advantages to the King of this system were that he received the income from the Customs in advance, and also saved the administration costs and the problems of collection—except, of course, for the appointment of his own comptrollers to oversee the farmer's collectors.

The farmers were able to exact a nice profit for themselves, for not only was the rent of the farm far less than the average yield of the Customs duty but they could increase their profit by the diligence of their officials, and in many cases by gross overcharging of the duty. They often received high interest rates on the sums advanced to the King. The farming of duties was in fact to be a feature of revenue-collection for almost four hundred years.

An illustration of this arrangement, farming, can be seen in an order issued to the Lord Mayor of London in 1275:

> [he is] to go in person to the said city and elect by the oath of good and lawful men thereof—two men of the City, who shall keep one part of the seal provided for the new Customs and shall seal letters of licence to take wool out of the city, together with the attorneys of Luke de Luk and his fellows, Merchants of Lucca, deputed to collect the Custom, to whom the King has committed that other part of the seal, so that such letters be sealed by view of the same.

The seal was known as the cocket, and today this term is used to signify that all Customs requirements have been met by the exporter. The possession of a cocket seal by a port virtually ensured its approval as a proper place for the landing and loading of goods. Only fifteen ports were assigned for the collection of this new custom. Once again in this medieval Customs administration we see a feature which will be carried forward to the modern administration—the approval of special ports for the discharge and loading of certain goods, making it easier to control the illegal landing of goods.

It is from the beginning of the fourteenth century that the surveyor, the fourth important official of the medieval Customs, makes an appearance. In 1303 a King's clerk was appointed 'to make a survey and examine the business of the Customs in all places beyond the Trent', and by 1316 'surveyors of the receipt of moneys' were appointed to various ports. Later their duties were extended to be 'Surveyors of Searches', and they virtually became supervisors or controllers of the searcher's activities.

In 1303 Edward I granted a new charter to the foreign merchants who had at this time a virtual monopoly of the trade both in and out of the country. The charter was called the Carta Mercatoria, and it granted large trading privileges to the 'foreign or alien' merchants. The price for these concessions was increased duties on the export of wool and woolfells, over and above the 1275 duties. To complicate matters, the duties under this charter became known as the 'new Customs', and the 'old' duties imposed in 1275 now became known as the 'ancient Customs'. In the same charter a duty of 3d. in the pound on all imported goods was imposed, and this was known as the 'Parva' or Petty Customs. Each of these duties had to be separately accounted and returned to the Exchequer, and in some ports separate officials were appointed for each duty.

The situation was further complicated in 1347 with the granting by Parliament of an additional duty of 2s. per tun on wine, and 6d. per £ on all other imports. These 'Tunnage and Poundage' duties were sanctioned for a brief period, but as throughout revenue history, temporary duties invariably become permanent. This was the case with Tunnage and Poundage; they remained the largest source of Customs revenue until the end of the eighteenth century.

During the fourteenth century collectors were chosen from the merchants at the ports, while in London many of the collectors had been or were Lord Mayors. Among the more famous names who served in the Customs in London were Sir William Walworth, Sir John Philpot and Sir Nicholas Brembre. All three were said to have been present at the insurrection at Smithfield in 1381, and Walworth is reputed to have killed Wat Tyler. The three were all members of a council to improve the royal revenue. Perhaps the most famous of all Lord Mayors of London, Richard Whittington, was appointed the Collector of the Wool Custom and Subsidy in 1401, but dismissed in 1410. In Hull the De La Pole family became prominent collectors. Richard finally became Chief Butler of England, and his brother William became very rich and powerful with trading in wool and had a son who later became the first Earl of Suffolk.

The collectors received no salary, and according to the records there is no evidence of them charging fees to merchants, although it is most likely that they did. However, they were still allowed to trade in their own right, so perhaps ensuring favourable treatment for their own goods was sufficient recompense. They all prospered, and there was no shortage of applicants for the 'unpaid' posts!

The comptrollers were appointed by the King, and seem to have been selected from the minor officials of the Court or Household. The posts were greatly sought after by well-educated laymen, as they were the only part of the King's service not dominated by clerks in holy orders. Comptrollers received a salary of £10 per annum, and an annual *regardum* or reward of 10 marks (£6 13s. 4d.). Although they took an oath not to receive any gift, there is no doubt there was collusion between them and the merchants; many of them prospered well enough to enter the trade themselves as merchants.

Probably the best-known Customs official was Geoffrey Chaucer; in June

1374 he was appointed Comptroller of the Custom and Subsidy of Wool, Woolfells, and Hides and the Petty Customs for the Port of London. Among the conditions of his employment were that 'he shall write with his own hand, the registers and entries belonging to his said office . . . and shall constantly act in person in his said office and not by deputy or substitute.' Chaucer's post was no sinecure, as that would be completely contrary to the medieval conception of his duties—as a constant check on the collectors.

Both Chaucer's grandfather and his father had been earlier employed in the Customs service. His father had been Collector of Butlerage in the port of Southampton. This family tradition was uncommon in those days, but such family connections were later to become a feature of both the Customs and Excise services. Chaucer served as an official for over twelve years, finally relinquishing his post in December 1386.

It was during Chaucer's service in the Port that John Churchman rebuilt the London Custom House on his quay at 'Wool Wharf in Tower Ward'. Certainly in 1341 there is reference to a Custom House on the site, with a tronage house or weigh-house on the ground floor and a computatorium or counting house on the first floor, for the collectors and comptrollers on the first floor. The building of Churchman's Custom House took from 1382 to 1386, and was originally planned to accommodate the officials of the Great Custom on Wool and Woolfells. As such it was named in the singular: 'Custom' House. Although it was later enlarged to house the officials of the Petty Customs, the name was not changed to the plural 'Customs' House. From that day all buildings have been known as Custom House, despite housing Customs officers.

From the date of Churchman's Custom House there has been a Custom House on or very near to the same site. The present London Custom House is slightly west of the original site. Three years after Chaucer left his post as comptroller he was appointed clerk of works, and for several years was involved with the repairs to Wool Wharf and 'the Custom Houses—nearby built by the Tower for weighing wool'.

The next hundred years was a period of stabilization for the Customs administration; the revenue continued to be farmed, mainly to foreign merchant houses, although the increasing prosperity of English merchants led to groups of English traders taking a more active part in the Customs farms. Slowly the dominance of Genoese and Florentine bankers in the Customs affairs dwindled, to be replaced by traders from the City of London.

There was one outstanding administrative problem which remained largely unsolved. This was the assessing of the correct value of goods liable to an *ad valorem* duty (a duty payable on goods as a percentage of their value). Values for the same goods varied greatly at the different ports. The current practice was to accept a valuation based on the sworn oath of the merchants. This procedure had led to considerable variations throughout the ports, with large under-declarations, and was open to collusion with the officers.

In 1506 a commercial treaty was signed with Spain which included an article which was to have a very important effect on Customs procedure. It provided for 'a table of all the subsidies, tolls and other payments, which may be legally demanded in either country, and shall be affixed on the doors of the Custom Houses in London, Bruges and Antwerp'. The following year the first official 'Book of Rates' was published.

The Book of Rates was the forerunner of the present-day tariff, but instead of listing the various rates of duty it laid down the official or notional values of imported goods. Not only was it an ideal instrument for simplifying the collection of duty, but it was still more important for the Exchequer as a revenue-raiser. It was only necessary to issue revised increased values to give a greater yield of duty, without altering the actual rate.

Much of the improvement and most of the reforms in the Customs administration in the reigns of Mary and Elizabeth were due to one man, William Paulet, Marquis of Winchester. When he was appointed Lord Treasurer in 1550 he inherited a Customs service hardly changed from its early formative years. The majority of revenue was collected in London, where the administration was elaborate and fairly closely controlled. However, in the out-ports the collection was rather informal, with the farms in many of the small ports in the hands of local merchants, who were in collusion with the district officers. There was no overall central administration to ensure a uniform system of control.

Winchester's first steps were to enter into discussions with the merchants on the production of a new Book of Rates; it had been nearly fifty years since the previous issue, and values had drastically changed. The new Book was issued in May 1558, and not only did it increase the values by an average of 75 per cent, but it also included very many goods not previously listed. It is of interest to note that the motives of the compilers of this new Book were 'to under-rate the most necessary commodities that come into the realm to draw them thither, and over-rate the superfluous commodities to drive them away'. A very early example of what modern economists would call 'demand management'.

Over the previous half-century there had been a gradual decline in the export of wool, which had been amply compensated by a large increase in the export of wool-cloth. In 1475 45,000 pieces had been exported, and by 1550 the trade had increased to 125,000. It was decided that the existing duty on cloth was insufficient, and an extra duty or impost was imposed on exported cloth. The duty on wine was also increased, and a new duty introduced on exported beer. This is the first instance of any duty being levied on beer in this country, although it is now of course a large revenue-producer.

In the same year as the new Book of Rates a link with the early days of the Customs disappeared. The old Custom House built by John Churchman was to be rebuilt; it had obviously fallen into bad repair, and was sadly inadequate for the increased staff in London. Wool Wharf and Custom House Quay were acquired by the Crown for the erection of the new building, which became the first Custom House to be built by the Crown. The building was intended for use by both the farmers and the officials, but was not completed until the early part of Elizabeth's reign, surviving until the Great Fire of London.

Winchester turned his attention to certain reforms in the Customs service itself. He appointed Sir Francis Englefield to a newly created post, Surveyor General of Customs in London, with overall control of all the collectors. Winchester had plans to extend this control to the out-ports and had devised a system of regular inspections, which included an audit of the collector's account. The return to farming after a short period of direct management by the Exchequer prevented these plans being put into operation.

By an Act in the first year of Elizabeth's reign strict conditions were imposed on the Customs control of vessels. The hours at which ships should discharge and load were regulated, and legal quays were appointed for the discharge of cargo. Masters of vessels arriving from foreign ports were required to report all their cargo at the Custom House before they were allowed to discharge it, and similarly for exports, details of cargo and destination were required before the loading could commence. Security of duty was necessary for all coastwise voyages. This basis of Customs control of shipping is, with certain modifications, the system in operation today.

The Court of the Exchequer had set up commissions, normally comprising certain gentlemen of the neighbourhood and one of the local Customs officials, to lay down for legal purposes the limits of the various 'Customs Ports'. Included in the limits were not just the ports themselves but areas of coastline, rivers and creeks, and also certain defined limits to seaward. The customers and collectors were required to provide deputies to serve in the small sub-ports and creeks within the limits of their port.

In 1565 the first consolidated rules and regulations for the Customs officials were issued. As well as embodying instructions on the new controls, they also included directions for the completion of 'The Queen's Books', or Port Books as they later became known. These vellum books contained details of both the overseas and coastwise trade of the ports, and were returned by the principal officers to the Exchequer. Where the Port Books have survived they provide an excellent picture of the trade of the port.

Despite the reorganization and the various reforms, the Customs was to remain in farm until the end of the century. It was during this period that one of the most famous Customs farmers emerges—Thomas Smythe. In 1559 he was Collector of Poundage in London, but by 1570 he had obtained the lease of the farms of London, Sandwich, Chichester, Southampton, Ipswich and Woodbridge for an annual rent of £20,000. At the end of his last lease in 1589 the rent had increased to £42,000, and he refused to renew the lease because the Lord Treasurer wanted to increase the sum further. Mr 'Customer' Smythe, as he was called, was given a very free hand in the management of his farm, and there is no doubt that he set up a very efficient organization in the ports he controlled. It was reckoned that in his later farms his annual income was over £8,000. His successful farm of six ports paved the way for a consolidated farm of all the Customs.

During the time of Smythe's farm the rest of the out-ports had been leased in total to Sir Francis Walsingham. Prior to this the out-ports had been leased on an individual basis to local merchants. Although a serious attempt was made to introduce good management into the ports by the employment of two deputies or surveyors general, the management was not successful, and when Walsingham died in 1590 he left considerable debts.

All the Customs were now out of farm and back in direct control. The first step in setting up a new system was the appointment of a Receiver General of Customs, who was responsible for all the receipts of duties and the various payments authorized by the Exchequer. The post of Chief Customer of London—a position held by Smythe—was given to Alderman Henry Billingsley, a prominent London merchant. The next important post, that of Surveyor General for London, went to Richard Carmarden, a very able administrator, who reported directly to the Lord Treasurer.

The control of the out-ports was entrusted to three surveyors general, all very experienced in Customs matters, having served under Walsingham. Surveyors were formally appointed to the ports, and they were to be fully knowledgeable concerning all 'matters in the office'. They were required to check the comptroller, and to 'keep their own books, walking the quays at their discretion'. The perennial difficulty in the management of all revenue services at this time was to find sufficient honest officials, who would abstain from extortion and bribery, and yet had enough financial skill to administer the large cash balances that accumulated at the ports.

The early experience of direct administration was not very encouraging: there were increasing difficulties in obtaining the duties from the ports; large balances of cash were being held by the surveyors. Also, there were widespread complaints of bribery and fraud; and although trade was increasing, the Customs revenues were diminishing. The system of direct control was obviously not working satisfactorily, and a return to farming seemed to be the only solution.

In July 1604 James I issued a notice that he was resolved to farm the whole of the Customs. Discussions on the farm continued throughout the year, a body of men called the Customs Commissioners meeting three times a week to hear and consider the various proposals. (These 'Commissioners' should not be confused with the Board of Customs established later in the century, for their function was entirely different.) Finally, a group of merchants headed by Francis Jones and Nicholas Salter were granted the lease for a term of seven years at an annual rent of £112,400. The 'Great Farm', as it became known, comprised all the Customs and Subsidies in force at the time, for both London and all the out-ports. There were some minor farms excluded, such as wines, silks and velvets, these being collected by individuals.

For the first time in Customs history, all the country was now included in one complete farm, providing a countrywide system of collection, with the added benefit of a regular income from the expansion of trade. For both James I and Charles I, the revenue from the Customs supplied over half their total income.

After long and at times acrimonious negotiations with the merchants, a new Book of Rates was issued in November 1604. Much of the final work on this was undertaken by two young and able Customs officers in London, John Wolstenholme and Arthur Ingram. Wolstenholme was destined to be involved in Customs affairs for the next fifty years. In this book there were for the first time separate sections for goods inwards and outwards, and detailed instructions as to the conduct of Customs officers.

The increase in values in the new Book was considered to be exorbitant. However, it was not on the question of values that Bates, a London merchant, brought his famous case against the King, but on the legality of increasing taxation without the consent of Parliament. The Books of Rates, of course, were issued under the Great Seal, and were not discussed or passed by Parliament. Bates lost his case, the judges deciding that 'he who has power over the cause must have power over the effect. The sea-ports are the King's gates, which he may open and shut to whom he pleases.' This is the earliest reference to the Portcullis in connection with Customs affairs, and many centuries before it was adopted as the department's emblem.

James I's abhorrence of tobacco is well known, and it is not surprising to find that he should select tobacco to bear a very heavy duty. In 1602 he charged a special impost of 6s. 6d. per pound on all imported tobacco. Prior to this date it had been charged at 2d. per pound, as 'other merchandise not specially mentioned'. The effect of this high duty was a vast increase in smuggling, and serious efforts were made to raise a crop in this country. In 1620 the duty was reduced to 1s. per pound, and it was decreed that all tobacco should bear a government stamp. The import was restricted to the London Custom House Quay, and tobacco-growing in this country was forbidden.

Charles I introduced a system of licensing for retailers, and allowed other ports, mainly Bristol and Plymouth, to share the trade. With the introduction of the Excise (see p. 13), a duty was placed on home-produced tobacco. Thus from these small beginnings grew the tobacco duty, which has figured so prominently in the Customs revenue over the years, and which is today the third biggest revenue-producer.

The great farm of the Customs lasted until 1641. During its existence it came under the control of various syndicates. Most of the farmers during this period were well-known London merchants; some of the most famous names of Stuart London—Lord Goring, Sir Paul Pindar, Sir William Cockaine and Sir William Russell—were all involved in the various farms. The rent had increased dramatically over the intervening years, and by 1638, the date of the last lease, it had reached £172,500. The Customs farmers were now a virtual banking syndicate, advancing money to the Crown on a scale unsurpassed previously. In 1641 the farmers were indicted by Parliament for connivance at the King's usurpation of Parliamentary rights. Their farm was sequestered, and to save their estates they agreed to a compromise fine of £150,000. This payment was in addition to £250,000 already advanced to the King in the previous three years—not a very profitable outcome for them.

With the demise of the farm the Customs went back to direct management, controlled by Parliament. The result was chaos. Many of the officials at the ports were dismissed and replaced by people with no knowledge of the Customs; the customers were labelled 'delinquents', and were strictly forbidden to act or collect the duties. It was reported that 'merchants land their goods, paying nothing'. This situation was not allowed to continue for long, several new Acts being passed in an attempt to regularize the position. In 1642 a new Book of Rates was issued, with an appended 'Rules and Directions for Customs officers'. It laid down that the officers should attend at the Custom House between nine and twelve in the morning, and that no fees other than those allowed by Parliament should be taken.

In the following year Parliament set up a Board of Commissioners to administer the Customs. This comprised four London aldermen and four London merchants, at a salary of £1,250 per year. Whether it was unsuccessful is not known, but two years later the members were all dismissed, and replaced by only five new Commissioners, once again all with connections with London. The establishment of a Central Board, responsible for the collection of Customs nationwide, was the first step towards the formation of a Customs department thirty-nine years later.

The Customs officers in the early Stuart period were mainly recruited from the merchant class. This was especially so in London, when the younger sons of influential merchants managed to obtain Customs places. Two examples were John Wolstenholme and Lionel Cranfield, who owed their appointment to their fathers' connections at Court, due mainly to their interests in the new trading companies. Once they were in positions of authority they were able to advance the careers of their younger relations. For instance, Robert Blackburne was Customs Secretary, his brother obtained the post of Collector at Plymouth and a cousin was given a minor appointment in Exeter.

In the out-ports the Customs officials came more from the local professional classes than from the mercantile families. In Boston the Comptroller was the son of a physician and mayor, his post on retirement passed to his son-in-law, and his son obtained the post of Searcher. In South Wales the Collector was the son of a lawyer, and owed his preferment in the Customs to a local landowner, who was also a high official of state. He served during the reigns of Charles I and II, as well as during the Commonwealth. When he retired the 'influence or patronage' passed to his wife's relatives, who held a variety of Customs posts in South Wales for the next seventy years.

Although the salaries were small, a collector received £30 per annum and £10 to cover 'riding charges'. His main source of income was the fees charged to shipowners and merchants for conducting the great variety of business. During the Commonwealth the post of 'waiter', the lowest official in the service, was said to be worth 'over £100 per year, more than a clerk in the Navy Department', but his 'official' salary was only £10. It is therefore open to conjecture just how much a collector's place was worth, with his vastly increased opportunities for obtaining fees and other payments. Initial entry into the service seemed to depend solely on patrimony and patronage.

The bitter struggle between King and Parliament was moving inexorably to a conflict of arms. In such a situation Parliament realized that it would require some new source of revenue to support its army. As we have seen, there were considerable problems in the collection of Customs in the early 1640s, while many of the out-ports were in Royalist hands. It was also felt that the collection of ship money had fallen too heavily on the maritime counties, and that a more evenly distributed form of taxation was needed. It was with this background that Parliament's—or more specially John Pym's—thoughts turned to other means of raising the necessary revenue.

Pym was one of the most experienced Members of Parliament, having entered the House in 1614. He had previously been a clerk in the Exchequer, and was thought by Clarendon to be 'a man of business'. In fact, in previous more settled times he had been considered by Charles I for the post of Chancellor of the Exchequer. Pym was certainly the financial theorist of the House of Commons, and his solution to the problem was the introduction of an Excise duty.

Several forms of Excise duties had been in existence on the Continent for many years, the most successful of which was in operation in the United Netherlands, and was known as the 'accijus'. However, the idea of an Excise was not unknown in this country. As early as 1592, an 'excise boll' was placed on salt imported into Scotland, while in 1626 Charles I set up a Commission 'to set forth an Excise in England'. The report from this Commission was brought before Parliament, but was firmly turned down. It was considered 'a foreign monster that would devour the nation'. In view of the additional and intense popular opposition, the idea was dropped.

In 1641 there were strong rumours of an Excise to be introduced by Parliament, which brought forth a most vehement denial: 'The Houses of Parliament receiving information that divers public rumours and aspersions are by malignant persons cast upon this house, that they intend to assess every man's pewter and lay Excise upon that and other commodities, the said House, for their vindication do declare these rumours are false and scandalous.'

However, Pym was quite prepared to wait until sufficient financial pressure was placed upon Parliament for them to accept this new and revolutionary tax. By April 1643 this position had been reached, and a committee was appointed to consider an Excise duty. Although no report of its findings has survived, it obviously now accepted the inevitable, and in the summer the House of Commons passed the first Excise Ordinance. The term 'ordinance' was used for what was primarily an 'unconstitutional' law, one not having the express decree of the King. Pym, the architect of the Excise, barely survived its introduction, dying in December 1643.

The Excise was introduced on 22 July 1643, its avowed intent being 'for the speedy raising and levying of monies by way of an Excise or New Impost for the maintenance of the forces raised by Parliament'. It was first levied for one year, and in its renewal was stated to be 'only for the duration of the war'. Like most temporary duties, it acquired the bad habit of becoming permanent!

It was basically a duty levied on *home-produced* goods, mainly beer and ale, strong waters (spirits), cider, and soap, but was later imposed on a wide range of imported goods. The goods liable to duty grew each year, thus confirming the worst fears of its opponents that an Excise lends itself easily to a general and widespread duty. Some of the goods later taxed were meat, salt, clothes, hats, drugs, paper, starch, glass, hops, leather, linens, tobacco, fish and various oils—a very comprehensive list. The duty was required to be paid by the 'first buyer', although other than in London, this rule appeared to be ignored.

The ordinance appointed eight Commissioners, all belonging to the City of London, who were allowed 3*d.* in the £1 of all duty collected. They were authorized to appoint the sub-commissioners (or collectors) and the 'inferior' officers. This privilege was unusual and important, and throughout their history the Excise Commissioners retained this right. Normally all appointments to the revenue services were made by the Treasury Commissioners, this certainly being the case in the Customs for the next 150 years.

From its inception the Excise aroused intense popular opposition. In 1645 a special Committee was established with very wide powers to prosecute 'persons obstructing the collection of the Excise'. The Excise Act of 1649 prescribed severe penalties for anyone attempting to corrupt Excise officers. These officers suffered considerable abuse, not only in London but throughout the country, the Excise Office at Smithfield being burnt down in 1647 during a riot against the Excise on meat. In various parts of the country the army was called out to protect the officers and assist in the collection of the duty. Despite this, by 1649 Parliament had described the Excise as 'the most useful and indifferent [fairly apportioned] levy that can be laid upon a people'.

Some of the reasons for this violent opposition were that the burden of the duty fell mainly on the necessities of life—meat, salt, leather, beer, and clothes—and as such was a greater burden on the poorer members of society. Almost for the first time, this section of the community were being taxed. Hitherto Customs duties, feudal and land taxes had largely fallen on the merchants and landed gentry. It was also distrusted because of its foreign

origin, and its express purpose of funding the army—the country
detested standing armies. Finally, and perhaps the most strong and
compelling reason for the hatred of the Excise, was the wide powers of entry
and search given to the Excise officers. At this time most excisable trades
were conducted from the trader's home, and such powers thus breached a
fundamental tenet of British life—the sanctity of one's home.

The unpopularity of the duty can be seen in the profusion of pamphlets
and broadsheets decrying it. There were more items on the Excise than on
any other duty or tax. One of the strongest opponents of the duty was the
pamphleteer William Prynne, who wrote a vehement protest against the
'accursed foreign impost' in 1654. (However, after the Restoration he
accepted a post as Commissioner for the collection of Excise arrears.
Presumably the salary of £100 per annum was adequate incentive to vary his
views!) The unpopularity of the Excise existed for well over a hundred years,
and greatly affected both the administration and the collection of the duty.

Although the Excise was considered a 'Parliamentary' duty, Charles I had
no compunction in raising his own Excise in the areas under his control. In
1644 Commissions were set up for Lichfield and Chester, followed by Oxford
and Worcester. The duty was required 'for a constant supply of moneys for
continuing the stores of Powder, Match, Bullets, Muskets, Pikes, and other
Ammuniations'. The King's Excise was levied on loads of hay and straw,
hops, 'larkes', eggs and fish—all items which were sold in the markets, where
the King's Excisemen collected the duty. Needless to say, these Excise
Commissions were short-lived, and when the towns were taken by the
Parliamentary forces no arrears of Excise were called for.

It is from one of these Commissions that the first of many famous literary
figures to serve in the Excise emerged; Elias Ashmole, founder of the
Ashmolean Museum in Oxford, was appointed Controller of Excise for
Worcester. Although he served only for two years, until the surrender of
Worcester, he had time (as he reported in his diary) to buy an 'ink-horn',
which was a small portable ink vessel. The ink-horn later became
synonymous with Excisemen, and even Samuel Johnson helping out at his
friend's brewery could be found 'bustling about with an ink-horn and a pen
in his button hole, like an Exciseman'. Ashmole was out of public office
during the Commonwealth, but at the Restoration of Charles II was
appointed Controller of Excise, and served in this post until his death in
1692.

Very little information has survived to show how the first Excise
Commissioners recruited a nationwide staff to collect and control the new
duty. Offices were set up in all market towns, and were open each weekday
for the various Excise traders to attend to make their weekly entries on oath
of the goods manufactured. At first no official check was taken of the trader's
declarations; it was not until 1660 that officers (or gaugers, as they became
known), went on a round of the brewers to check 'the gage in the cask'. The
offices were normally situated in inns, where a room was set aside to conduct

the Excise business. Some years ago when an very old inn was being renovated a wall was uncovered with a mass of Excise receipts for beer stuck to it. All the receipts related to the mid seventeenth century. Inns were used as Excise offices right up to the nineteenth century.

By 1653 Commissioners of Excise Appeals were established to hear and judge Excise cases in London; in the country Justices of the Peace were made 'the final judges in excise cases'. Prior to this it was a complaint that the Excise officers 'had been judges in their own cases'. In the same year most of the Country Excise (as opposed to the Town, or London, Excise), was farmed to local landowners, but by 1657 the whole of the Excise was farmed as one. The political problems of the time meant that this great farm was short-lived, and by September 1659 in the chaos of political unrest the Excise returned to direct administration.

The Customs had remained in direct management for a large part of the Commonwealth, with the officers still appointed by patronage. In 1653 none other than Oliver Cromwell wrote to the Committee for regulating the Customers on behalf of 'a friend of mine'. He had obviously written once before with no success, and once again proposed his friend for 'a post, if not in the city, by reason of the multiplicity of suitors, a place in the out-ports, and I doubt not his utmost abilities will be improved to the faithful discharging of such trust as you shall impose on him'. (It is not known whether Cromwell's friend was ever appointed.) In 1657 it was decided to include the Customs with the Excise in one large farm. The syndicate comprised London financiers headed by Martin Noell, who had previously controlled the majority of the Excise farms.

With the Restoration of Charles II in 1660 it was felt that the very unpopular and revolutionary Excise, with its doubtful legal backing of barely seventeen years, should disappear. While discussions on the King's settlement were progressing the existing Customs and Excise duties continued to be collected. When the settlement was announced the Excise was retained, and formed an essential part of the King's settlement. The 'new' Excise was levied on home-produced and imported liquors. The duty was raised on beer, cider, mead, and strong waters, and also on coffee, tea and chocolate per liquid gallon, as sold in the coffee-houses. Half of the Excise was granted to the King in perpetuity, and became known as the Hereditary Excise (and after the establishment of a Civil List was formally renounced by each new monarch on accession). The other half of the Excise was granted to the King for life only, and thus became known as the Temporary Excise. The new duties came into force in December 1660, when the old Commonwealth Excise was allowed to lapse.

As far as the Customs were concerned, a new Tonnage and Poundage Act was introduced, which formed the basis of Customs legislation for over a hundred years. Charles II was well aware of the importance of foreign trade; he commented, 'The thing which is nearest the heart of the nation is trade and all that belongs to it.' The Act was accompanied by a new Book of Rates and a set of rules for the conduct of Customs officers. Both services had a change of Commissioners; the Customs Commissioners were all men who had been Customs farmers under Charles I back in 1641. The fresh Excise Board again consisted of new men, who would feature prominently in the farming of the Excise in the coming years. The administration of neither Customs nor Excise altered, although the majority of posts in the Customs out-ports changed hands, as royalists petitioned for lucrative places for services rendered. The new Excise administration appeared to take over the existing staff with very little change.

There were considerable problems in the direct administration of both revenues, and especially so in the Excise, where the anticipated yield of £300,000 per year did not materialize. By 1662, therefore, both Customs and Excise were placed back in farm. The Customs became a total farm for the whole of the country, again largely in the control of London merchants, but now with the introduction of two goldsmith-bankers, Sir Robert Viner and Edward Backwell. There was a very low opinion of Customs officers. Ashley Cooper, Earl of Shaftesbury, remarked, 'When anyone fails in business or a gentleman wants to part with an old servant, interest is made to get them into the Customs as if into a hospital.' Despite this, the revenue from the Customs improved rapidly in the early years of the reign.

There were still inherent problems in collecting the Excise; it was still universally unpopular, and reports of opposition to the Excise officers came from places as widespread as Dorset and Durham. The officers were frequently attacked and abused, and received scant help or support from the Constables, or the Justices of the Peace. The Collector at Monmouth was brutally attacked by a victualler in the presence of the Constable, who was severely reprimanded by the Treasury Lords for 'neglect of duty'. Despite this continual opposition, the progress of Excise improved, and it averaged nearly a quarter of a million pounds per year. Overseas trade quickly recovered from the turmoil of the Restoration, and as a result the Customs revenue increased. The first setback to this progress was the Plague of 1665. By mid-July London was like a dead city—10,000 houses were empty and 200,000 people had fled. All shipping stopped, no port in Europe would allow any goods from London to be landed and those masters foolish enough to smuggle goods ashore were shot if caught. Defoe remarked that there was grass growing on the deserted riverside quays—not a vessel to be seen. As London dealt with over half the trade of the country, the effect on the Customs revenue was dramatic.

The Excise also suffered greatly, all business ceased in London, and even in Kent 'the plague raged so much that one-third of the receipt (of the Excise) has failed'. Throughout the country the various local Excise farmers petitioned the Treasury for large 'defalcations' (allowable deficiencies) on their rent 'due to the dreadful pestilence'. In fact, all future leases for the Excise included a clause for allowances 'in time of plague'. The disastrous Excise returns resulted in some of the smaller local farmers becoming bankrupt, who were then bought out by the London farmers, thus bringing a total farm of the Excise that much closer. As a precaution against the plague the Excise Commissioners moved their office in St Bartholomew's Lane in the City to a large mansion called 'Faux Hall' (Vauxhall). They were still there in December, when the Treasury Commissioners (writing from the relative security of Oxford) ordered them to return to the City.

Both services had hardly any time to recover before they suffered an even greater setback in the following year, when both the Custom House and the Excise Office were completely destroyed in the Great Fire. All the records, ledgers and accounts perished in the fire, causing particular problems in the Customs, where it was normal practice to allow merchants considerable credit on Customs duties. Many of these merchants were made bankrupt by the fire, and thus the unpaid duties were never recovered.

The Customs moved their headquarters to temporary accommodation in Mark Lane, a large house belonging to Lord Baunis, which was strangely enough on a site not far from the present headquarters of the department. The Excise were unable to find suitable accommodation in the City, and they 'reluctantly' moved out of the City for the first time to rooms in Southampton House, near Holborn. This move was very temporary, because in the following year they obtained small but suitable premises in Aldersgate Street, back once again in the City.

A Royal Warrant was issued for the rebuilding of the Custom House, on the same site in Thames Street. It was in this warrant that the term 'Great Fire' was used. The Customs farmers were required to pay £6,000 towards the cost of rebuilding, although the final cost was £10,000. The architect was Sir Christopher Wren, and the new building was completed in March 1671, it being the first public office to be rebuilt.

The most striking feature of the new building was the 'Great Long Room' on the first floor, running the whole length of the central river front. This was the public room, where all the import and export business was transacted. Because of this room, all other public rooms in Custom Houses throughout the kingdom, and later throughout the world, became known as 'Long Rooms', irrespective of their size or shape. Defoe was very impressed with the Long Room; he reported 'It is like an Exchange every morning, and the crowd of people who appear there, and the business they do, is not to be explained in words, nothing of that kind in Europe is like it.'

In 1671 both farms were due for renewal. The Excise farmers headed by William Bucknall, acting on behalf of the Corporation of London brewers, had a renewal clause in their contract. They remained in possession of the valuable London farm, but also managed to obtain control of over half of the other county farms. This meant that they were now responsible for nearly three-quarters of the entire Excise.

Negotiations for the new Customs farm had commenced in the previous year. Tenders were received from two groups, one headed by Sir Richard Ford and the other by William Bucknall, the Excise farmer. The decision to award the farm to Bucknall's group was probably due to his important connections at both Treasury and Court and the family's widespread interests in the revenue of the country. One brother was an Excise farmer in Yorkshire and Sussex, another a revenue farmer in Ireland and another relative an Excise collector.

However, despite apparent full agreement being reached, and £60,000 being advanced by the new farmers, the lease was abruptly cancelled, and it was announced that the Customs would be placed into direct management. A contemporary report gave the reason for the volte-face as follows:

> The new farmers, upon confidence of the money they had already paid and the interest they had, thought that they might make better conditions and add some other causes for defalcations. The King did not like this and being more than ordinarily moved, told them that he should never have an end with them at this rate, nor any certainty in his Revenue, and if they would not accept the terms agreed upon, they may leave it.

It is also possible that both the King and the Treasury were concerned that over three-quarters of the Customs and Excise revenue would pass into the control of virtually one man, William Bucknall. It would appear that a new group of farmers were sought, but because time was so short it was decided 'to have it done by Commission'. The farmers were informed that their advance would be reimbursed 'when the King has money but the money for bribes is certainly lost'.

The return to direct management was a matter of expediency rather than a deliberate change of policy, but once made was final. The change was popular with the merchants:

> they are well pleased with the alteration, upon the presumption that they should meet with nothing but hardship from the farmers, some of which are ready enough and design nothing but their advantage. Time will show, what will be the effect of this sudden change.

However hasty the decision, it set a precedent for the ultimate departure from farming in all the revenues. As far as the Customs was concerned, it marked its coming of age as a government department.

CHAPTER TWO

Coming of Age

On 18 September 1671 the *London Gazette* carried a report in these terms:

> that whereas His Majesty has been pleased to take His Customs and Duties,
> arising by the last Wine Act, into his own hands, from the 27th September inst,
> and put them into Commission, their Lordships do expect and require all His
> Majesty's said Officers, both in the Port of London and Out-ports, that they
> and every one of them, do diligently attend, execute and perform the Duty of
> their respective Places; and that they do obey and observe such rules, orders
> and instructions, as from time to time they shall receive from their Lordships,
> or from the Commissioners appointed by His Majesty for the managing,
> levying and collecting His Majesty's said Customs, and the duties arising by
> the said Wine Act; and that they do not trade as Merchants for themselves, or
> as Factors or Agents for others, according as by law in those cases is provided;
> and that whoever of them shall offend against these Rules, their Lordships will
> suspend them from their Employment, and put others in their stead.

The Royal Warrant effecting the change was issued on 24 September, for a
patent under the Great Seal to appoint the new Commissioners. From this
date there has been a continuous·succession of Commissioners appointed by
the Sovereign by Royal Letters Patent. Six Commissioners were appointed
at a salary of £2,000, a princely sum in those days. They were given wide
powers in the supervision and control of shipping, and were authorized to
administer oaths on all Customs matters. However, they could appoint inferior
officers only on nomination from the Treasury or Exchequer, and could
move or displace them only by a similar warrant.

The most famous of the six Commissioners was Sir George Downing, who
although he had been born in Dublin had been brought up in Salem in
America, and had been educated at Harvard. He returned to England to
seek his fortune and served under Cromwell. For a short time Pepys acted as
his clerk. At the Restoration he changed sides swiftly and successfully, finally
being made Secretary to the Treasury Commissioners. At the time of his

appointment as Customs Commissioner he was serving as Ambassador to The Hague, but had so enraged the Dutch that he felt it politic to return to England; whereupon he was placed in the Tower for deserting his post, thus gaining the dubious honour of being the first and last Commissioner to be imprisoned in the Tower. He was removed from the Commission, only to be reappointed the following year on his release, and served as a Commissioner until his death in 1684. Perhaps his greatest claim to fame was his development of land near St James's Park, by the erection of four houses, as he put it, 'for superior persons to live in'. These houses were named after him—Downing Street.

The Commissioners were fortunate in taking over a well-organized service, which had served the farmers very well. In fact, in the last year of the farm, so confident were the farmers of the renewal of their lease that they issued printed instructions to the officers, which were termed Index Vertigelium, and which embodied all the rules and practices to be used in the ports. This was the first formal attempt to regularize the vastly different procedures used at the various ports.

Wisely, the Commissioners retained the majority of the existing officers. They did, however, find it necessary to establish some new posts. Three surveyors-general were appointed to travel the country and inspect the ports, to ensure that the uniform system of control was being adhered to and that the officers were not taking exorbitant fees. The men appointed to these posts were well experienced in Customs matters, having figured prominently in the previous Customs farm. A Receiver-General was appointed to receive all monies from the collectors and account the sums weekly to the Exchequer, as well as paying the disbursements allowed by the Treasury. Finally, a post of Comptroller-General was established to check all the accounts and supply a balanced account to the Treasury.

As well as taking over the staff and making no virtual changes in procedures, the new Commissioners even followed the precedent of the farmers in signing all their orders to the officers 'Your loving Friends'! For the next hundred years or so the Board's letters, even when they violently censured or dismissed one of the staff, were always subscribed 'your loving friends'.

The staff in the out-ports consisted of a number of 'patent officers', together with a number of executive officers. The posts of customer, comptroller and searcher were allowed to continue, but the holders of these posts invariably employed deputies, to whom they allowed part of their salary. The old post of customer lost much of its executive power, and became virtually a sinecure.

It was in the Port of London that there were the greatest number of patent posts, and there the opportunities for patronage were extensive. The two most important and profitable appointments were 'collector inwards' and 'collector outwards'. In 1675 the Duke of Manchester was granted the hereditary patent as collector outwards, considered to be worth over £2,000 per annum, and the family held this appointment for over a hundred years. There were also numerous minor collector's posts—for example, John Dryden was collector for the duties on wool from 1683 to 1692 at a salary of £5 and 'all the other fees and profits thereof'. His pension as Poet Laureate was paid out of the Excise. Besides these posts, there were also six patent searchers, one of whom was William Dockwra, who founded the first penny post service in London.

The main Customs official in the port now became the collector. He was appointed by the Commissioners under Treasury warrant, although in many ports he also acted as deputy customer. The collector was responsible for the collection of all duties and the control of all business and staff. The controllers continued their old role as checking officers, although this was now a check on the collector rather than on the customer. The controller also shared with the collector a responsibility for the port. The post of searcher was normally included with that of land waiter, and dealt with the general supervision of the landing and examination of imported goods.

These three main grades formed the basis of the staff at the ports; there were also tidesmen and tide waiters, who as their name suggests, boarded vessels on the tide to ensure that there were no illegal landings of goods before the vessels arrived at the quays. Clerks were employed in the Custom House, and the senior clerk would deputize for the collector in his absence.

Throughout the service the salaries were very small, but they were made up with a system of fees, which were paid by merchants on every Customs document and transaction. These fees were the main source of income for the officials. Even the patent officers were entitled to a share. The scales of fees were so considerable that most officers were on average able to increase their salary tenfold. As these fees were paid by the merchants and importers, they formed a 'hidden taxation' element, and in fact until they were abolished in the early nineteenth century a large proportion of the cost of the Customs administration in the ports was virtually being borne by the trading community. As Pepys wisely remarked, 'It is not the salary of any place that did make a man rich, but the opportunity of getting money when he is in place.'

The system of patent officers proved to be very detrimental to the service, for the privileges held by the patentees often conflicted with the administration of the Commissioners. The Board had no control over the appointment of deputies, and the very existence of a set of separate officials greatly interfered with their administration. Many of the problems of the Customs service in the eighteenth century stemmed from this relic of the medieval system. The abolition of these posts in 1786 proved to be a turning-point in the history of the department.

Within the first year of the Commissioners taking office, they tried to replace some of the older officers, who had served for many years under the aegis of the farmers. Many of them were too old and inefficient, and also too many were corruptible. However, the Treasury Lords were quick to remind the Board that all commissions for officers, except those of tidesmen (virtually the lowest grade) were 'to be passed and granted only by the Lords'.

Some months later it was decided by the Treasury that Customs officers should be 'protected' from serving on juries and inquests. The main reason for this exemption appeared to be the prevention of smuggling runs at a time when the officers would be fully occupied elsewhere. In Swansea the local people, thwarted by this order, attempted to co-opt the local officers as churchwardens—a post to which in those days many onerous duties were attached. The Board issued a writ of privilege to prevent this happening. The reply from the local stewards was that they would 'pursue the Customs officers to the utmost—even to excommunication'. The exemption as to jury service still applies to the Customs and Excise.

It also proved necessary to afford Customs officers some protection from the attentions of the press-gang. It would appear that some officers at Liverpool had been pressed for service in the Navy, and it was felt by the Treasury that this was gravely prejudicial to the safeguarding of the revenue. The Treasury instructions to the Admiralty did not seem to resolve matters, because it was found necessary to issue Customs boatmen with certificates absolving them from naval service. As we will see later, both Customs and Excise officers were to become involved in the administration of the dreaded press-gang.

During the next ten years the Board took steps to ensure the greater efficiency and economy of working in the ports. The activities of the Surveyor-Generals were extended, and soon Commissioners were embarking on prolonged tours of the ports. These inspections became a feature of both services, and were carried out by the Commissioners, until the establishment of the Chief Inspector's Office. In 1682, in the hope of improving the efficiency and honesty of the staff, the salaries of all officers were increased. However, they still fell far short of the income derived from fees. The Commissioners also attempted to introduce a promotion scheme for the inferior officers based on merit, but it proved of very limited effect, as it could only work in the larger ports like London, Bristol and Southampton, where there were sufficient numbers of staff to warrant supervisory grades. Nevertheless, the efforts made by the Commissioners, with the active support of the Treasury, demonstrated that the Board were at least trying to establish an efficient Customs service.

Despite the change to direct management in the Customs, the Excise continued to be farmed. By now the annual yield had increased to over £400,000. In June 1674, when the lease came up for renewal once again, agreement was made for a total farm of the Excise. The sums involved were now so great that the local landowners could no longer compete with the wealthy London merchants. Thus for the first time the Excise was under the full control of a group of London financiers and merchants, headed by George and Samuel Dashwood, members of an influential City family and supported by the large London brewers. The amount required to be advanced annually had now reached a quarter of a million pounds; the farmers received 6 per cent interest on this sum, which in addition to their various 'management' fees and allowances made the whole enterprise very profitable.

Nevertheless, there were very many rumours circulating of the 'extensive frauds by the farmers to the great detriment of the King's Revenue'. It was therefore decided to set up a commission in 1676 to examine the problem. As a result of this inquiry, extra accounting controls were imposed on the farmers. Ashmole as Comptroller was required to check all the ledgers and accounts monthly, and four deputy controllers were appointed to inspect the local administration and submit independent accounts to the Commissioners of the amount of revenue collected. A new departure was made, with the secondment of a cashier from the Navy Office to inspect the current cash accounts and report directly to the Treasury. The man appointed must have impressed the Treasury, because later he was appointed Customs Collector at Rochester. For the first time with these extra controls the Commissioners were in a position to know the exact amount of Excise that was collected.

This closer control on the accounts of the farmers resulted in them exhorting their officers to become more strict and exact in the collection of the duty. Evidence of this closer enforcement can be seen in the wave of very strong opposition to the farmers and their officers, which reached a climax in these years. There were reports of riots and disturbances up and down the country. The farmers complained to the Treasury about 'the abuses offered to their officers' and the lack of support from the Justices of the Peace. There were incidents in virtually every county and most large towns. In the Forest of Dean, for example, 'persons were animating the people from paying the Excise . . . and officers threatened to be driven out of the Forest, in fear of their life'. The Treasury sent letters to Mayors and Justices reminding them of their duty to assist the Excise officers, and judges going out on circuit were specially instructed 'to put down these Excise tumults'.

The opposition to the Excise was slowly declining, and by 1681, as the date for the renewal of the farm came close, it was intimated that the King was considering 'to take the Excise in his own hands'. This he in fact decided to do, but was not prepared to put it into action immediately. A further lease of two years only was offered to the farmers, who gladly agreed to the new terms. It would therefore be midsummer 1683 before the Excise would come into direct management.

Certainly there had been growing suspicion that the farmers' administration and control was becoming less efficient. The revenue had not improved sufficiently, considering the increased trade and prosperity of the country. In 1682 the farmers were directed 'to examine what officers employed in the Excise have manifested disloyalty to the King and are not capable for their duty and forthwith dismiss them'. With the successful example of the new Customs Commission, it is not surprising that the Treasury advised the establishment of direct control in the Excise.

The new Commissioners were appointed, like those of the Customs, by Royal Letters Patent, and took over full control with effect from 24 June 1683. Four of the existing Commissioners, Sir Denny Ashburnham, Francis Parry, Robert Huntingdon and Charles Davenant, were retained, and were joined by two of the Excise farmers, Felix Calverd and John Friend—both brewers—and Nathaniel Hornby, a goldsmith-banker. They were granted, unlike the Customs, powers to appoint officers and sub-commissioners, pay salaries and incidental expenses, enter ships to search for brandy, and generally to proceed in all business left unfinished by their predecessors. For these duties they received a salary of £1,000 per annum, which was £200 less than the Customs Commissioners were now receiving. However, they had the satisfaction of far greater control over the service, with less opportunity for Treasury 'interference' in the general management of the Excise.

They took over the existing officers with very few changes at first. However, they did feel it necessary to improve the control of the local administration, and, following the example of the Customs, appointed a 'general rider' and two riding supervisors to inspect the country Excise. Within a short space of time they too were involved in tours of inspection. Slowly over the next few years they weeded out the inefficient officers, and carefully replaced them with their own selected men.

The Country Excise was divided into thirty-nine areas which were called collections. These areas were loosely based on county boundaries. Wales was divided into four ridings, East, West, North and Middle. Each collection was headed by a collector, with a number of districts under the control of supervisors. The officers—or gaugers, as they were still called—were normally centred in the market towns, with some of the larger towns having more than one officer. The area in a town was called a 'division', whereas the country outside was called an 'out-ride'. In London the officers were grouped into brewery and distillery gaugers. Each gauger was responsible for a small number of brewers or distillers in his area. This system of concentration of staff was a feature of the reorganization of the Excise in the 1960s.

The build-up of an efficient organization commenced with an increase of salary from £40 to £50 per annum for gaugers. The increase was stated 'to encourage the better collection of duty and discourage frauds'. It is interesting to note that the London gaugers received £2 extra, an early example of what is now termed 'London weighting'. A system of training new entrants was introduced. This was undertaken by the older and more experienced officers, who were allowed to charge each pupil 30s. for 'instruction in the art of gauging'. Promotion by merit was introduced, and it was possible for officers to reach the highest grade of collector by recommendation and reports.

In 1687 a 'Charity Fund' was established to support 'old and disabled' officers. This was the earliest example of a superannuation scheme in the Civil Service; it predated a similar Customs fund by about sixty years. A deduction of 3d. in the £1 was made, and a pension of £10 was granted to gaugers. The only conditions were that the officer had to have served at least seven years and not be in receipt of any income equal to the pension. These improvements in salary, pension, and training produced what Davenant, the Excise Commissioner, was proud to call 'such a set of men as perhaps no prince had ever better employed in his revenue'.

The Board of Excise had their Head Office in the City of London. In the late 1670s they had moved from the 'small house' in Aldersgate Street and obtained the lease of Cockaigne House in Broad Street. The property belonged to Sir Eliab Harvey, brother of Sir William Harvey, the famous physician. In fact Ashmole records that his office in Broad Street 'had been the chamber of the Doctor where he dyed'. The Excise seemed particularly attracted to Broad Street: their first office had been set up in Lord Cottingham's mansion there, and they were destined to return to the street later in the next century.

In some of the earliest surviving Excise records there is an account dated 1683 which records the monthly payments made by the Excise on behalf of the King. Besides the various sums paid to bankers and the 'secret service', there are regular monthly payments of £500 to Mistress Eleanor Gwynn, sometimes described as Mistress Nelly or Noll. It would appear that she could not even manage on this sum, and frequently asked for an advance. Her annual payment of £6,000 was at a time when the Excise officers were paid £50 per year, and out of this sum had to provide for a horse!

Within a year of the new Excise Board being formed the collection of hearth-money was placed under their control. The duty on hearths and stoves had been introduced in 1662, at a rate of 2s. for each hearth. It was intended to make up the deficit of revenue due under the King's settlement. The duty was very unpopular, even more so than the Excise. One of the main reasons for its unpopularity was that the Act gave the officers (or chimneymen, as they were called) powers to enter all houses, to ensure that the correct number of hearths had been declared. Previously, like the Excise, this duty had been farmed, but with very little success. It was hoped that bringing the collection under direct control would improve the yield. However, it was not destined to survive for very long, being abolished by William and Mary in the first year of their reign. The reason given for its repeal: 'in order to erect a lasting monument of their Majesties goodness in every hearth in the Kingdom'.

During October 1688, while the preparations for the invasion of the country by William of Orange were in hand, Samuel Pepys, Secretary of the Navy, issued a letter to all the collectors at the out-ports. It instructed them to place an embargo on all sailings from English ports to prevent assistance being rendered to the 'foreign invader'.

On 5 November 1688 (which happened to be a Custom House holiday) an agitated letter came from the Customs officer at Brixham to his Collector at Dartmouth. He reported that about 300 Dutch sailing vessels had come into Torbay, many of them landing soldiers. The Collector had already forwarded the following report to Pepys:

> This morning, being very hazey, foggie and full of raine, cleared up about 9 of the clock, at which time appeared the Dutch fleet, consisting of about four hundred or five hundred sails as neere as we can guess, all standing to the Eastward with the wind at W.S.W., a moderate gale.
>
> The capital ships are off Torbay about four leagues from the shore, the small shipps and fly-boats, between the Start and Dartmouth about a league and a half offe.

This letter was the first confirmed report of the landing of the Prince of Orange. Pepys received the report on the evening of the 6th, which considering the distance involved was a remarkable postal feat.

By the 20th of the month 'The Excise officers in the West' were instructed to go to the Commanders-in-Chief of the King's forces 'to guide them to any places whither they are to march, being well acquainted with the course of the country'. The officers in Cheshire and Lancashire 'were to take great care that the King's money do not fall into the hands of any persons in the insurrection'.

In the uncertain times of the Interregnum several merchants were unsure to whom they should pay their Excise duty. They settled on a compromise, and decided to collect it themselves and place the money 'on trust' for the Crown, until the matters of state were finally settled. The 'trust money' was deposited with a London financier, and even as late as 1731 over £18,700 was still held 'on trust'. (In fact this sum was never handed over to the Excise Department.)

The outcome of the 'Glorious Revolution' was virtually settled by 23 December, when James II left the country with almost indecent haste. Tradition has it that he made his escape from Rochester in a Custom House vessel. Certainly there were three Customs vessels—or smacks, as they were called—stationed in the vicinity, but there is no evidence in the Customs records to substantiate the story.

In February 1689 William issued a public order that there would be a cessation of all offices until their beneficiaries were authorized to act by fresh powers. As a result of this order two new commissions were appointed in April. Only one of the Customs Commissioners was retained, the control of the Board passing to a group of London financiers, Sir Robert Clayton being the most well known. The Excise Board fared little better, two Commissioners being retained. The new Excise Board did not last long, and was changed in October of the same year, leaving no pre-1688 Commissioner in post. Both Boards had the salaries reduced by £200 per year, although the Excise received an allowance of £300 for 'special services'. The old Commissioners came to realize, as had Pepys, that strong political and religious convictions

were not compatible with a long Civil Service career. The exception to this
rule was Ashmole, who had survived as Comptroller through four reigns, and
who died in post in 1692 at the age of seventy-five.

Even by May 1689 there was obviously still much uncertainty in the
service about the political situation—so much so that the Commissioners
issued the following letter to all collectors:

> Whereas we hear false rumour has been spread abroad upon the revolution, a
> General Change is designed by us of all the officers in all ports. We desire you to
> acquaint them of your port that it is not the intention to make any such change
> or any further than what we shall find just and necessary for the King's Service.

At the time of the Revolution the Customs duties amounted to £788,000,
with the Excise slightly lower at £733,000. Both revenues had greatly
developed and increased since the days of the farming. The revenue system
which had been established was, despite many faults, well devised and
administered. It would not change greatly over the next hundred years, and
many historians consider that its development and success was one of the
greatest achievements to come out of the troublesome times of the late
seventeenth century.

The most immediate result of the Revolution was that the country was
drawn into war with France. There was also a need to maintain a large army
in Ireland to prevent invasion by James. Such policies demanded a large
amount of revenue, and naturally led to a vast increase in both Customs and
Excise duties.

High import duties were placed on 'luxury' goods, such as silks, wines,
brandy, lace and spices, and a few years later additional duties were imposed
on French goods. These new and high duties ushered in the smuggling age:
the success of the smugglers reduced the anticipated yield in revenue, which
resulted in further increases being imposed, which only gave a further
incentive to smuggling—a vicious circle. By 1695 an additional duty of 25
per cent was placed on French goods.

Parliament was still forced to look elsewhere for extra revenue, and the
increases in the existing Excise duties were only a partial solution. The duty
on beer was doubled, and a new duty imposed on 'low wines' (spirits
extracted from the first distillation). However, the feature of the period was
the number and variety of articles taxed. Duties were placed on salt, glass,
paper, tobacco pipes, malt, stone bottles, leather, hackney carriages, and
windows. Perhaps absurdity was reached with a registration duty on births,
marriages and deaths. The rates were carefully graded according to social
position; for example, commoners paid four shillings for a funeral, whereas
in the case of a Duke the duty was fifty pounds. Although the Excise officers
were not directly involved in the collection of this last impost, they were
requested 'to give every assistance to the Surveyors and Inspectors for the
ascertainment and improvement of the Revenue'.

Some of the new duties were of a temporary nature, but the majority survived for many years. Most of the new duties were placed under the control of the Excise Commissioners, and were to form the basis of Excise work for the next hundred and fifty years. The duties on malt, paper, glass and leather brought the officers in contact with a much greater section of the trading community, and complicated their work because of the highly technical nature of the new excisable goods. In the case of salt, hackney carriages and windows, new commissions were established, thus affording extra opportunities for further Treasury patronage. The duty on windows 'replaced' the infamous hearth tax. It was slightly less unpopular than its predecessor, the officers having no powers of entry—the number of windows could be counted from outside. However, many householders bricked up windows rather than pay the tax, and several instances of this can still be seen in old houses.

It is not surprising to find that there was an increase in the Excise staff to cope with this extra work. New collections were formed, based on county boundaries, and a system of general supervisors to cover the whole of the country was established. For the first time ever, Excise duties exceeded a million pounds. One could truthfully say that the Excise Service had come of age.

The method of collection of Excise hardly changed for the next two hundred years. The collectors went on the 'rounds' of their collection eight times in the year. They held 'sitting days' at each of the market towns, when the sittings were held in the Excise office, which was almost always an inn. The innkeeper was called the 'office-keeper', and received a 'deputation' from the Commissioners to receive entries and notices submitted by the Excise traders. The traders were required to attend these sittings to pay the duties which had accrued in the previous weeks. The amount of duty to be paid had been calculated by the officers, who visited the trader's premises regularly to check the amount of goods produced in the period. The trader was issued with a voucher stating the amount of duty payable, which was presented to the collector at the sitting. In 1702 a system of permits was introduced to prevent the illicit removal of goods liable to duty. In the early days these permits were issued to traders at the sittings.

One of the many problems faced by Excise collectors was the safeguarding of the duty which they collected on their rounds. Although they were normally armed with pistols, and were attended by a clerk or a supernumerary to carry the money bag or portmanteau, they were frequently attacked and robbed by highwaymen, and in one instance a collector was murdered. The situation became so serious that they were expressly forbidden by the Board 'to ride between dusk and dawn'. This was not so much for their protection as to ensure they were aware in which 'hundred' they had been robbed, because each of these administrative divisions was itself responsible for recompensing travellers for any money stolen within its bounds.

Even if the collectors managed to arrive back safely to their office, they had the further complication of sending the money to the Head Office in

London. Since the early days of the Excise, collectors had been encouraged to use bills of exchange—basically an early form of cheque. Frequently they were forced to resort to obtaining bills from merchants whose businesses failed before the clearance of the bill, or from drovers and itinerant traders who sometimes absconded without clearing the bill in London. In 1696 a notice was fixed to the Excise Head Office door, to the effect that such defaulters would be prosecuted.

The Customs had none of these problems, for the duty was paid directly to the Custom House and, in the absence of safes, lodged in a large chest, which was known as the King's chest. The design of these wrought-iron chests was based on the strong-boxes used by the Hanseatic League. Their main feature was the very complicated lock mechanism, located under the lid, which had a spring of great power operating up to eleven bolts. Some of these chests are still preserved by the department. Much of the duty collected was either paid out directly to support Army and Naval forces stationed in and around the port or was disbursed as salaries or expenses. What money remained was normally transferred to London by convoy, strongly guarded by troops.

The relations between Customs and Excise officers were not at all cordial, especially at the out-ports; there Excise officers were employed to collect the Excise duty on imported goods, mainly spirits. There were continual fierce disputes as to the rights of reward for seized goods, and whether Excise officers could board ships to rummage for smuggled articles. There were many instances of attacks by both sets of officers, and on one occasion an Exciseman was thrown overboard by the Customs officers. This instance occurred in Newcastle, and was perhaps due to the choleric nature of the Collector, Henry Brabant, who was dismissed from his post 'for associating with papists and other abuses'. Brabant demanded satisfaction from Sir John Lowther, the Commissioner who 'had turned him out'. A report of the duel suggested that 'they went in a hackney coach to the park and fought, Sir John was wounded in the shoulder and disarmed. The other escaped in being in great misdemeanour to challenge a privy councillor.' Brabant was taken 'prisoner in the King's Bench' and was forced to surrender his other Customs patent post of 'Wine taster in London Port'!

The situation between the two services so deteriorated that the Treasury was forced to intervene, and called the two Boards together to discuss the problems. (This was the first example of co-operation between the two revenue services, although in later years they would meet frequently to discuss various common problems, such as smuggling.) As a result of this first meeting certain procedures were established concerning rummaging, seizure of smuggled goods and exchange of information. Although both Boards issued instructions to their officers, they were not adhered to, and the rivalry continued almost to the amalgamation of both services.

It was during this period that both services were first employed on what is now termed 'agency work'. Broadly speaking, this is the employment of staff on duties for another official body or department, not directly concerned with the main functions of both departments—the collection of revenue. Agency work figures prominently in the history of both services, and nowadays covers a wide range of activities.

In 1693 the Excise were called upon to provide statistics for the Secretary of State for War. Because they had officers in every market town, and their activities covered villages, they were asked to compile a return of the number of beds and the extent of stabling facilities in all inns and taverns in England and Wales. This return, which became an annual task, was 'for the more equal distribution of forces'.

Both Customs and Excise officers were involved in the administration of the dreaded press-gang. The officers were empowered to pay 12d. per man as imprest money, 6d. per man per day to maintain them 'til sufficient number be gotten together', and 8d. per day when 'they are marching to the place of embarkation'. The officers were enjoined to ensure that 'no decrepid, crazie or unhealthy men were taken but such that are young and healthy with able bodies fitt for service'. For the whole time the press-gang system was in operation, the financial administration was undertaken by both services, on behalf of the Admiralty.

The collection of light dues dates from 1696. It was during that year that Trinity House agreed with the mercantile community to construct a lighthouse on the now famous Eddystone rock. In return the merchants agreed to pay one penny per ton on all vessels entering and leaving a port. During the eighteenth century, as the number of lighthouses grew, there were many separate accounts for the various lights. The collection of the light dues was entrusted to the collectors at the various Custom Houses around the coast, the receipts being transferred to the Trinity House. However, in the nineteenth century, in some of the larger ports, the work was undertaken by patentee clerks for light dues. These were allowed a seat in the Customs long room.

Also in 1696, the Government created a new Commission for Trade and the Plantations, which was the forerunner of the Board of Trade. One of the duties of this Commission 'was to enquire, examine into, and take account of the state and condition of the general trade of England'. To assist them in this work the Customs Commissioners were called upon to supply an annual return of imports and exports showing the balance of trade. It was decided, in view of the amount of work involved, that there should be appointed an officer of 'Skill and Experience to be known as the Inspector-General'. The person selected for the post was William Culliford, who had been in the service for over thirty years, and had been a Commissioner for a short spell in 1688. So successfully did he establish the office, and the principles of trade statistics, that in 1702 he was rewarded with a seat on the Board again. The collection of trade statistics has been continuous since 1696, and is now the responsibility of the Statistical Office of the department, based at Southend.

It was at this time that the Commissioners took notice of the numerous complaints concerning the lack of technical knowledge of their officers. They issued an order that no officer above the rank of tidesman should be employed until he had attended in a temporary capacity to receive the necessary practical instruction. In this matter of training certain instruction ports were approved, mainly the larger ports like London, Bristol, Hull, Whitehaven and Southampton, and during the next forty years the formal training was extended to fifteen large ports. It was stated that no collectors should be appointed 'unless bred to Clerkship and other business in the customes', but this order was universally ignored, the posts of collector and controller being filled by 'Country Fox-hunters, Bankrupt Merchants and Officers of the Army and Navy—without the least knowledge of the business of the Revenue'. It would be nearly a hundred years (till 1787), before they were required to be formally trained for six months before taking up their appointment.

With the large increase in trade with the Colonies—or Plantations, as they were then called—in 1696 the Customs Commissioners were given far greater control over the Customs officers overseas. In 1672 a special plantation duty had been introduced, not so much for augmenting the revenue as to prevent direct trade with Europe. In the early days the amount of duty collected was small, barely enough to cover the expenses of maintaining the Customs staff. However, the West Indian trade, especially in sugar, had greatly increased, and the West Indian merchants now formed a powerful lobby in Parliament. The number of collectors was increased, and considerable improvements were made in the conditions of service. From this date until the early nineteenth century the control of the Customs in the Colonies was vested with the Commissioners in London.

During the last decade of the seventeenth century the Excise passed through very troublesome times. There were serious accusations of extensive frauds and abuses throughout the country. Samuel Dashwood, the late Excise farmer, and now Collector for Norfolk, was found guilty of 'widespread frauds' and dismissed from his post. A supervisor in Wales detailed many irregularities, which implicated two of the Commissioners. The worst area was the London Brewery, where it was considered that 'The King is defrauded by about £50,000 per year'. Here collusion between the brewers and officers was thought to be widespread.

Certainly the yield from the Excise on beer had drastically decreased; however, the reason for the fall in revenue could more likely be attributed to the very high duty, which had caused a reduction in consumption, rather than gross mismanagement. This is somewhat borne out by the reduction in the numbers of brewers and brewing victuallers, with a compensatory large increase in home brewing (which was not liable to Excise), which occurred in these years.

Nevertheless, the Excise Commissioners heeded the complaints and took steps to improve the efficiency of the service. They were mainly concerned with the London Brewery. John Danvers, a recently appointed Commissioner, and Thomas Everard, a promoted officer, were selected as 'the reforming officials to root out the frauds and abuses in the Brewers'. They had a very drastic effect on the London Brewery officers, Everard being the direct cause of the first industrial action in the Civil Service.

In August 1695 thirty supervisors and officers of the London Brewery met 'in a clubbe neer Holborne' to discuss the 'intolerable conditions under the new regime'. They decided that they would not work under Everard, and 'laid down their commissions', which was tantamount to a strike. So seriously did the Treasury view this action that they called several of the officers to explain in person their reasons for the 'strike'. Edward Dennison, a supervisor, and apparently the spokesman of the group, placed most of the blame on Everard's reforms. He had moved officers from one division to another without thought of their place of residence, the hours of attendance had been greatly extended, supervisors had been demoted and officers from the Country Excise had been brought in and 'put over them and did not understand the business and cannot even take gauges'. Finally, Everard had 'greatly abused the officers with foul oaths'.

All the 'striking' officers were dismissed, and furthermore were informed that they would never again be employed in the Excise. For his services Everard was made Commissioner, but for the officers also there is a happy ending to the story. In 1699, because of the vast increases in the Excise duties and the shortage of suitable recruits, all the offending officers were re-employed. Dennison was subsequently promoted to surveyor-general, and in 1705 was rewarded with £50 for 'discovering frauds in the distillery at St Katherine's'.

Perhaps more serious were the complaints that the Excise was full of avowed Jacobites (supporters of the Stuart cause). Many officers were removed for disloyalty to the King, invariably on evidence provided by their fellows. The Commissioners were not immune from the accusations. Sir John Friend, who had been a Commissioner from 1683 to 1689, was implicated in a conspiracy to overthrow the King, and was beheaded for treason. His brewery was sold, and the proceeds went to the Crown. Everard and Danvers were accused of Jacobite views by fellow-Commissioners, and were brought before the Treasury Commissioners to refute the allegations. Both managed to survive, while their accusers were removed from the Board.

The Excise Service was in disarray, and deeply divided by the internal struggles. It is not surprising to find that in 1700 the Treasury seriously considered several proposals to farm the Excise. Francis Parry, one of the recently deposed Commissioners, headed one of the groups of prospective farmers. The discussions on the farm lasted for about three months, each group promising 'to improve the Revenue' but requiring too many allowances and too large 'management fees'. They were also not prepared to advance the considerable amounts required by the Treasury. The King took an active part in all the discussions, and by the middle of June it was reported that 'it was now too late to think anymore about the proposals to farm and it was absolutely necessary to have good Commissioners, that will indisputably improve the Revenue with their skill and Industry'. The incumbent Board had successfully defended their management, and the last serious attempt to farm the Excise had failed. The question of farming was never again seriously proposed for either service.

There was no shortage of recruits for either the Customs or the Excise; despite the hazardous nature of the work and the general unpopularity of their calling, life was not too unattractive. Compared with similar posts, revenue officers were relatively well paid. With the possible exception of officers of the armed forces, it would be difficult to find a trade or profession with salary and prospects comparable with the Excise, with the added attraction of a pension scheme—unique in those days. The posts in the Customs were especially lucrative owing to the system of fees, which were now considerable because of the large increase in trade. In addition, officers of both services were exempt from direct taxation, their assessments being paid by the departments. (Unfortunately, this no longer holds good!)

Although there were no formal leave arrangements, both Boards were very liberal in their approval of absences caused by sickness or 'private affairs'. The Customs had the advantage of forty-four Custom House holidays each year, in addition to all Sundays. Both services demanded security ranging from £200 to £2,000, which effectively barred entrants without land or wealthy connection. They therefore attracted the sons of wealthy maltsters, brewers or merchants and the more substantial tradesmen. Frequently, although entrants were following a family tradition, many of their relations were already in the revenue services.

The more complicated work of the Excise, with the diversity of manufacturing processes to be controlled, demanded a higher standard of education from its entrants than did the Customs. Applicants were required to understand 'the first four rules of arithmetick and write with a fair hand'. Their application had to be supported by a person of substance, and they had to obtain training in the art of gauging, normally from the local officer. Thomas Everard, the Excise Commissioner, had written a book on gauging, which ran into many editions and was the precursor of similar works on gauging in the eighteenth century. He also ingeniously devised a slide rule, based on a logarithmic scale, which enabled the officers to solve a multitude of gauging problems. This rule was used in the Excise for over a hundred and fifty years. Perhaps as a result of Everard's book, the Customs officers were ordered in 1707 'to make themselves masters of the art of gauge'.

Certainly both departments were endeavouring to improve the technical knowledge of their officers. The Excise, as new duties were imposed—for example, leather and glass—looked for their new recruits from people 'well versed in the business'. The Customs also recommended to the Treasury persons with knowledge in the shipping trade, and collectors frequently employed their sons as 'supernumerary clerks' at the age of twelve years, in order that they might gain experience of Customs business, thus obtaining a more lucrative post when they were older. The Treasury offered 'two professors of book keeping' to the Customs Commissioners to assist with their accounts!

The most important event of Queen Anne's reign, as far as both departments were concerned, was the Union with Scotland. Early in 1706 commissioners from each country were appointed to examine the problems involved in such a Union, and to agree the terms of the treaty. The committee resolved 'That there be the same Customs and Excise and all other taxes and the same prohibitions, restrictions and regulations of trade throughout the United Kingdom of Great Britain.'

When the committee looked at the figures from the two countries they found that the English Customs averaged £1,350,000 and the Excise £950,000, whereas the Scottish revenues, which were farmed to 'tacksmen', amounted to only £30,000 and £35,000 respectively. Much of the English revenue was charged to the large and quickly growing National Debt, and it would therefore be grossly unfair to saddle the Scottish people with a share of this burden. A scheme of 'equivalents' was arrived at, whereby Scotland would receive a cash payment of £398,085, with a further instalment in seven years' time, to balance the increased taxation due to the Union.

A further complication arose with the various Excise duties; some were of only a temporary nature, and it would be pointless to impose them in Scotland for their short duration. However, the main duties on liquors were introduced, and straightway the different Scottish measures caused considerable confusion. The other main Excise duty, on malt, was not to be imposed until seven years after the Union, when its introduction led to riots which threatened the latter's stability.

Separate Boards of both Customs and Excise were established in Scotland in June 1707, on much the same lines as the English Boards. Many of the Commissioners and Head Office staff in Edinburgh were recruited from England; also, officers from both English services were sent to Scotland as experts to establish a unified system of collection. The more numerous were the English Excise officers, who were stationed throughout Scotland, and the attempts of these officers to impose the English system of control caused considerable trouble, and their presence was a source of bitterness for many years. The term gauger was used in a more derogatory sense in Scotland than elsewhere.

During the greater part of Queen Anne's reign the country was involved in expensive wars on the Continent; the cost in 1709–10 being over £13 million. Such a large expenditure demanded increased taxation. Excise duties were introduced on soap, candles, hops, calicoes, dice and playing-cards. The last-named duty survived the longest, not being abolished until 1960. Cards were originally liable to a stamp duty of 6d. per pack, the revenue stamp being embossed on the Ace of Spades, and forging this stamp was an offence punishable by death. Because the 'duty card' was different to the touch, it lent itself to card-sharping. The mode of payment was therefore changed to a duty-paid wrapper, and later to a label.

The most unpopular duty introduced at this time was that on candles, which were an essential part of life for both rich and poor alike. The duty of 1*d*. per pound on tallow candles (wax candles were 8*d*. per pound) fell heavily on the poorer sections of the population, especially those in the towns and cities. The way in which the Excise Department tackled this new duty gives an interesting insight on eighteenth-century administration, and shows some relation to present-day controls.

All chandlers were required to register their business, as were retailers of candles. The Excise officers were requested to make their own list of chandlers and retailers in their area and send it to Head Office in London, where a comparison was made with those registered. There proved to be over 4,000 manufacturers and almost 6,000 retailers. The chandlers were compelled to notify the Excise before starting a course of candle-making, and were limited to prescribed hours of working. All the manufacturing vessels were locked by Crown locks, which meant that the officer was compelled to attend early in the morning and late at night to lock and unlock the vessels. The sale of candles was prohibited other than by a registered retailer, and private manufacture at home was allowed on payment of a fee of 1*s*. per head of the family. The Excise had even made inquiries in the mines to 'ensure that the revenue may not suffer in that direction'.

The extra officers for the new duty were recruited from within the trade as specialists, most of the new posts established at the Head Office going to men 'well versed in the candle business'. Much of the work in the country was undertaken by malt officers, released after the malting season had finished. The new duty averaged over £135,000 per year, and the cost of collection was estimated at £3,500 (or little over $2\frac{1}{2}$ per cent). This was a very low figure judged by the standards of the day, and demonstrates the efficient organization of the duty.

In less than forty years both services had endured and survived the traumas occasioned by the change from farming to direct collection, with all the associated problems. They had developed into recognizable government departments with a considerable amount of central control. During the next hundred years they would face even greater problems and many reforms, before emerging as fully fledged departments of state in the modern sense.

CHAPTER THREE

Owlers and Free Traders

For the majority of people the most interesting and exciting aspects of the history of the Customs and Excise are those relating to smuggling. The origins of the illicit trade can be traced to the first imposition of Customs duties and the formation of a system of officials to collect them. The word smuggling is probably derived from the Low German *smuggeln*, although cognate forms are found in all the Scandinavian languages—for example, *smuga*=hidey-hole. The smugglers themselves never used the word (which in any event dates only from the seventeenth century); they considered they were 'free traders'. Even at this period, however, the views of the authorities were somewhat different:

> (1661) Proclamation 9 Aug. A sort of leud people called Smuckellors, never heard of before the late disordered times, who make it their trade . . . to steal and defraud His Majesty of His Customs.

The smugglers and the majority of the public considered the revenue fair game, and in no way thought their activities criminal. As Charles Lamb wrote in the early nineteenth century, 'I like the smuggler, he is the only honest thief. He robs nothing but the Revenue, an abstraction I never greatly cared about.' An old Deal boatman recalling his old smuggling days summed up the general attitude to the trade: 'Good days then, when a boatman might smuggle honest, didn't go astealing and wasn't afraid to die for his principles.' I would venture to suggest that even today many people with a high standard of conduct in other affairs see no great harm in smuggling, and often recount tales with obvious delight of passing through the green channels with the extra cigarettes or bottle.

Over the years many artists and writers have perpetuated the romantic view of smuggling. They have conjured up pictures of moonlit caves, hidden caves and secret tunnels, lanterns and lights flashing on cliff-tops, ponies laden with tea, brandy and tobacco trotting up dark lanes, led by jolly 'gentlemen' with eye-patches and wearing striped jerseys. The revenue men have invariably been depicted as taciturn and cold-hearted, natural opposition for the daring free traders. Many towns proudly boast their connections with smuggling, their guide-books abounding with 'typical smuggling bays and famous old smuggling inns'.

However picturesque and romantic these images may appear, they were very far from the truth. For over a hundred years, from the late seventeenth up until the early nineteenth century, smuggling was a major crime conducted on a colossal scale, the execution of which was violent, ruthless and bloody in the extreme, even when judged by the brutal standards of the time. The smugglers were encouraged and financed by the local gentry, protected by compliant magistrates, condoned by the clergy, aided and abetted by the ordinary people and at times facilitated by venal revenue officers. The illegal trade extended throughout the country and permeated every level of society; the smuggled goods found their way into virtually all households, from the most lowly to the highest.

The earliest references to smuggling are to be found in the latter half of the thirteenth century, due in no small measure to the imposition in 1275 of the 'new custom' on exported wool. This new and high export duty (equivalent to 40 per cent *ad valorem*), and the presence of officials at the ports to collect the duty, gave the merchants the incentive to avoid payment of duty on their shipments. Unlike later smuggling, this early free trade took the form of the illegal exportation of wool.

In the same year as the new duties were introduced a group of Florentine merchants were charged with the illegal export of over 4,000 sacks of wool. They pleaded guilty, and were apparently quite content to pay the fine of £2,200 imposed by the King, providing they could continue to trade. The earliest known smuggler was operating at this time. He was Henry of Arderne, and appeared to be a wool merchant of some importance. Not only did he trade in his own right but he also 'arranged' shipments for fellow-merchants. His various activities came under suspicion, and he was watched very closely—so much so that he felt it best to leave the country. In 1297 he left for Flanders, but he was not safe there, being eventually captured to stand trial in the Exchequer Court. He pleaded guilty to several smuggling offences, and was sent to Fleet Prison. After paying a ransom fee of £200 in instalments, he returned to the wool trade, and no doubt smuggling, for in 1302 he was imprisoned in Ghent 'arrested with his merchandise'.

During the fourteenth century the smuggling activities of the Lombard merchants in London were so extensive that references to 'their frauds' are to be found in monastic manuscripts. It was estimated that their nefarious trade had caused a loss to the King of over £3,000. They were all imprisoned in the Tower. One of the leaders, Nicholas Sardouche, had all his goods confiscated until he paid the fine of £2,000. He had been involved in 'wool and divers merchandise frauds', but was also concerned in the illegal export of gold and bullion.

In 1374 Geoffrey Chaucer, then Comptroller in London Port, received the sum of £71 4s. 6d. as his share of the proceeds of the sale of wool forfeited by John of Kent, for exporting it without payment of the duty. This seizure reward was a princely sum, considering that Chaucer's salary only amounted to £16 13s. 4d. per annum. At about this time there was great concern over import smuggling; the Mayor of Bristol was directed in 1387 'to investigate English smugglers entering the Severn and running goods into Wales'. Three years later it was reported that there was extensive smuggling around the Isle of Wight and 'the unguarded coasts of North West England'. Investigations were extended to Devon and Cornwall.

During the next forty years the laws relating to smuggling were strengthened. In 1404 stringent penalties were imposed 'for the prevention of frauds in the Customs committed by Merchants smuggling wools in empty casks and stealing abroad with cargoes un-customed'. By 1432 it was a felony to export wools except from the lawful ports. These were the various staple towns and ports, which had been appointed in 1353, and had a monopoly of the wool trade. The towns had varied between Antwerp, Bruges, Middleburg and St Omer, although by the end of the fourteenth century the Company of Staplers had set up their headquarters at Calais.

From the early fourteenth century the recorded instances of smuggling greatly diminished for a period. It would be unwise to attribute the apparent decrease in smuggling to either the increased penalties or the greater vigilance of the officers and the merchants. The port of Southampton was a good example. It was an important medieval port, trading with the Continent and Mediterranean, and was the outlet for the staple town of Winchester. In 1333 the tronours (weighers of wool) were dismissed for 'those more diligent in the service of the King'. In 1345 three officers were dismissed and fined heavily for allowing certain evasions. By 1398 the situation was so bad that a full inquiry was made into the frauds and abuses in the port. Nicholas De Mordenant, the Collector, was found guilty of allowing goods to be shipped without payment of the Customs. Thirty years later John Pole, the Searcher, was convicted on various frauds. Again, in 1444, another inquiry was set up to examine the Italian and Spanish trade, and heavy fines were imposed on both merchants and officials. There is no reason to suggest that Southampton was worse than any other port in the kingdom.

Another factor to be borne in mind in the apparent decline in smuggling was the use made by merchants of the small ports and harbours, where there were no Customs staff to bother or hinder them. For many years Bristol merchants had used Chepstow and other South Wales ports for the discharge and loading of goods. Many ports also claimed 'ancient liberties', which they considered exempted them from certain duties. The merchants of the Cinque Ports argued that these privileges predated the imposition of the new duties. When the King refused to renew these privileges they took the matter into their own hands. This spirit of independence led to open smuggling, and it is not coincidental that these ports later became the centres of intense

Two fine examples from the collection of coats of arms held by the Customs and Excise. *Top:* Charles II *Bottom:* William and Mary   *HMSO*

King's Lynn Custom House, built 1683
HMSO

Below: Poole Custom House, built
1813–14   *HMSO*

Right: Old Preventive Station near
Margate (p. 104)   *HMSO*

Below right: Excise Head Office,
Broad Street (p. 66)   *HMSO*

Notice at Custom House, Yarmouth (1809)   *HMSO*

King's Chest at Customs and Excise Museum   *HMSO*

'Quarantine' or 'Plague' bible   *HMSO*

smuggling activity. Ports like Berwick and Queenborough claimed such 'rights' as late as 1575.

During the sixteenth century, with the introduction of the Book of Rates and the consequential increase in all duties, evasion of duty became a more attractive and profitable enterprise. Greater supervision was imposed on the Customs staff, and they were encouraged to exert their authority. The effect of the increased vigilance of the officers can be seen in a riot at Lyme Regis in 1576; most of the vessels there were suspected of smuggling, and the keenness and efficiency of a new officer caused a riot. The mayor had to intervene to prevent bloodshed. In the same year John Vaughan, the Customer at Milford Haven, hired a gang to make seizures. He reported, 'I am so hated and contested in words that I cannot execute my office for fear of danger.' One collector admitted in 1596 that there were so many things wrong with his port that he could not hope to reform it even if he had five hundred men.

The West Country ports were particularly difficult to control. The independent Elizabethan 'sea-dogs' were not only active in piracy but in smuggling as well. Men like Sir John Gilbert, Richard Grenville and Richard Hakluyt used ports like Dartmouth, St Ives, Exeter and Penzance as virtual free ports. Their smuggling exploits were impossible to control, as they had the encouragement and support of the Court. As long as recognized trade provided the Exchequer with a reasonable profit the task of tackling the problem of smuggling was left to another day.

Considering its subsequent importance in the smuggling trade, tobacco was at first lightly taxed following its introduction into the country in the 1560s. It was James I who termed it the 'pernicious weed—abomination of the devil', and attempted to tax it out of existence. He raised the duty from 2d. per lb to 6s. 8d. per lb. This step put legal tobacco out of the reach of the general public, and gave a great incentive to smuggling. Although the high duty was later reduced, some form of government control was attempted. It was decreed that all tobacco must bear a government stamp. By 1625 grocers and retailers in London were complaining of 'the amount of tobacco which is uncustomed, for sale in the various ale-houses'. It was being sold for 1½d. per lb—much less than the duty on the goods. When restrictions were placed on Spanish tobacco smuggling increased, the tobacco being landed in Jersey and Guernsey for onward shipping in small vessels to England and Wales.

The illegal export of wool, or 'owling', was still a constant problem. The term 'owling', and 'owlers' for the wool smugglers, is said to derive from the latter working at night, although another source suggests that the word is a corruption of 'woolers'. Except for isolated instances elsewhere around the south and east coasts, the owling trade now seemed to be concentrated on the Kent and Sussex shores. During 1669 the House of Lords debated the problem; some of the officers at Dover gave evidence, and expressed their views on the trade. They reported that the numbers of owlers had increased, and that they were now in large gangs, and well armed. They advocated that troops be stationed in every village along the coast to keep a constant watch and patrol every night, and commented on 'the number of fights and affrays between the owlers and the Revenue men'—a fairly new feature—which were ominous signs of the battles to come in the next century.

The West Country appeared no better, a traveller to Bristol in 1679 reporting 'the roads jammed with waggons laden with French wine and hundreds of tuns of wine being brought by day in open defiance of the laws'. The area between Lymington and Poole was full of landing-places where 'vast quantities of French goods are landed . . . the merchants combine to hire great numbers of men to come around to assist to unload the vessels and to convey them into the country'. The Collector in South Wales complained 'of the number of pirates and smugglers in the Channel, landing tobacco and other merchandise in all the creeks along the coasts'.

Although the East India Company had only received its charter in 1661, already there were considerable problems through the Company's vessels off-loading goods to small vessels which met them as they came up the Channel. 'These evil practices of late were so great' that a commission was granted to Richard Ward to place men on board the East Indiamen at Falmouth to accompany them to London. Later revenue vessels would be required to escort the vessels to the Downs, when tide-waiters would be placed on board for the journey to London.

The last decade of the seventeenth century saw a dramatic increase in smuggling, which can largely be attributed to two factors. Perhaps the most important was the development and introduction of the 'fore and aft' rigging, which completely revolutionized sailing techniques. Vessels could now tack, and when close hauled beat into the wind. They could now sail into any creek, discharge their cargo and leave, irrespective of the wind being in the right quarter. Within a short time vessels were being built specially for the smuggling trade, their main features being speed and a shallow draught to come in close to the shore.

This technical break-through in sailing technique came at a time when there was a vast increase in import duties of all kinds, both Customs and Excise, as well as the introduction of various trade restrictions and prohibitions. These changed conditions heralded a new era of smuggling, which would engage the combined efforts of the Customs, the Excise, the Army and the Admiralty in what was virtually a civil war.

It was left to a private individual to take the first steps to control the owlers in Kent and Sussex. This man, William Carter, was a clothier by trade, and during the years 1685–90 he waged a personal battle with the owlers. He achieved a modicum of success in seizing some wool consignments, and managed to bring some prosecutions. Few of these private prosecutions brought convictions, which he felt was largely due to the dilatory attitude of the Customs Board. He continually exhorted the Customs Commissioners for assistance, money and a vessel to patrol against the illegal trade. Not unnaturally, he became a marked man with the owlers, and suffered considerably at their hands. On one occasion he was violently assaulted by the smugglers' wives! It is unlikely that he conducted his one-man campaign out of public spirit, and nor did he gain much financial reward. His motive appeared to be the appointment to a high and well-paid post in the Customs service, but this he never achieved.

The Customs Board must have heeded some of his advice, because in 1690 a special inquiry was set up to investigate the illegal trade in Kent. As a result of the report eight riding officers were established 'to prevent the carrying of wool to France and bringing over uncustomed and prohibited goods by the French privateers'. These riding officers were paid £60 per annum, and were stationed at Lydd, Romney, Hythe and Folkestone. They replaced the two sloops *Enquiry* and *Observator*, which had patrolled the coast since 1689. The reason given for the change was that the sloops 'are not strong enough to prevent the French privateers from bringing in the goods'. By this change over £1,000 was saved, but this policy seemed short-sighted as the smuggling increased, to the obvious detriment of the revenue.

By 1698 the owling trade had reached a new peak. The main centres were Folkestone, Lydd, Rye and Romney, 'where every house was an owlers', although every town and village on the coast and many inland were involved in the trade. Drastic action was required, and in 1698 the famous 'Wool Act' was passed. This Act decreed that the owners of wool within ten miles of the coast in Kent and Sussex were to give an account of the number of fleeces and where they were stored. Wool registers were set up at the various Custom Houses, and no person could sell wool within fifteen miles of the coast unless it were registered first at the Custom House and a certificate issued for its removal. The Act also applied to the Borders of Scotland.

To enforce this a 'land-guard' of riding officers was established in 1699. They each received a salary of £90 per year, to include the cost of a servant and a horse. They were allocated an area of coast to patrol, normally about ten miles in length, and were stationed from the Isle of Sheppey right around to Chichester. At places like Folkestone, Hythe, Lydd, New Romney and Guildford four officers were appointed. The total cost of the establishment was just under £5,000 per year. The scheme of officers had been proposed by Captain Henry Baker, who had fought in the recent wars and was also a Treasury Solicitor. He was appointed Surveyor-General of the Riding Officers. He brought to his task a tireless enthusiasm and much zeal. He was ruthless in removing those he considered to be useless officers, his comment on one such being that he was 'of no more use than a gull on the beach'. By 1703 Baker reported to the Customs Board, 'I do believe the neck of this owling trade is in great measure broke, especially in Romney Marsh, as well as the spirit of the owlers'. To a certain extent he was correct, since owling had appreciably decreased, only to be replaced by a far greater trade in import smuggling.

As well as the new Land-guard in Kent and Sussex, the Customs Board, also in 1698, decided to increase the protection around the rest of the coasts. 'Customs sloops' were established at Weymouth, Dartmouth, Fowey,

Penzance, Padstow, Cardiff, Ilfracombe, Aberdovey, Holyhead, Whitehaven, Newcastle, Grimsby, Yarmouth and Wivenhoe. For the first time
their commanders were appointed directly by the Customs Commissioners,
rather than by the Admiralty. At the same time extra staff were appointed
along the coast from Portsmouth to Padstow, some receiving an allowance of
£10 for a horse, and in other ports for keeping a boat. However, only three
riding officers and a surveyor were appointed to patrol the border with
Scotland, and they were allowed 'fire arms for their defence, as are the
officers in Kent and Sussex, which is all that can be done to prevent this
clandestine trade without the assistance of a military force'.

In London a force of seventeen land carriage men were appointed. Their
specific duties were to watch the inns and to examine the various carriages on
arrival to ensure that no smuggled goods had been carried from the port.
They also had powers to search the inns and their warehouses. Originally they
were confined to London, but were later extended to other large ports such
as Bristol and Newcastle. One of their earliest successes was in 1705, when
they seized over 2,000 dollars and bullion and plate from 'a carriage in
Holborn'. The Excise officers were given similar powers to the Customs men,
and their commissions were extended to include the right to board and
'rummage' (search) ships for smuggled spirits. This considerable increase of
staff had the appearance of formal battle lines being drawn, ready for the
impending conflict.

In 1712 an Excise officer on a beach near Conway, North Wales, watched
'the whole country-side turn out with carts and wagons full of salt'. The large
gang of smugglers were led by Sir Griffith Williams, Bart. and Justice of the
Peace! The officer was discovered, soundly beaten, bound and blindfolded
and taken away to spend 'a day and a night in Sir Griffith's henhouse'.
Although he reported the incident to the Excise Commissioners, no action
could be taken, because all the smugglers were 'the tenants or servants of the
great man', and thus nobody was prepared to give evidence. This is an early
example of how the gentry involved themselves in smuggling, although it
was rare to find them taking such an active part. A few years later Lady
Sunderland's carriage was stopped at Harwich and wines from Holland
valued at £250 were seized. Even Sir Robert Walpole engaged in the trade:
he arranged with Josiah Burchett, Secretary of the Admiralty, to have wine
brought up the Thames by Admiralty launch without paying duty at the
Custom House.

The east coast of England was a particularly notorious area for
smuggling. In 1718 a 'run' of brandy had been interrupted by the King's
Lynn officers, and the smugglers attempted to rescue their seized goods. A
riot had broken out in the town which required the militia to restore order,
and the smugglers and rioters were captured and convicted, and were
'whipt around the town'. The magistrates were thanked by the Commissioners for their assistance, so unusual was the occurrence. The violence
and lawlessness of the east-coast smugglers almost surpassed that of the

notorious gangs of Kent and Sussex. However, an incident off Yarmouth in 1709 shows a certain naivety considering the violence that was to occur some years later. Captain Darby of the Yarmouth smack boarded a Dutch vessel and attempted to seize forty half-ankers (an anker was about $4\frac{1}{4}$ gallons) of brandy, which the Dutchmen were trying to land. He and his crew were badly beaten, and he called out for help from a passing boat from Gorleston. The commander reported, 'they only laughed at him and would not come nigh him. . . . Your Honours should take some course in this for fear of growing into an ill.'

Less than twenty years later an Excise officer near Snape came upon a gang of smugglers. He challenged them to halt, and a fight ensued. Since he was greatly outnumbered, he was disarmed, and had his nose cut off with his own sword. He manged to crawl into a hedge to hide, when later the smugglers returned with the intention of killing him. It was reported that the Suffolk smugglers went around in such force and are so well armed and violent that even the dragoons 'could not come up with them'. However, they did not have it all their own way, and a very great number ended up in Chelmsford Gaol. It was said that every seaboard parish in Essex and Suffolk had its representative in this gaol—many managed to escape. One of the most active and dedicated officers in the area was William Lisle, who was Surveyor of the Riding Officers from 1733 to 1750. Much of the scanty success achieved by the Customs in the area was due to his activity.

For sheer brutality, the gangs operating in Kent and Sussex were unsurpassed in the whole history of smuggling. Defoe writes in 1724 of the scene he witnessed while passing through these counties:

> As I rode along this coast [Romney Marsh], I perceived several dragoons, riding officers and others armed and on horseback, riding always as if they were huntsmen beating up their game; upon inquiry I found their diligence was in quest of owlers, as they call them and sometimes they catch some of them; but when I come to enquire further I find too, that often times they are attacked in the night with such numbers, that they dare not resist them or if they do, as it were, to stand still and see the wool carried off before their faces not daring to meddle.

As Defoe travelled further westward to Lymington he did not 'find any foreign commerce except it be what we call smuggling and roguing, which I may say, is the reigning commerce of all this part of the English coast, from the mouth of the Thames to Land's End of Cornwall'.

Defoe's assessment of the situation was not exaggerated. It is therefore not surprising that very few collectors were prepared to make a determined stand against smuggling. Indeed, the problems they faced seemed insurmountable. The officers were greatly outnumbered, and many were in collusion with the smugglers or were related to them, and were thus not dependable. The revenue vessels were also too few, and were generally out-sailed and out-gunned by the smuggling vessels. There was a general disinterest among the dragoons and their officers, and invariably their sympathies lay with the smugglers. Finally, virtually the whole population sided with and actively assisted the smugglers. In spite of all this, the fact remained that too many collectors were weak, some were corruptible and the majority accepted the situation as hopeless, and turned a blind eye to the vast illegal trade. One of the first officials to make a vigorous and determined stand against the smugglers was John Collier. He was a solicitor by profession, and was Surveyor-General of the Riding Officers in Kent during the period 1733–50. What little success was achieved in this area was because of his zeal, dedication and courage.

The extent of smuggling in Kent and Sussex was staggering, and the most ominous feature of the trade was the number of well-armed gangs of up to two hundred men who operated it, and who were prepared to use extreme violence and brutality in its execution. These gangs terrorized the whole countryside with a Mafia-like omnipotence. In 1720 the Mayfield gang, which operated in the Eastbourne area, murdered a Customs officer, but although the Customs were aware of the culprit, no person would come forward to give evidence. By 1734 Lydd, Hastings, Folkestone, Deal and Dover were virtually in the control of the smuggling gangs. These worked both by day and by night. They were never less than forty to fifty in number, although at times there were as many as two hundred gathered on the shore, unloading tea, brandy and tobacco from vessels that made regular trips to Holland and France. These vessels brought in tea by the hundredweight, and perhaps 250-half-ankers of brandy and geneva each trip.

By 1740 the vessels used in the smuggling trade were so large and well armed that they easily repulsed any attack from the revenue vessels. As the commander of the Dover sloop reported, 'we are actually in danger of being run down and sunke by them, who have not only threatened to do so, but also attempted it'. One gang called 'The Transports' from Hastings captured two officers who had the audacity to challenge them and transported them on the next vessel to France. The riding officer from Lydd was driven from his house by the vicious attacks on him and his family. The gang threatened to murder him if he returned. The Surveyor at Hythe witnessed a gang of smugglers armed 'with pistols, muskets and fuzees' loading sixty horses with tea at Lydd; they then 'took over' two inns in the town to have breakfast and left in a long train through the town, 'to make a show to the inhabitants'. He was much concerned with the sight, 'which nothing but a military power can prevent'.

Even when the military were called out in support of the officers, they were still outnumbered, and many bitter and bloody battles ensued. In 1740 Thomas Carswell, a Rye officer, with a detachment of dragoons, seized a cargo of tea. In the battle with the smugglers which followed Carswell was killed and two dragoons seriously injured, the smugglers escaping with their tea. Only three years later a notorious gang from Groombridge fought a pitched battle at Bulverhithe, between Hastings and Bexhill. The smugglers had been surprised unloading goods on the beach, and in the battle two of them were killed and many badly injured. The Groombridge gang, according to John Collier, was 'the most notorious and desperate gang concerned in smuggling . . . they struck terror into the inhabitants of that part of the country, although their violence is alienating the sympathies of the people'.

Of all the gangs that operated in the eighteenth century, without doubt the most violent and brutal was the Hawkhurst gang, led by Arthur Gray and William Kingsmill. This had its centre of operations at the village of Hawkhurst, about ten miles north of Hastings, and just inside the Kent boundary, although their operations covered the whole coastline from Deal to Portsmouth. It was reported that they could assemble up to five hundred men within the hour. Farmers in fear hired them horses and wagons, and the gang established a series of 'warehouses' for the smuggled goods all over the Weald. They appeared to reign supreme in the area, and especially so after an incident in March 1746, when they co-operated with a small gang from Folkestone and Deal in running a cargo of tea. There were eleven and a half tons of tea to be loaded onto 350 horses, a massive operation even for the Hawkhurst men. Before the job was completed they were disturbed by Customs officials, and the Folkestone gang disappeared, with the result that some of the tea 'belonging' to the Hawkhurst men was seized. Kingsmill gathered together a force and marched on Folkestone to take his revenge on the other gang. A bitter fight resulted, leaving Kingsmill and his men victorious, and they took over forty horses from the rival gang.

Perhaps the most graphic description of the state of the coast at this time is given in a letter written by Admiral Vernon to the Admiralty in 1745:

> I can't but think it is a seasonable time to suggest to your Lordships that there are said to be in the town of Deal, no less than two hundred able young men and sea-faring people, who are known to have no visible way of getting a living but by the infamous trade of smuggling, many keeping a horse and arms to be ready at all calls.
>
> At Dover it is conjectured that there may be found four hundred at a time ready to smuggle, at Ramsgate and Folkestone three hundred each; and it is said that within these three weeks no less than nine cutters at a time have gone off from Folkestone to Boulogne; and that it is conjectured that from the town of Folkestone itself, a thousand pounds a week is run over to Boulogne in the smuggling way; and about six or seven days past, a Dover cutter landed goods in the night under the castle, that was carried off by a party of sixty horses, and the cutter supposed to have done it came into Dover pier next day; and although most believed it was she, no one proceeded against them to make inquiry about it. This smuggling has converted those employed in it, first from honest, industrious fishermen to lazy, drunken profligate smugglers, and now to dangerous spies on all our proceedings, for the enemy's daily information. As this passes within my observation, I should think it criminal in me not to inform you of it; I can't but think it a national reproach upon us, to have let their villainy and treachery run to such extensive lengths.

The smuggling trade was not confined to the east and the south coasts, it was carried on extensively in the West Country, Wales and North-west England. Although the amount of the goods run on these coasts was almost as great as in the Kent and Sussex area, for some unaccountable reason the trade was far less violent and brutal. The Collector in Caernarvon reported in 1740 that the town 'was full of smugglers, not an honest trader'. Much of the goods smuggled into Wales and North-west England came from the Isle of Man, which had become a virtual magazine of tobacco, spirits and tea, waiting to be shipped to the mainland. It was reported that 'ten to twelve boats are almost every week seen in a fleet leaving the Island for Whitehaven, Cheshire and Wales'.

The island had been granted to Sir John Stanley and his heirs in 1406, and remained in private jurisdiction, with its own insular duties, which were far lower than those on the mainland. For instance, tobacco was liable to duty at $\frac{1}{2}d$. per lb, and there was no limit on its export. Brandy, tea, silks and other goods were specially imported from France and Holland for re-export. A number of merchants from Liverpool had set up a company in Douglas to take advantage of the illicit trade. The majority of tobacco used for smuggling was 'diverted' tobacco, which had been re-exported from Liverpool and Glasgow on payment of drawback (refund of duty) for the Continent. It was landed on the Isle of Man, and within a week or so was being smuggled back into England or Wales. The island had become 'a nest of smugglers, who glory in their treasons, the whole island lives on smuggling'.

The Liverpool Collector reported in 1764:

> Foreign ships run no risque in landing their goods by open day, no person there dare not offer to molest them, since some of Captain Dow's crew [of the revenue vessel *Sincerity*] were most cruelly beaten and wounded and imprisoned for seizing a Dutch vessel in Ramsey Bay with spirits from Holland, and the ship and goods rescued from them.

The Customs Commissioners considered the situation to be hopeless: smuggling had reached enormous proportions, and was estimated to be to the extent of almost a third of a million pounds per year. The only solution appeared to be the outright purchase of the fiscal rights of the island. Negotiations were opened with the Duke of Atholl—the family acquired the island in 1736—who offered the rights for £70,000 and an annuity of £2,000. Parliament readily agreed to the terms, and the money was appropriately paid out of Customs funds, the warrant being granted on 30 April 1765.

Within a fortnight officers were sent to the island 'to prevent any illicit commerce'. The system of Customs control on the mainland was extended to there, with Collectors being established at Douglas, Peel, Ramsey, and Derbyhaven. In less than twenty years the Collector at Liverpool reported that 'there has not been any information received of an avow'd smuggler coming within the limits of this port since the Isle of Man was annexed to the

Crown'. It is unlikely that this sweeping statement was correct; the presence of a Customs staff on the island for such a short time could hardly have changed the lifetime habits of the islanders. However, what was evident was that the island's smuggling trade was never again so extensive as it had been before the purchase.

Other off-shore islands were havens for smuggled goods, and became the habitual haunts of smugglers. This was especially so with those in the Bristol Channel; Lundy Island, which had long associations with piracy, now became the centre of operations of smugglers in the Channel, particularly when Thomas Benson, a rich and apparently respectable merchant and also a Member of Parliament for Bideford, obtained the lease of the island. He established there a very successful and lucrative smuggling business. Not only did the ships coming to Bristol discharge goods on the island, but a much more profitable trade was established by outward-bound ships discharging tobacco for ultimate smuggling on the mainland. Like the Isle of Man, it had become 'a magazine for smugglers'. The Collector at Cardiff believed that 'There never lived yet a man on the Island of Lundy, who was not connected with smuggling.' Benson was placed in charge of the transportation of convicts to America; he pocketed the passage money and shipped them to Lundy to assist in his smuggling empire.

The Commissioners felt they had a special problem with Lundy; it was not within the limits of any port, and was almost twelve miles from the shore, which made the legality of any seizures doubtful. Furthermore, it was very difficult to patrol, as the smugglers had erected a platform with cannons to prevent the Customs vessels landing on the island. Once again the only answer seemed to be the outright purchase; however, this was not pursued, and thus Lundy was always a thorn in the flesh of the Customs in the Bristol Channel.

Barry Island near Cardiff, now a popular seaside resort, was for a number of years the strongly fortified centre of the 'notorious smuggler Knight', who traded in a well-armed brig from Ireland and Jersey. According to the Collector, 'all the country people are in fear of Knight'. He was eventually driven away from the island by the diligence of the Cardiff staff, only to re-establish himself in the same business in Lundy. Flat Holm was used as a centre by a smuggler from Guernsey, whose vessel was most distinctive 'painted red with a mermaid on the bow'. He traded 'vast quantities of tea, brandy, rum and tobacco' on to the coasts around Bristol. These smugglers had virtual freedom of the Bristol Channel, as there was no revenue vessel stationed at any of the Channel ports. Almost continually the various collectors pleaded with the Board for a vessel to patrol the Channel, as the only way to stop the 'pernicious trade'. Their appeals were in vain; the Board felt it was more important to deploy their limited resources to protect the south coast. This, of course, resulted in the smugglers increasing their efforts and activity to the West Country and Wales, where there was less chance of capture.

As the Customs—and to a lesser extent the Excise—struggled to try to contain the smuggling trade Parliament continually brought out new legislation or reframed existing Acts in an attempt to combat it. Each successive Act became more drastic, the penalties harsher, with the result that the legislation became self-defeating. In 1718 it was enacted that any vessel of fifty tons or under, laden with tea, brandy or French silks, found 'hovering' within two leagues (six miles) of the coast was liable to seizure. This was the first of many 'Hovering Acts' passed during the eighteenth century. Three years later it was enacted that any boat of more than four oars found on the coast would be forfeited and destroyed by 'cutting in three'. Receivers or purchasers of smuggled goods were liable to three months' imprisonment, and convicted smugglers were transported to the Colonies for a term of seven years. Smugglers in this Act were defined as any person 'who carried firearms or wore any vizard, mask or any other disguise when passing with such goods'. Frequently convicted smugglers transported under this Act were only taken as far as France, and within a month or so were back in the smuggling trade. For instance, in December 1738 the Customs put out a poster proclaiming a reward of £50 for the apprehension of six smugglers transported three months earlier.

The first of many Parliamentary Inquiries into the smuggling trade sat in 1736, under the chairmanship of Sir John Cope. This report conveyed to Parliament (possibly for the first time) the extraordinary extent of smuggling:

> The smugglers being grown to such a degree of insolence, as to carry on their wicked practices by force and violence, not only in the country and the remote parts of the Kingdom, but even in the City of London itself, going in gangs armed with swords, pistols and other weapons, even to the number of forty or fifty, by which means they have been too strong, not only for the officers of the Revenue but for the civil magistrates themselves. . . . The number of Custom House officers who have been beated, abused and wounded since Christmas 1723 being no less than 250, besides six others who have been actually murdered in the execution of their duty.

The result of this report was even sterner legislation; an Act called the Indemnity for Smugglers was passed in 1736. Under this legislation any smuggler could obtain a free pardon for past offences, providing that he disclosed them fully, and named his associates. The Act also brought in the death penalty for wounding or hindering revenue officers, while those persons assisting smugglers by unloading goods or making warning signals were liable to a month's hard labour. The Act was not very successful; few smugglers were prepared to give information, for the retribution meted out to informers was normally death.

The next inquiry into smuggling was held in 1745, and its report was followed by fresh legislation, which made the death penalty the only punishment for smuggling. Largely because so few smugglers were caught, the law was amended to make the judgments automatic. Those failing to surrender within forty days of their names appearing in the *London Gazette*, and the very many 'wanted' posters issued by the Customs Commissioners, were adjudged to be guilty. Persons hiding smugglers were similarly judged to be outlaws and felons, with the punishment of death. These draconian Acts did little to combat the extent of smuggling, and in fact greatly exacerbated the situation as far as the officers were concerned; smugglers used far greater violence to ensure that they were not taken, as capture automatically meant the death penalty.

Very few serious studies have been made into the economic effects of smuggling on the trade of the country. This 'black' economic activity has been estimated at £2 to £3 millions of goods being illegally imported each year, and this at a time when the legal imports only amounted to £12 millions. Thus the country was losing at least a quarter of its revenue each year. For most of the eighteenth century the staple commodity of the smuggler was tea (or 'dry goods', as they called it). The high value of tea in proportion to its bulk—plus, of course, the high Excise duty—made its smuggling very profitable.

Much of the smuggled tea was bought in Holland for as little as 6d. per lb, depending on quality, and this tea could be sold for as much as 3s. to 4s. per lb. The cheapest legal tea to be bought in London cost 5s. per lb, so that it can be seen how profitable the smuggling of tea became. By 1750 it was estimated that 3 million lb were smuggled annually, more than three times the legal trade. By 1773 this figure was thought to have risen to 7 million lb. The majority of smuggled tea went to London: in fact, most London grocers were taking up to two hundred pounds of smuggled tea each week. Large consignments of tea were seen regularly being carried through the City escorted by strongly armed men, who resisted any attempts the Excise officers made to seize the goods. Large caches of tea were stored in Epping Forest and Clapham Common, while Stockwell was reputed to be the centre for the distribution of smuggled tea to regular customers in London.

In November 1742 Excise officers went to the Fleet Prison to search for smuggled tea. They found over a hundredweight but were unable to seize the goods, because they were 'mobbed and beaten by the prisoners'. Returning some weeks later with forty soldiers from the Tower, they were denied access by the Warder, while the tea was being removed by the back door. All they found when they were allowed entry was 'an empty room smelling as strong as any tea warehouse'. Three years later Excise officers attempted to seize 'a large quantity of tea' near Holborn. Not only were they attacked by the smugglers but they were mobbed by the public, to an extent which forced them to retreat unsuccessful.

The whole smuggling trade was very profitable, from the financial backer right down to the merest labourer. The 'merchant' who supplied the finance to purchase the smuggled goods was frequently one of the local gentry, who acted through an agent. He viewed the financing of smuggling as no different to any other investment, other than that it was more profitable. (He also received his tea free, and his brandy and wines at very reasonable prices!) It was estimated that over £1 million in coin was exported each year to pay for the smuggled goods. The shipmaster who arranged the purchase and brought the goods over in his vessel was paid handsomely for what was a relatively small risk—certainly so in the early days, when there were very few revenue vessels and most of the seizures were made on land.

The lion's share of the profits was taken by the 'master smuggler' on land, who arranged the unloading, dispatch and distribution to customers. He took the greatest risks, but the profits were so high that it was suggested that he could afford to lose two shipments out of three and still show a handsome profit. As the revenue officers were never this successful in making seizures, providing the smuggler could avoid being taken he quickly became very rich. Arthur King of the Hawkhurst Gang was reputed to be worth over £50,000, and had built a large country house in Sussex. Even the locally recruited labourers found the trade profitable; they received 10–15s. for a night's work, as well as free tea and gin. (This was at a time when the average weekly wage for a farm labourer was 8–10s.) The tubmen who carried two half-ankers of spirit slung over their shoulders, and the batmen, who received their name from the bats they carried—stout wooden staves, often iron-tipped and at least six feet long, to enable them to ward off the swords and cutlasses of the Customs men—both received about one guinea for the few hours' work. Even the farmers who supplied the horses and carts were paid in kind; tea and brandy was left when the carts were returned. It was reported in 1733 that the farmers in Kent and Sussex were obliged to raise the wages of their labourers, and were still unable to get sufficient hands at harvest-time, because of the great number employed in smuggling.

When the duty on tea was reduced in the mid-century (which made it less profitable to run) the smugglers concentrated more on brandy, geneva and wines. The profit on spirits was even greater; the half-anker tub, which was made specially for the smuggling trade, could be purchased abroad for £1 and could be sold for at least £4, a price which was half the cost of legal spirits. The trade could be quite profitable for the Customs officers, other than those who were in collusion with the smugglers. A seizure of smuggled goods would result in a reward, which was shared by the seizing officers. In 1752 seized tobacco was worth 2d. per lb, and tea worth 1s. 6d. per lb. A good seizure could mean that the officer might receive a reward almost equal to his annual salary. These rewards gave a very necessary incentive to follow what was a very unpopular and hazardous occupation.

By 1747 there was a glimmer of hope that the extreme violence and brutality of the smuggling gangs was beginning to alienate the sympathy and support of law-abiding citizens. The small village of Goudhurst, which was situated very close to the centre of operations of the Hawkhurst gang, decided to defend itself against the continual lawlessness of the smugglers. Led by a young man named Sturt, the inhabitants formed themselves into a band of militia for the protection of their village. The gang heard of the proposed defence, and sent word that they would attack Goudhurst. So confident were they of a victory that they even stated the precise date (20 April 1747), when they said they would burn every house and murder every man, woman and child.

Sturt was well aware that this was no idle threat, and the village prepared for the attack. Trenches were dug, firearms were distributed and the men were drilled by Sturt. The gang were as good as their word, and led by Thomas Kingsmill—who had been born in Goudhurst—they attacked on the allotted day. The villagers, however, were now well prepared for the attack, and were concealed in windows, on rooftops and even in the church tower. In the first volley Kingsmill's brother was killed, and after a sharp bout of fighting the smugglers beat a hasty retreat. They were pursued by the villagers, who managed to capture two of them and hand them over to the authorities. This battle was unique in smuggling history, and has all the flavour of a story written for a Western film.

Undeterred by this setback, the Hawkhurst gang next perpetrated the most barbarous outrage committed in the century. In September 1747 a smuggling cutter called *The Three Brothers*, carrying a large quantity of tea destined for the Hawkhurst gang, was seized by the revenue vessel *Swift* based at Poole. The smugglers led by Richard Perrin managed to make their escape in an open boat, and the seized tea was brought back to port and secured in the Custom House, Poole. Meanwhile Perrin and his crew had arrived back home and, obviously angered at the loss of such a valuable cargo, decided to attempt to retrieve what they felt was their own property.

On the night of 6 October 1747 a gang of about thirty strong, including Kingsmill, Fairall and Perrin, attacked and broke into the Custom House. They loaded the tea on to a train of horses and triumphantly carried the cargo inland, being cheered as they passed through the various towns and villages. As they passed through Fordingbridge Daniel Chater, a shoemaker, recognized one of the gang as Jack Diamond (sometimes known as Dimer). Dimer passed a bag of tea to Chater for old time's sake. When the reward for information about the persons involved in the outrage was posted Chater—no doubt encouraged by the £200 reward offered—came forward with the information as to the identity of Dimer. As a result Dimer was arrested and placed in Chichester Gaol.

It was required that Chater be examined by the Justice of the Peace in Chichester, and it was decided that he should be escorted by a revenue official. The Collector at Southampton chose an elderly tide waiter by the name of William Galley for the duty. He was given a letter by the Collector, explaining the case for the J.P. During the journey the two men stopped for the night at an inn at Rowland's Castle near Havant. This inn was a notorious haunt of smugglers, and the innkeeper, a Mrs Payne, soon realized the identity of the two travellers and informed the local smugglers; they arrived at the inn, questioned the two men and the incriminating letter was

found. It was now clear that Chater was the informer on whose evidence
Dimer had been arrested. The Hawkhurst gang were apprised of the
presence of Chater and Galley, and when members of the gang arrived at the
inn they had obviously decided that Chater must be killed.

Both Chater and Galley were severely beaten, but because the innkeeper
refused to allow the murder to take place in her inn the two men were taken
outside. They were tied to horses and taken away to the country, being
continually beaten with whips and sticks. After they had gone about six miles
Galley fell from his horse senseless. He was virtually dead, so he was dragged
into a field and buried. Chater lasted somewhat longer; his nose and ears
were cut off, but he still managed to stay alive, and was finally thrown down
a dry well, large stones being dropped on him until his cries could no longer
be heard.

Even in such lawless days the disappearance of the two men could not go
unnoticed, and another reward was offered for any information. A smuggler
captured while trying to escape to France thereupon confessed to the
murder, and gave evidence concerning the rest of the gang. The bodies of the
dead men were not recovered for seven months, but one by one the
murderers were captured, including the innkeeper and her two sons. The
trial was held in Chichester in 1749, and caused considerable public interest.
The government had ensured that the proceedings would gain maximum
publicity, for the capture of these men was one of the most successful
achievements in the smuggling war. Seven smugglers were convicted of
murder and executed, their bodies hung in chains in prominent smuggling
places, as a grim warning to other smugglers. Kingsmill, Fairall and Perrin
and others were tried at the Old Bailey for their part in the attack on the
Poole Custom House, and again all were found guilty and executed.
Kingsmill's body was hung on a gibbet at Goudhurst. Thus at long last the
most notorious smuggling gang was destroyed.

The attack on the Poole Custom House appeared to set a precedent,
because in April 1748 a gang of twenty smugglers in 'disguise', but believed
to be part of the infamous Hadleigh gang, armed 'with pistoless and
blunderbusses' broke into the Colchester Custom House. They used 'a crow
and large blacksmith's hammer', and carried off over sixty oil bags
containing 1,514 lb of tea. Despite a reward being offered for their capture,
no information was received. No doubt people were only too aware of the
vengeance meted out to informers.

Although the last two incidents were unusual for their extreme violence
and effrontery, they were by no means isolated cases. During the period
1746–9 there were more violent attacks on officers than at any previous time.
At Brighthelmstone (Brighton) an officer and two informants were attacked
and shipped over to France. The East Anglia area, and more especially that
around Yarmouth, was particularly active with smugglers. Large and
heavily armed gangs operated around Benacre Warren and Kesland Haven.
The Collector plaintively reported that without dragoons the officers

'cannot stop this pernicious practice'. In December 1747 a force of 140 soldiers was stationed in the area, and almost immediately achieved some notable seizures.

In August 1746 John Corbolt, alias 'Giffling Jack' (to giffle was Suffolk for 'to be restless'), a notorious smuggler, was being escorted by a party of riding officers to Norwich Castle, when within six miles of Norwich they were ambushed by a group of smugglers. The officers were 'severely beaten', one losing a 'hat and wigg as good as new, which cost him £1 2s. 6d.'. The prisoner escaped and was never recaptured. A much more audacious escape occurred in November 1747, when a party of thirty smugglers attacked Maidstone Gaol, wounded the keeper and his assistants and released six 'dangerous smugglers'. Even in Newgate Gaol in London the smugglers were not secure. Two smugglers disguised as pedlars obtained entry, and by 'knocking down the turnkey and his assistants', achieved the release of two fellow-smugglers. It must have been particularly galling to the officers to find their efforts in capturing the smugglers largely nullified by these escapes.

The Excise officers also were not immune from the violence of the smugglers, and they suffered their fair share of assaults. Two particularly vivid reports stand out. One concerned an Excise officer in Scarborough, who with other officers was seizing a quantity of smuggled goods. They were attacked by the smugglers, and 'some person deliberately and maliciously presented a pistol close to the breast of the said John Smith and killed him on the spot'. The other incident happened at the unlikely place of Chislehurst Common. The officer—from St Mary Cray in Kent—was set upon by smugglers who 'beat him with whips and repeated the blows until the whips broke into pieces, of which blows the officer now lies dangerously ill'.

However, judging by the entries in the *Gentleman's Magazine* for the years 1747 to 1749, the numbers of smugglers convicted was increasing greatly. Hardly a week went by without the report of a trial, followed by due execution at Tyburn. Some of the sobriquets of these smugglers are amusing. There was Thomas Puryour, alias Black Tooth, and one who rejoiced under the nickname of Nasty Face, along with John Mills—Snoaker—Thomas Winter, alias One-Eye, and Richard Rowland—Little Fat Back—to mention a few. With the capture of so many smugglers and the break-up of the more notorious gangs, one is tempted to conjecture that at long last the authorities were gaining the upper hand. However, in retrospect it is obvious that the improvement was only transitory, merely a temporary respite before the bitter and bloody battles of the next hundred years, a period which became known as the heyday of smuggling.

CHAPTER FOUR

Riots, Rebellions and Revolution

The eighteenth century was a period of continual strife for both services; not only were they faced with a prolonged, bitter and bloody battle against smuggling, but they also encountered considerable opposition in their day-to-day work. The Excisemen particularly suffered the violence of mob riots on numerous occasions, and throughout the period were faced with open hostility because of the unpopularity of their calling. It is against this background of strife that both services struggled manfully to administer a mass of largely unworkable legislation, and at the same time attempted to improve the management of the revenue.

With the death of Queen Anne on 1 August 1714 the advent of the Hanoverians was heralded by an instruction to the Customs in London, in September of that year, 'to carefully examine the King's baggage on his arrival, to ensure that no customable or prohibited goods were imported'. Subsequently, on the arrival of the King's mistress from Hanover, her goods should be passed 'with all possible civility and dispatch'!

The Jacobite threat at this time was very real. Both the Customs and Excise services were subjected to a rigorous inquiry into the political affiliations of their staff. All those in government service who were suspected of Jacobite sympathies were removed from office. By November both Boards of Commissioners in England had been changed. The majority of the Customs Commissioners were removed, including Edward Gibbon, grandfather of the historian, and were replaced by men who had served on the Board in the 1690s.

There were wholesale changes of staff in the out-ports, new collectors, controllers and searchers being appointed. Among the new appointments were William Congreve the playwright, who became one of the five 'under-searchers' in London Port, and John Oldmixon the historian, as Collector at Bridgwater. There were less changes in the Excise, perhaps because it had undergone such a radical upheaval in the latter years of the previous

century. The officers of both services were in a difficult position: they were
open to accusations of 'disaffection to the King', and many were discharged
on very flimsy evidence that they had 'drunk the health of the Pretender'.
Frequently the information was supplied by merchants and Excise traders,
who obviously wished to gain revenge on officers who had prosecuted them.

As might be expected, the changes made in the two Scottish
administrations were far more comprehensive; the number of removals
suggested a virtual 'witch-hunt' for Jacobite adherents. The tenor of the
times can be judged from the case of a Customs officer in Scotland, who was
allowed an ex-gratia payment of £50, on account of being 'barbarously
assaulted and maimed for expressing his affection to the Government of the
times, on the occasion of the King's Coronation'.

The first ill-fated Jacobite Rebellion of 1715 was partly financed by the
collection of Excise duties during the progress of its forces through the
northern counties. The Excise Commissioners reported:

> the rebels in their passing through the Counties of Cumberland, Westmore-
> land and Lancashire, extolled from several victuallers, malsters and chandlers,
> several sums of money, being the duty then charged upon them and which had
> been collected at the following sittings and had by one Ossington and
> Louthwaite, whom they called their Collectors, given receipts to the people for
> the same.

The interesting point in this report is that the Excise traders were given
receipts. It was obvious that many of the 'rebels' were from the revenue
services; they were well versed in the Excise system of collection. In Kendal,
for instance, 'they compelled the belman to go and give notice to the
innkeepers and chandlers to come and pay what Excise is due'. Certainly
Ossington, the main collector, had been an Exciseman.

As the rebels appeared to be sure of collecting the Excise duties as they
moved from market town to market town, this obviated the necessity of
foraging in the surrounding countryside for supplies. Thus the movement of
the rebel force caused very little disturbance to the people. The Excise
traders also did not suffer, as they had receipts for the money they had paid to
the rebels. After the Rebellion the officers endeavoured to collect some of the
'arrears'; eventually the total sum of £379 collected by the rebels was
remitted to the Excise by the Treasury. It was not, however, until 1729 that
the traders who had paid twice were finally reimbursed.

The aftermath of the Rebellion resulted in the Customs at the ports being
enjoined 'to search diligently for escaping rebels'—especially 'General'
Foster, the commander of the Jacobite force at Preston. He had been
captured, but had managed to escape from Newgate prison. A description
was issued to all ports, and a reward of £1,000 offered for his capture. The
description was so vague that it is not surprising that he managed to escape.

This type of work, which would now be properly called Special Branch
duties, became a feature of both Customs and Excise over the next hundred

years. Descriptions were issued for all manner of political rebels and escaped convicts, although the majority of wanted men were either smugglers or highwaymen. In 1717 the Receiver of Land Tax in Somerset had 'gone off with a great deal of public money'. The officers at Dover and Harwich were issued with the following description: 'He is a tall man with light brown complexion and wears a periwig.' Although they had orders to stop and secure him, there is no record of his capture. In 1752 the Scottish Customs were issued with a description of Allen Breck Stewart, a suspected murderer. (Breck was featured in Robert Louis Stevenson's famous story *Kidnapped*.)

On 13 January 1715 some gunpowder stored in a chandler's shop in Thames Street near the London Custom House exploded, and within a very short time a fire had spread to the adjoining shops and wharves. It soon reached the Custom House, and so badly damaged the building that all the staff had to be evacuated. Besides the serious structural damage, 232 hogsheads of sugar, valued at over £2,000, were destroyed; this was the payment of plantation duty, which had been received in kind. Also 'lost' were 80 gallons of brandy and wine, part of a seizure. This liquor had been distributed to the people helping to fight the fire, so perhaps this explains why so many properties were destroyed (including the Trinity House in Water Lane, where Pepys had been a frequent visitor).

The Commissioners met the following morning at Garraway's Coffee House, one of the most famous in the City, to assess the damage and to find new temporary premises. For a few weeks they met at Somerset House, later to be the headquarters of the Excise. The Commissioners considered an offer from the Clothworkers Company for the hire of their hall, but felt that the rent of £500 per year was prohibitive. They eventually settled for a large house in Fenchurch Street, where they remained for nearly ten years while the Custom House was being rebuilt.

Thomas Ripley, who had been 'master carpenter' to the Board, was appointed surveyor and clerk of works for the new building project. He submitted plans to extend the building greatly, and much time and effort was expended in obtaining the necessary adjoining land. It was finally decided to settle on a less grandiose plan, although the new building did have an extra floor and fine large cellars. Ripley retained as the central feature the now-famous Long Room; in fact, the whole edifice was planned to resemble closely Wren's Custom House. (Incidentally, this latter building was the first of Wren's works to be destroyed during his lifetime.)

Pavilions were erected at right angles to the ends of the main building, forming a piazza on the quay. The temporary boatmen who collected there daily to wait for employment became known as piazzamen. The original estimate for the building had been £8,000, but the final cost was over £11,000. Ripley was called to the Board to explain the large discrepancy. His explanation was that 'the price of lead had increased as had many other articles too numerous to mention'. The building, after several delays, was ready for occupation in 1725.

The piazza became a fashionable promenade for the wealthy members of the City society to gather and stroll in the evenings. In 1725 the Commissioners allowed bonfires to be continued as before, on the anniversary of the King's Coronation. (They were, however, very conscious of the risk of fire to their new building, and gave strict instructions to the housekeeper 'to make a fire not exceeding forty oistry faggots and ensure that no firebrands are thrown about or any squibs fired'.)

The area around the Custom House was a maze of small streets, lanes, wharves and warehouses, serving the whole business of the Port of London. This relatively small area, from the Tower to London Bridge, was continually congested with traffic and the myriad of people involved in the shipping trade. A writer in 1766 described the scene:

> It is astonishing how much business can possibly be carried on in a place, which is so extremely crowded and consequently perpetually confused. Those only can form an idea of it whose business or curiosity prompt them to become spectators of this scene of hurry and confusion.

Largely because of this congestion and 'confusion', the Commissioners appointed Constables to keep the area around the Custom House and its quay free of traffic. They later decided to extend the Constable's duties to the streets, lanes and wharves in the vicinity. These 'street watchers', as they were known, patrolled the lanes and quays in an attempt to prevent the extensive pilferage and theft prevalent in the area. Although they were employed by the Customs, they were in fact sworn in before the Lord Mayor. As they were full-time professional watchers—as distinct from the unpaid Ward watch—they could be considered the earliest form of police in the City. It was some years later before the merchants appointed their own watchers, who were called merchant constables.

Perhaps it was the expense of the new Custom House that concerned the Commissioners, or maybe they felt the need to set an example of economy to their officers; whatever the reason, the Commissioners resolved in future to pay for their breakfasts, rather than charge them to the Crown, which had been their practice previously. Furthermore, they also decided to pay for all their books and pamphlets, although the hay and straw for their horses was paid out of the public funds. The Excise Board felt no such compunction to follow suit, and happily continued to breakfast and read at public expense, until stopped by the Treasury in 1811.

Judging by an account given in 1736 by an Excise Commissioner, life on the Revenue Boards was certainly not uncongenial, or for that matter particularly arduous. They met every weekday (except Sundays and public holidays) at nine in the morning, and had 'full employment 'til one, never arriving home 'til two in the afternoon'. The only afternoon both Boards were compelled to work was Wednesdays, when they attended the Treasury. At these times the Customs Commissioners were always called in first. During the summer months, when business was quieter, each of the Commissioners had several weeks' leave to pursue 'private affairs'.

The Customs Commissioners had more formal duties than the Excise Board. As well as being called more frequently to the Treasury, they also attended the House of Commons on numerous occasions, to answer questions on new Bills that were being introduced, or to defend their management of the revenue, especially on smuggling matters. Every morning one Commissioner was required to attend the Long Room to sign cockets and warrants, and to mediate in disputes between the officers and merchants. They were often called upon to undertake a variety of tasks; in 1739 two Commissioners were ordered by the Treasury to travel to Portsmouth and make account of the treasure taken on board a Spanish prize and accompany it to London under a proper guard.

It is not surprising that with the high salaries, minimal duties and boundless opportunities for patronage, a position on the Revenue Boards was one of the most coveted prizes of eighteenth-century political life. The majority of places on the two Boards went to persons with influential connections or local political influence. Sir John Evelyn, grandson of the famous diarist, who was a Customs Commissioner from 1721 to 1769, besides having great political influence in Surrey was connected by marriage to the all-powerful Godolphin family. Many Commissioners were appointed to release seats in the House of Commons (since the beginning of the century Commissioners could not sit as Members of Parliament). Papillon Senior vacated his seat for a supporter of Walpole, and was rewarded with a place on the Excise Board; when he retired his seat on the Board passed to his son, another method in which the posts were filled. Often Commissioners were appointed at the end of their political career or after long Royal service. Thomas Boone, who had experienced a difficult time as a Governor in the American colonies, was appointed to the Customs Board, and served for thirty-six years.

It was not until the mid-century that some able administrators were appointed to the Boards. Men like Sir William Musgrave, Customs Commissioner 1763–85, who was probably the most able Commissioner ever to serve on the Customs Board, and George Lewis Scott, Excise Commissioner 1758–81, who was a distinguished mathematician, who brought new ideas to the Board. Slowly persons who had worked their way through the services were appointed to the Boards. Samuel Mead of the Customs and Stamp Brooksbank of the Excise added a much-needed touch of professionalism to the Boards. Unfortunately, few men of this calibre and ability were appointed, and the majority of Commissioners felt like Sir Thomas Robinson that the position was 'an employment for life, unless I should misbehave in it'. The system of privilege appointments, without the necessary expertise and management experience, greatly impaired the efficiency and development of both services for most of the eighteenth century.

The dangers of the plague being introduced into the country by vessels from infected ports had concerned successive governments since the days of the Great Plague. Considering the lack of suitable precautions, the country had been fortunate to avoid the various epidemics which had raged on the Continent. In Queen Anne's reign there had been an outbreak of the plague in the Baltic countries, and an Act was passed to establish a quarantine procedure for all vessels arriving from infected ports.

The control of quarantine was firmly placed on the Customs service. In 1720 there was a more serious outbreak on the Continent, and as a result more stringent legislation was introduced. Masters of vessels were compelled to bring their ships to approved boarding stations and make a health declaration on oath. The Customs officer handed to the master at the end of a boat-hook a bible enclosed in an iron cover; after the declaration had been made the 'Quarantine or Plague Bible' was dragged through the sea-water, in order to cleanse it!

In 1720 the plague had reached the Isle of Man; the Customs Commissioners directed that nobody from the island, whether infected or not, should be allowed to land. A party of 'gentry of the Island', in an attempt to escape the infection, sailed to Whitehaven. The Collector and his officers 'beat them out to sea'. They tried to land farther down the coast at Lancaster, but there had to contend not only with the Customs but also with a crowd of angry townspeople. Troops were finally called to prevent any bloodshed. The party was not allowed to disembark, and the vessel returned to the Isle of Man.

The general concern in the country over quarantine was so great that in 1722 the Commissioners were called before the House of Commons to report the efficiency of their control. They gave a satisfactory account, but complained bitterly of the extra work to the service. As a result they were each granted an annual allowance of £220. There is no record, however, of the officers who were directly involved in administering the control receiving any extra remuneration.

Imported goods were still being charged according to the values laid down in the Book of Rates, which dated from Charles II's time. Not only had values greatly increased but many goods not listed in the Book were now being regularly imported. The value of these 'unenumerated' goods was based on the sworn declaration of the merchant. For some time there had been misgivings about the undervaluation of such articles. By 1748 'a Custom House oath' had became a proverbial expression for something not to be regarded as true.

It was therefore decided to introduce a new procedure, whereby if the collector felt the goods were undervalued he could by law purchase them on behalf of the Crown at the declared value plus 10 per cent, to allow for a reasonable profit for the importer. They were then sold at the next Custom House sale, and in most cases their sale price brought a handsome profit for the revenue. One importer who suffered under this procedure was Thomas Chippendale, the famous furniture-maker. He was a regular importer of partly made chairs from France, which he seriously undervalued. The collector purchased one consignment of five dozen chairs for only £20! Quite a bargain even then, although unfortunately the final sale price is not recorded.

Since the vast increase of Excise duties in the early part of the century, no new duties had been introduced. Early in 1725 an additional duty was placed on malt. The extra imposition caused no outcry in England, but in Scotland the opposition to the extra duty was so great that the rate had to be reduced to one-half. Despite the reduction, it was the opinion of the Scottish Lords that it would need a regiment of dragoons to collect the duty.

These fears were fully justified when the additional duty was first imposed in June 1725. When the Excise officers in Glasgow tried to collect the duty the maltsters refused them entry to their warehouses to take stock. Mobs thronged the streets, their cry being 'No Union, No Malt Tax.' The revolt quickly spread to the rest of Scotland. In Edinburgh the Excise officers were forced to hide from the mob for fear of their lives, and at Inverness the maltsters were forced to comply only by the severity of General Wade's dragoons. The riots spread as far as the Orkneys, where the Collector reported that his officers were beaten back by 'a mob of riotous women' when they attempted to survey the malthouses.

However, it was Glasgow where the most serious riots occurred. Excise officers were beaten and stoned, and their office was ransacked. It was only when two regiments of troops were brought in that order was restored. Many of the rioters were publicly whipped, some members of the Corporation were imprisoned and the City was forced to recompense the Excise Commissioners for the damage sustained to their property. The malt tax was eventually enforced, with some relaxation: it was agreed that some of the revenue would be applied to improving the Scottish commerce and trade.

Robert Walpole, who had been instrumental in the introduction of the malt duty into Scotland, turned his attention to the considerable abuses and frauds prevalent in the Customs. In 1732 he set up a committee to look into the problems. The report revealed a disastrous state of affairs, especially in the tobacco and wine trades. The duty on tobacco was 6½d. per lb, which produced a gross yield of £754,000, but the net receipt was only £160,000. The enormous deficit was the result of various frauds and forgeries.

One of the favourite methods of fraud was for the merchants to secure—by false certificates or false weights—a greater amount of drawback of duty (repayment of duty on export of the goods) than they were entitled to, and in many cases in excess of the duty they had originally paid. It was estimated that in London alone the loss on tobacco duty was over £250,000. The disquieting aspects of the report were the extent of the implication of the Customs officers in these frauds, the vast amount of smuggling, and the complete inadequacy of the Customs to prevent this free trade.

Walpole's proposals to correct these abuses were to reduce greatly the Customs duty on tobacco—to a nominal amount, just sufficient to secure an entry for the goods—and to replace it with an Excise duty. The tobacco on importation would be removed to a bonded warehouse, under the control of the Excise, and secured by both the Excise and the merchant. Thus the worst abuses of the trade would be avoided, the Excise duty being collected when the tobacco was taken from the warehouse. Walpole claimed that the Excise was a relatively more efficient service, and that his scheme would be simple and effective, and detrimental to none but the smugglers and unfair traders.

The reaction to these proposals was immediate. It was thought that the scheme was the first step to the imposition of a 'General Excise' on all manner of goods. Such was the fear of the Excise that the opposition to the scheme gathered momentum rapidly. The horrors of the Excise were pictured in such lurid detail by the pamphleteers that soon the country was as perturbed about the Excise scheme 'as it might have been about the approach of a pestilence'.

By the time Walpole presented his Excise Bill in 1733 the country was ablaze with opposition to the 'odious Excise'. As support for his scheme dwindled, and the public frenzy over the scheme reached a height, Walpole withdrew the Bill, saying, 'In the present inflamed temper of the people, the Act could not be carried into execution without an armed force.' The Queen had told Walpole that though she thought his scheme 'the best in the world', yet seeing the people expressed such a dislike of it, 'she would not have them displeased'.

When the news of the withdrawal of the Bill became known London became delirious with joy, bonfires were lighted, crowds thronged the streets and the bells pealed all night. As the news spread through the country similar outbursts of rejoicing took place in most major towns and cities. It was reported that no victory over a foreign army had ever been received with greater acclaim. In fact, in 1734 on the first anniversary of the defeat of the Excise the mob assembled in the City in several places and 'committed riots'. The Lord Mayor was compelled to repel them, and was wounded in the head. For several years after the event these celebrations were continued on each anniversary, such was the fear and dread the word 'Excise' engendered in the people. It was to be a long time before any Minister ventured to impose any extension to the Excise. Thus the bonded warehouse scheme, an admirable reform, was regrettably delayed until almost the end of the century.

The continued unpopularity of the Excise can be seen in Dr Johnson's opinion expressed in his dictionary, first published in 1755. His definition of 'Excise' as 'a hateful tax levied upon commodities and adjudged not by the common judges of property, but by wretches hired by those to whom the excise is paid' was noticed by the Excise Commissioners, and they asked the Attorney-General whether it was to be considered a libel, and if so should they proceed against the author, printer and publisher. The opinion they received was

I am of opinion that it is a libel: but under all the circumstances, I think it better to give him an opportunity of altering his definition; and in case he don't, threaten him with an Information.

29th November 1755.

The Dictionary was revised in 1773, but the definition remained unaltered, and the Excise Commissioners took no action; perhaps they were chary of challenging such a formidable opponent! A copy of the *Dictionary*, open at the offending page, was on display in the Custom House Library, and during the bombing in 1940 a shell-splinter fell on the book, completely obliterating the definition of the word Exciseman. Vengeance is mine, saith the Lord!

One of the gravest social problems of the period was drunkenness. In 1727 five million gallons of spirits were produced, and by 1733 the amount had doubled to over eleven million gallons. These were official Excise statistics, and it was estimated that if one included the illicit spirit distilled the true figure would be closer to twenty million gallons. The cause of the dramatic increase was the introduction of a new spirit called geneva (from the French *genièvre* = juniper), which was perhaps better known as gin.

Lord Hervey, commenting on the state of the nation at this time, said:

> Drunkenness of the common people is so universal by the retailing of a liquor called Gin, with which they could get drunk for a groat, that the whole town of London and many towns in the country swarmed with drunken people from morning to night, and were more like a scene of a Bacchanal than the residence of a civil society.

The introduction of geneva into the country owes much to the accession of William III. As a Dutchman, he was naturally partial to the spirit, it being basically a Dutch drink, but he also encouraged its manufacture. Moreover, by his prohibition on French brandy and foreign spirits, demand for English varieties was greatly stimulated.

The English distillers found the compounding (redistilling) of raw spirit with juniper berries an easy and cheap process: little plant was required, and there were as yet no Excise restrictions on either its production or its sale. At first sales of gin were slow, but with the steady increase in beer and malt duties the hitherto traditional drinks of the country, beer and ale, were becoming relatively more expensive. A contemporary writer suggested 'that gin gained such universal applause, especially with the common people, that by a moderate computation, there is more of it in quantity sold daily in many distiller's shops than of beer'. Soon gin could be bought almost anywhere, even from street barrows and carts. The sign 'Drunk for 1*d*., Dead Drunk for 2*d*., Straw for nothing' appeared in the windows of inns and shops all over London. The straw was for sleeping off the effects of the spirit. Gin was now the drink of the working classes of all ages.

In 1728 the death rate in London exceeded the birth rate, and gin-drinking was the main cause. There were now over 10,000 gin or dram shops in London alone. The government decided that some action was needed. They imposed an Excise licence of £20 on all retailers of spirits, and placed a duty of 2s. per gallon on gin. This action had the opposite to the desired effect; it put the legitimate shopkeepers out of business, and opened the way for the illicit producers.

By 1736 it was clear that more drastic action was necessary. The licence duty was raised to £50, with a fine for non-compliance of £100, and the duty was increased to 20s. per gallon. The intention of the Act was to price gin out of the reach of the working classes, but most politicians considered that the laws could not be enforced, and would thus lead to yet greater production of illicit spirit. A way was in fact found to evade the new law by mixing gin with wine (a wine licence cost only 3s.). The resultant drink was often sold as medicine, and went under various exotic names, although the most popular name was Parliamentary Brandy.

As predicted, the Excise officers were unable to cope with the legitimate side of the business, let alone the vast illicit trade. In an attempt to control the problem the Excise imposed fines for unlicensed production or sales. In the first two years there were over 5,000 convictions, but to achieve these the Excise had to resort to paid informers. However, the violence shown to these informers, to the Excise officers, and even to the magistrates, was such that after 1739 there were virtually no convictions. Only three licences were taken out, and the revenue from spirits had fallen to almost nothing. The situation was completely out of hand; as the Excise Commissioners reported, 'the law has become odious, contemptible and unworkable'.

Although originally the problem had been largely confined to London and the other cities, the Excise were also experiencing much opposition in the country areas, and soon illicit distillation was widespread. In 1738 a gang of over 1,000 colliers in Kingswood Forest, Bristol, was engaged in making large quantities of gin and selling it in Bristol and the surrounding area. These colliers had so terrorized the Excise officers in the area that, far from the Excise moving in to break up the illicit distillation, a detachment of dragoons were needed to accompany them on their normal visits.

In the intervening years certain minor changes were made in the laws—for instance, the duty on beer was reduced, in the hope that the populace would change their drinking habits. This did not succeed, and increasing pressure was placed on the government to introduce some form of realistic control. The dramatic effect of Hogarth's print *Gin Lane*, and of Fielding's treatise on crime, had some influence on the government and a new Act was introduced in 1751. The system of licensing was greatly improved; so much so that within a few years the Excise Commissioners were able to report that the situation was now under 'complete control'. Some years of bad harvests, which greatly increased the price of the spirit, also had their effect. Towards the end of the century gin had advanced to become a middle-class drink; it had achieved respectability.

The second Jacobite rebellion in 1745 caused even greater disturbance to both services than had the earlier one. The Highland army on its march to Edinburgh broke into and ransacked the Custom House in Aberdeen and

Montrose, but did not find any public money. However, at Montrose they took the Customs weights to melt down for shot. Following the pattern of the earlier rebellion, they again collected the Excise duties as they advanced through the northern counties. By the time they had reached Derby they had appropriated over £2,000—a much better haul than fell to the earlier rebel force.

During the approach of the rebels the Collectors of Customs at Whitehaven and Liverpool were much concerned for the safety of the Customs money at their ports. The Collector at Whitehaven decided to send his cash by armed guard to Newcastle, where General Wade was in command, and at Liverpool the 'entire King's chest' was placed on two new warships which had been built in the port.

After the defeat of the Rebellion the officers in Scotland were instructed 'to examine all strangers to ensure that no rebels escaped', and the Excise officers were given the invidious task of compiling a list of persons who had sided with the rebels. Even as late as 1752, seven years after the uprising, several officers were required to explain their actions during the time of the Rebellion. The collection of public money was considered a serious offence. A judge at one of the trials ruled that 'the acceptance of a Commission of Excise from the Pretender was an overt act of Treason'. It was not until December 1752 that the Treasury allowed the Excise Board credit for the deficit of £2,441 16s. 6½d., so that as before no Excise trader lost any money.

Since the renewal of its charter in 1708, the East India Company—or as it was more familiarly called, 'John Company'—enjoyed many privileges and concessions, especially in Customs matters and procedure. The Company had its own landing berth at Blackwall, numerous private warehouses in the City and duty deferment on imported goods, and was allowed to conduct its own sales, which established the import values for dutiable purposes. The vast trading empire, with its monopoly of Indian and Chinese goods, demanded close Customs supervision; over five hundred Customs officials of varying ranks were directly involved in the Company's activities.

From the first arrival of the East Indiamen in the Downs near Deal, the vessels were closely controlled by the Customs. In the early days tidesmen had been placed on board to accompany the ships to Gravesend. By the mid-century this practice had ceased, and the fleet was escorted to the Thames by Customs cutters. From Gravesend the vessels would proceed to Blackwall with tidesmen on board. There the goods would be loaded into hoys or lighters, for discharge at the legal quays around the Custom House. The Company's goods and the 'private trade' goods—those on freight for other merchants—were taken direct to the East India warehouses near Crutched Friars. The goods belonging to the master, officers and crew were placed in the King's Warehouse at the Custom House. The Company allowed its servants to trade privately, and it was reported that a captain might make over £1,000 on a single voyage. At all stages of these operations full accounts of all the goods landed were taken by the Customs officers.

Most of the sales of goods were conducted by auction in the East India House in Fenchurch Street. For many years the sales were conducted by 'candle inch'—that is, a candle was lighted at the start of the auction, and the bidding continued until an inch of candle had burnt, and at that precise time the highest bid secured the goods. As the Company had a monopoly in many goods, such as pepper, spices and of course tea, the prices obtained at these auctions determined not only the value for duty but also the selling price in the country. At some of these sales over 200,000 pounds of tea would be sold in a single day. Such was the size of the Company's operations that it paid over £1,000,000 in Customs and Excise duties.

There were several inquiries into the Customs dealings with the Company over the years. One of the earliest had been at the start of the century, when Richard Score, the Collector at Penzance, spent over eighteen months investigating frauds, ultimately saving the Customs £40,000. He was given £1,000 for his labours. Slowly, as the various inquiries disclosed widespread collusion between the Company servants and the Customs officials, much more control and greater restrictions were placed on the activities of the Company. By 1772, when the arrears of duty outstanding were so large—about a quarter of a million pounds—the Customs Commissioners decided to put the Company's bond in suit. The very high incidence of smuggling of tea was blamed for the Company's inability to sell their tea at a competitive price. (At this time there was sixteen million pounds of tea stored in their warehouses!) The Commissioners extended the period of warehousing, and the Treasury allowed the Company to ship large quantities of tea to the American colonies duty-free. This decision was one of the indirect causes of the Boston Tea Party. By December 1772 the Company must have resolved some of its financial problems, since they were able to pay off some of the outstanding duty. The sum of £205,400 was deposited at the Custom House 'in one banknote'!

Thirty years after the riots and furore occasioned by Walpole's Excise Bill, the Excise found themselves faced once again with bitter opposition and hostility on the imposition of a new extra duty on cider. For some time it had been considered that the high malt duties were largely unproductive in the west of the country, where the traditional drink had always been cider. It was therefore proposed, in order to equalize the position, to increase the existing duty on cider, and furthermore to extend it to include cider made in the home. The head of each household was required to declare all the members of the family over the age of eight, and to pay 5s. per person as an Excise licence.

The 'Cyder' Bill was introduced in 1763 by Lord Bute's administration, and at first the opposition to the duty was confined to the cider counties in the west of the country, and was largely that of interested parties. However, within a very short time the whole country was in ferment over the Bill. Once again the unrest arose from the hatred of the Excise, and the fear that this new duty was a prelude to the introduction of a 'General Excise'.

The mob attacked Excise offices, and effigies of Excise officers and Lord Bute were burned in the streets. One of the caricatures of the time was *The Roasted Exciseman or Jack Boot's Exit*. Despite the storm of protests, the Bill was passed, but a week after the Royal Assent Lord Bute resigned. A further attempt to repeal the Bill in 1766 was defeated, and the cider duty remained on the Statute Book until the general repeal of the old beer duty in 1830. However, once again Ministers had been given a painful reminder of the dangers of introducing any new Excise taxation.

At the start of the century the Excise Head Office was situated in Broad Street, but with the rapid growth of the department larger premises had to be found. The Excise Commissioners rented 'a large mansion' in Old Jewry, which had originally been the home of Sir John Frederick, a Lord Mayor of London. By the mid-sixties even this building was insufficient for the increase of staff, and the Excise Board were once again searching for suitable accommodation somewhere in the City of London.

In 1766 they started negotiations to purchase the Bishop of Ely's palace and grounds in Holborn. The discussions were so well advanced that a draft Bill was presented for Parliament. It is interesting to note that one of the provisions in the Bill was to make the land at Holborn part of the City of London. Suddenly, and for no apparent reason, the negotiations with the Bishop were suspended, and no further action was taken. About six years later the Treasury purchased the property to house the Stamps and Hackney Carriage Commissioners.

The Excise Board turned their attention to Gresham College in Broad Street. It was reported that on 17 March 1767 'the City members, attended by Mr Dance, the surveyor, waited on by the Lords of the Treasury with a plan of the ground on which Gresham College stood, for the purpose of pulling down the old building and erecting an Excise office in its stead'. In 1768 they finally purchased the site from the Mercers Company for an annual rent of £500. During the excavations some fine Roman remains of a large house were uncovered, including a well-preserved mosaic floor, which was taken up and preserved, and many years later was put on display in the Crystal Palace. The building was completed in 1772, and an eye witness describes it thus:

> On the east side of Broad Street stands the Excise Office, a handsome plain building of four stories high, with an entrance through the middle of it into a large yard, in which is another building of brick nearly the size of the principal one. The front building stands on the site of ten alms-houses founded by Sir Thomas Gresham in 1575, and the back one with the yard occupies the space on which Gresham College formerly stood.

During the rebuilding of the Royal Exchange the Excise courtyard was used by the shipping and mercantile interests in the City as a temporary Exchange. Once again the Excise had returned to Broad Street, very close to the site where it was first housed in 1643.

The Customs duties had so increased in number, and the laws, regulations and exemptions had become so involved, that no merchant was competent to unravel the intricacies of the system. The documents required to enter the goods and account for the duty were so complicated that very few Customs officers even were conversant with all the regulations. There was an obvious need for some explanatory handbook. In the early years of the century Henry Crouch, 'an officer in London', published *A Complete View of the Customs*, which became the authoritative manual on Customs procedure. It received virtual official status when collectors were told to 'consult Crouch' on various procedural matters. By 1757 another London Port officer, Henry Saxby, had produced his *British Customs*, pointing out the many errors in the earlier publications. Saxby's book became the vade-mecum of all the officers; none would attempt to calculate the various duties without first consulting this book.

The Excise officers also faced similar problems; the new duties, with the different manufacturing processes and the intricate gauging operations, created a demand for a comprehensive manual. This need was supplied by a guide called *The Royal Gauger*, first published in 1739, and running into seven editions up to 1779. The author was Charles Leadbetter, sometime Excise officer but more famous as a mathematician and astronomer. *The Royal Gauger* gave instructions in the theory and practice of gauging, as well as providing a guide to Excise laws and controls. For over fifty years it was an essential reference work for all Excise officers.

As the plantations in America and the West Indies flourished and their trade prospered, so the Customs control from London was regularized. Eventually a separate Plantation Department was set up in the London Custom House. Appointments to the ports in the plantations were similar to the English service, mainly by patents; the salaries were nominal, and the main remuneration was by way of fees. The officers were instructed in London, prior to leaving for the colonies, but they were not paid until they arrived at their respective ports.

Many duties were imposed on articles into the American colonies, which met with strong opposition from the colonists. Large new territories passed to Britain after the wars in Canada, and the problem of control of this large area by long distance from London was proving almost impossible. It was therefore decided to establish an American Board of Customs. They were appointed, like their English counterparts, by Letters Patent, and had the same wide powers, although at a salary of £500 they were grossly underpaid by English standards.

The new Board set up their headquarters in September 1767 at Boston. With hindsight, the choice of Boston seems most unwise, as it was the centre of strong anti-British feelings, as well as being famous (or infamous) for the Stamp Act riots. Furthermore, it was not the main port in America, both New York and Philadelphia being larger and more loyal to the Government. Perhaps the credit for the selection of Boston should be given to Charles

Paxton, the Surveyor of Customs at Boston. He was in England during 1766–7, and certainly had some influence with Government officials, especially Charles Townshend, the Chancellor of the Exchequer, who would listen to his advice. On his return to America he became a Commissioner on the new American Board of Customs. Paxton was considered by a contemporary to be 'every man's humble servant but no man's friend'.

From the start the American Board met strong opposition; they were a constant resident reminder of the 'tyrannical' London government. The many new and unpopular duties imposed on the plantations made their job very difficult, but it was perhaps their stricter application of the laws and their vigorous collection of the duties that gave rise to the most fervent opposition. Particularly unpopular was their use of Writs of Assistance, which were an authority to empower officers to enter any house, warehouse or shop to search for uncustomed goods. Such writs had been in use in England since 1662, but had been moderated by a certain regard for private property. However, in America the Customs authorities had attempted to make the writs open and general, or as James Otis, one of the opponents of their use, called them, 'a carte blanche to the invasion of property'. John Adams, remarking on the opposition to the use of writs, commented, 'Then and there the child Independence was born.'

So strong was the opposition to the American Board that frequently they had to leave the Custom House at Boston and take refuge in Castle William, a fortified island in Boston Harbour, returning only under the protection of the Army. The Tea Act of 1773, which imposed a duty of 3d. per pound on tea exported from the East India Company in London, caused the most serious opposition to the Customs administration. The Company were allowed to ship large quantities of tea in order to clear their large stocks, and also to attempt to stimulate demand in America. Cargoes were sent to the main ports in America. Three vessels arrived at Boston and remained undischarged, while the townspeople decided what action to take. It was agreed to return the tea to England, but a small number of citizens took the matter into their own hands, and on 16 December 1773, 340 chests of tea were thrown into the harbour.

The Government in England retaliated by closing the port of Boston, and removed the Customs Board to Salem. The Board did return to Boston, once again under the protection of the Army, but their return was short-lived. The relations between the colonists and the Government were deteriorating, and moving inexorably to outright war. Finally, on 17 March 1776, Boston was evacuated by the Army and the American Commissioners took ship for Halifax and arrived back in England in September, never to set foot in America again. (They received their salaries, however, until their patent was revoked in 1783.) The officers in the loyal ports dealt directly with the Treasury, and frequently paid their duties direct to the military forces. After the War of Independence all the remaining ports in the British colonies were controlled by the English Board in London.

Despite few new duties being introduced, the revenue from the Excise in
1770 amounted to £5 millions, almost double the amount raised from
Customs duties. The Excise collected this figure with less staff than the
Customs. Nevertheless, there were over 10,000 persons employed in both
services—a fair percentage of the literate population. Neither was short of
applicants; the Excise maintained a list of appointees waiting for the next
vacancy, and at one stage had to close the books to fresh applicants.

The Excise still suffered considerable public opposition, and in 1787 this
manifested itself with the so-called riots over the collection of malt duty in
Ware, Hertfordshire, which was the centre of a large malting area. A new
Excise supervisor, Robert Guard, was appointed to the town, and within a
very short time he and an officer named Veal had brought a number of
summons for minor Excise infringements against some of the most
prominent maltsters in the town. All the cases were dismissed by the local
Justices, which only encouraged Guard's vigilance. The officious manner of
the Excisemen was 'so obnoxious to the people that they were hooted
wherever they went, and even a little street dirt was thrown at them'.

According to Guard's report to the Excise Board, he 'was regularly
assaulted and insulted by the rioters and his officers were prevented from
doing their duty'. He asked the Board for some protection for himself and for
his officers. As a result troops were moved in, and the town was placed under
military law. Malting virtually ceased, and the situation between the
townspeople and the Excise worsened. The troops stayed for almost five
months, and it was only on the written assurance of 'gentlemen of the
neighbourhood that the inhabitants are willing to suffer the revenue' that
the military force was withdrawn. In the official inquiry after the 'riots'
Guard and Veal were found to have 'exceeded their authority', and were
downgraded and removed to other areas.

There was a sharp rise in prices in the 1770s, but the Customs officers were
cushioned against this inflation with their system of fees. The Excise officers
were not so fortunate, since they relied solely on their salaries, which had not
altered since the beginning of the century. By 1772 there was some agitation
among them for an increase, many petitioning the Board and Members of
Parliament on their plight.

Perhaps the most famous address was published in a pamphlet entitled
The Case of the Officers of Excise. It was written and circulated by Thomas
Paine, the author of *Rights of Man* and *The Age of Reason*, who found fame but
not fortune in America and France. Paine entered the Excise in 1762 as an
officer at Alford, near his home town of Thetford. In 1765 he was discharged
from the service for 'stamping his ride'—showing in his journal that he had
visited traders, when in fact he was absent from his area. The following year
he wrote a most abject letter of apology, requesting to be reinstated. The
Board agreed, and offered him a post in Cornwall, which he refused, finally
accepting a post in Lewes in February 1768.

His pamphlet on pay was published in 1772, and was signed by himself and seven other officers, who were reputed to be the Committee representing the 3,000 or so Excise officers. Over 4,000 copies were printed, an expense which suggests some formal organization to finance the project. The petition cogently argued the case for some increase in salary, maintaining that when tax, the Charity Fund and hiring expenses were deducted the officers were left with £46 per annum. Further, most had to purchase and maintain a horse, the expense of which brought their take-home pay to only £32.

The petition was sent to Members of Parliament, the Excise Commissioners, and certain influential people—Oliver Goldsmith was one example. The reply from the Treasury was short and sharp—no increase. Perhaps Paine was not unduly surprised at this answer, as he is reported as commenting, 'A rebellion of the Excisemen, who seldom have the populace on their side, is unlikely to succeed.' Paine's Excise career came to an end in 1774, when he was discharged once again, this time for being absent from his work without the Board's leave.

Another famous literary Exciseman, Robert Burns, found the salary more congenial. 'I find £50 per an., which is now our Salary, an exceeding good thing—People may talk as they please of the ignominy of the Excise, but what will support my family and keep me independent of the world is to me a very important matter; and I had much rather that my Profession borrowed credit from me, than that I borrowed credit from my Profession.' Burns was an Excise officer in Dumfries from 1789 to his death in 1796. His view of his duties show the arduous life of the Excise. 'Five days in the week, or four at least I must be on horseback and very frequently ride thirty or forty miles ere I return; besides four different kinds of book-keeping to post every day.' Despite his reputation, Burns acted well as an Exciseman; the entry in a character book (staff report) read 'The Poet, does pretty well.' He was recommended for promotion to supervisor, and at the time of his death was waiting for a vacancy to arise in the area. His widow, Jean Armour, received a pension of £8, later increased to £12, right up to her death in 1834.

The Scottish Customs service of the time also had an eminent literary man—Adam Smith, the author of *The Wealth of Nations*. This classic work was first published in 1776, and reached five editions in Smith's lifetime. Adam Smith was appointed Commissioner of Customs in Edinburgh in 1778, a post he held until his death in 1790. He had a Customs background, for his father had been Comptroller and his uncle Collector in Kirkcaldy.

Both services had survived a most difficult period in their development. The Excise, particularly, had demonstrated a keen efficiency in administration and control in the face of almost constant opposition. However, it was not beset with the inherent defects of the Customs service, which had to contend with a marked expansion of trade encumbered with a medieval system of patent posts and intricate laws and duties. Both Boards had made very genuine attempts to improve their respective services, but many of the solutions to the problems were beyond their control, and the reforms lay with Parliament. Certainly the time was ripe for change.

CHAPTER FIVE

The Wind of Change

The last decades of the eighteenth century and the early part of the nineteenth century can be largely considered as the watershed between the old revenue services and the modern revenue departments. The changes and reforms were so sweeping and comprehensive that within a relatively short time the appearance of both services had been radically altered.

The one person largely responsible for these changes was William Pitt the Younger, who abounded with economic talent and was full of very progressive ideas. He inherited a Customs service with a very involved system of duties and fees, a mass of laws, an administrative chaos of revenue accounts and smuggling at an unprecedented level. During his Ministry he managed to achieve many of the much-needed changes, but also—and perhaps more important—he laid the foundations for other reforms undertaken in the next thirty years.

Early in 1780 a Board of Commissioners were appointed to inquire into the public accounts of all departments of state. Somewhat hopefully, their initial authority was limited to one year only, but it was to be over five years before they presented their various reports. They highlighted the very involved and intricate system of accounts in the Customs, as well as the number of archaic patent posts. In London the Duke of Newcastle was Patent Comptroller at a salary of £375, plus fees to the value of £1,300 per year, and the Duke of Manchester was still Patent Collector (Outwards) collecting his normal £2,000 fees. In the out-ports were the various patent customers, searchers and controllers with virtually no duties, sharing their salaries with their deputies and collecting their percentage of the fees.

As a result of the Committee's reports, the customer and other patent posts were abolished in 1798. There was no sudden disappearance of these ancient posts; the process was gradual—the posts not being filled as the patents came up for renewal. The question of fees in the Customs was passed to another committee, established solely to gauge the extent of the problem. This separate committee reported in 1789, and showed in great detail the number and amount of the fees that were paid. In some instances a merchant was required to pay sums to nine different officials to enter and clear one consignment of goods. The report recommended that a list of the 'official and allowable' fees should be exhibited at every Custom House, and that the Commissioners ensure that no 'exorbitant fees are charged'. Noticeboards were erected at Custom Houses to list the scale, especially for the sale of documents on which importers entered the goods: the receipts from these were a major portion of the officers' remuneration. (Until fairly recently the Crown received an income for various Customs documents, which were called Sale forms.) One such noticeboard dating from 1809 gave the notice that 'all Officers and Persons in the service should give every Facility, Despatch, and Accommodation to merchants, traders and others that the Faithful Discharge of the Duties of such Officers and persons will permit'.

Fees were not finally abolished until 1806, first in London Port and a year later in the out-ports. Prior to this the Treasury had sent forms to all officers, asking them to disclose full particulars of all the fees they received. The officers, suspecting some form of extra taxation, greatly under-declared the amounts, only to find to their chagrin that the Treasury based the amount of compensation on these forms when the fee system was abolished. The practice of fee-taking did not cease overnight, for even ten years later there were complaints that 'certain sums were still being charged by the Customs officers'. At the same time the opportunity was taken to reduce the number of Custom House holidays from 45 to 10 days, and the hours of attendance at the Custom Houses were extended to four o'clock in the afternoon.

The growing trade of London Port, and the very limited number of legal quays—which had not been added to since the days of Charles II—had resulted in complaints of congestion in the Port, many vessels having to wait for days and even weeks before they could load or discharge at the legal quays. This had led to collectors allowing 'sufferances'—for a fee, of course—for the vessel to discharge at a place other than the legal quays. Usually these 'sufferance wharves' were a distance from the Custom House, which made supervision and control difficult. In 1789 the Commissioners decided to regularize the situation, and listed various wharves as permanent sufferance wharves, open to all importers. The proprietors were required to give a bond 'as a security for their fair dealings with the revenue', and were further required to pay for the attendance of the officer. Although this procedure only applied at first to London Port, it later spread slowly to the out-ports.

About fifty years had elapsed since the defeat of Walpole's Excise Bill before any Minister ventured again to consider any new Excise duties. A rather abortive duty had been placed on household plate, specially designed to tax silver teaspoons, which were rapidly coming into general use. The duty was very difficult to administer, since its control depended mainly upon servants informing on their masters. The Excise Board wrote to all persons suspected of owning articles of plate which had not been declared. John Wesley, the Methodist minister, received such an inquiry. His reply was succinct: 'I have two spoons in London and two spoons in Bristol, which I have at present and I shall not buy more, while so many round me want bread.'

Pitt was determined to use the Excise service as the best and most efficient means of collecting the revenue. In 1784 he imposed an Excise duty on bricks to pay the interest on debts incurred by the American war. The duty was 5s. 10d. per thousand on common bricks and 10s. per thousand on large bricks. To complicate matters, many bricks were of unusual shape, and the moulds for these bricks were checked by the Excise officers to determine whether they were liable to the higher rate of duty. After testing, the approved mould would be stamped with a branding iron with the word EXCISE, and kept by the brickmaker. Many of these irons are still in existence, for the brick duty was not repealed until 1850. Pitt also introduced the principle of a licence duty for all retailers of beer, wines and spirits, which varied according to the extent of their business or the value of their business premises. Hitherto licences had been issued for a nominal sum, just as a formal recognition of the Excise trader—a type of registration fee. The new system of licences was brought in primarily as a source of revenue, and established the very complex system of Excise liquor licences which survived until after the Second World War.

Pitt, no doubt encouraged by the relative ease with which these duties were accepted by Parliament, now felt assured that he could successfully carry out measures which Walpole had been compelled to abandon. In 1786 he proposed to transfer the greater part of the duties on wines from the Customs to the Excise. This was a means of preventing the extensive frauds in the wine trade, especially smuggling. It was estimated that the annual losses on wines amounted to £280,000. The new Act empowered Excise officers to have access to the premises of all wine dealers and retailers, and despite considerable opposition from the wine trade, the Bill was passed.

He now turned his attention to the tobacco trade, which suffered even greater abuses in fraud and smuggling. It was again proposed that the main control of the duty should be passed to the Excise. Instead of the duty being levied at import as a Customs duty, it was proposed that part would be paid at import and the rest be raised as an Excise duty on removal from warehouses for home consumption. Elaborate arrangements were made to set up bonded warehouses, and all tobacco-manufacturers, dealers and retailers were required to take out licences, and submit to control by Excise officers. In an attempt to combat smuggling, stringent regulations were brought in to control the import of tobacco. It could only be carried in vessels of a certain size, the allowances to crews were drastically reduced, and vessels found hovering near the coast with a hundred pounds of tobacco were subject to seizure.

There were great protests from the tobacco trade at these measures, which they considered savage. So vociferous were the complaints that a Parliamentary Committee was formed to hear the objections. However, the new measures were already showing some success; the revenue from tobacco had increased by nearly £300,000. This was sufficient reason for the new system to be retained. The duty on tobacco now stood at 1s. 3d. per pound (equivalent to almost a 400 per cent duty by value), but during the next twenty years would rise to 4s. per pound, thereby establishing itself as the most productive of all revenue duties, a position it retained until 1968.

The successful introduction of wine and tobacco warehouses laid the foundations for more general warehousing for many other goods. Although warehousing before payment of duty had previously been allowed on some goods—for instance, pepper as early as 1714, rum in 1742 and sugar in 1766—all other goods were liable to immediate payment of duty on importation. This was proving a great hardship to trade, and especially to the small importer, who was compelled to pay large sums of duty before he had sold the goods. In 1803 an Act was passed which allowed all types of goods to be placed in warehouses pending payment of duty. New warehouses were speedily constructed in nearly every port, and although the ports themselves had to be authorized by an Order in Council, approval of the new warehouses was delegated to the Customs Commissioners.

The increasing expenses of the war required continual new finance. The list of articles and services taxed seemed endless, and included hats, hair-powder, armorial bearings, carriages, auctions, as well as additional duties on spirits, tea, malt, paper, glass and salt. The latter duty was transferred to the control of the Excise, and the Salt Commissioners were disbanded. Perhaps the most famous tax to be introduced in this period was income tax, which was brought into being as a wartime measure in 1799. The rate of tax was 2s. in the £ on total income above £200, and was criticized for its complexity, but the main cause of its unpopularity was the fact that every taxpayer was required to make a return of his total income. It was controlled by the Board of Taxes, which later was amalgamated with the Excise to form the Inland Revenue.

One of the most urgent reforms needed in the Customs was to consolidate and simplify its laws. The whole system had grown into one of bewildering and utter chaos. The laws had been recently reprinted, and made up a total of twenty large volumes. This edition was for the use of the Commissioners and senior officers in London; no copies were available for public sale. The majority of goods were liable to duty under twelve to eighteen different Acts, dating from Charles II, irrespective of the many and varied Acts dealing with special goods, plantation trade, East India, coasting and smuggling. There were no less than a hundred different branches of duty, each requiring separate values, imposts and accounts. A Commissioner wrote in 1784:

> The computation has become so intricate and extensive, that there are very
> few people who understand the business properly, nor is it easy to procure

assistance . . . the duties are so complicated that it is hardly possible for a general merchant to know what duties he may be liable to pay.

The first steps to consolidation were taken in 1781, when the work was given to a Customs Committee led by James Hume, the Deputy Comptroller at London, who later became a Commissioner. The work of the Committee lasted for almost six years before they managed to produce a draft Bill. The draft was sent to the large ports to obtain not only the collectors' comments but the reactions of the merchants to the proposed new legislation. The consensus of opinion was overwhelmingly in favour; it was considered that the Bill would be of 'the greatest advantage to the mercantile world'.

Pitt introduced the Bill into the House of Commons in February 1787, saying in his introduction, 'We wish to remedy this great abuse now subsisting in this confused and complex manner, by substituting one single duty for each article.' The Bill was designed to repeal all the existing Acts and values and to reintroduce a new duty article by article. This mammoth task required no less than 2,615 different resolutions of the House, and despite the large number all were passed at one sitting! One further complication was that the Customs revenues were appropriated to anything up to twenty-five different funds, causing endless accounts not only in the Customs, but also in the Exchequer. At one stroke the Bill changed the mass of confused accounts, by directing that all the revenues, both Customs and Excise, should be carried forward to one fund only, henceforth to be called the Consolidated Fund.

Despite the inestimable value of the new Act, it was basically a reform of only the duties and accounts, and not of the procedure when new and additional duties were introduced. The same causes which had brought about the confusion were therefore still in operation. During the next ten years fresh duties were introduced, additional duties imposed, and old ones augmented, with the result that a new consolidation of the duties was once again required. This was done in 1797, and again in 1803, 1809, 1813 and 1819. The later Acts virtually established the system of the modern tariff.

The laws and rules governing Customs procedure were equally as complicated, and if possible in a more chaotic state than the Customs duties. They filled 'six large folio volumes unprovided with any index'. In 1810 it was decided to have at least a digest of them produced, and this work was entrusted to Nicholas Jickling, the Collector at Wells, a small port on the Norfolk coast. He had already spent much of his official life assimilating and indexing the mass of Customs laws. After working assiduously for five years he produced his *Digest*, a massive tome containing 1,375 pages; he received £4,000 from the Board for his labours. Despite this excellent volume, the laws still required long and patient study, before the precise legal basis of much of the Customs procedure could be traced.

In 1822 James Hume, one of the officers in the Long Room in London

Port, conceived the idea of repealing all the extant laws, consolidating them and re-enacting the operative sections into a series of new statutes. Sanction for this immense undertaking was obtained from the Treasury, perhaps helped by the fact that Hume was the son of James Hume the Customs Commissioner and instigator of the earlier 1787 Act. Hume spent three years on the work, and even drafted the Bill, which was passed by Parliament in July 1825. It was praised as a 'great triumph of industry and skill—for the first time, neither the meaning nor the application of the Customs laws can be no longer mistaken'.

The procedure pursued by Parliament after the 1825 Act was to present a Bill annually, embracing all the changes in Customs laws enacted during the year, as an amendment to Hume's standard Act. Hume was appointed Controller of London Port, but his obvious ability had been noticed by William Huskisson, then at the head of the Board of Trade, and he created a special post of Joint Secretary of the Board of Trade for Hume, who became closely concerned with the various reforms of Huskisson, notably those related to Free Trade.

Like the Customs, the Excise Department was subjected to rigorous scrutiny by the Parliamentary Committees during 1781–6. However, unlike the Customs, the Excise on the whole escaped relatively unscathed from the ordeal, and even received some credit for its able administration. The inquiries revealed virtually no sinecure posts, and hardly any fees. The Excise Commissioners were justifiably proud of the low cost of collection of the many and varied duties, and were constantly alive to the possibilities of even further economies. However, they were being continually petitioned by their officers for some improvements in their salaries; the salary problem had not been resolved since Paine's famous petition.

Early in 1788 the Excise Board saw a way to achieve some consolidation in posts and accounts, thereby obtaining a substantial saving of salaries, and at the same time to increase the salaries of the remaining officers. After 'a careful enquiry by persons of skill and integrity', a report was produced that proposed redundancies of almost 760 officers, which was nearly a quarter of the staff working in the collections. This figure was mainly achieved by enlarging the officers' areas. The gross saving was close to £46,000. The scheme appealed to the Treasury, who 'greatly approved' of the proposals, and they were introduced immediately. It became the biggest reorganization ever introduced into the Excise.

The very meagre salary increases—on average only £5 per year— did little to assuage the officers' demands for a 'respectable remuneration'. Literally hundreds of petitions for increases were received from all over the country. They were all accompanied by detailed cost of living tables and annual budgets for families, the figures quoted being remarkably similar, which suggested some form of central committee organizing the petitions. In addition to the low salaries, the other main complaint was the frequent compulsory moving of staff on grounds of efficiency. It was claimed that these removes, normally every five years, exposed the officers and their families to considerable personal disturbance, as well as making them suffer exorbitant rents for fresh accommodation.

The Treasury, faced with such a forceful case—presented by a very unified staff, from collector down to the most junior assistant—spent some time deliberating the matter. It was well aware that 'those who are entrusted with the protection of the revenue should have proper encouragement to excite themselves to a due discharge of the trust committed to them'. Finally, in December 1800, it capitulated and agreed to some increases, which ranged from £15 for officers to £30 for collectors. The Commissioners, who had not supported the claim, did not receive an increase. The Treasury was adamant in its refusal to abandon the removal system, which was destined to remain for another fifty years.

One of the results of the improved salaries was a far greater demand for Excise positions. Soon there were over 300 qualified persons on the waiting lists, and it was found necessary to restrict future nominations. The Commissioners issued an instruction 'that only the relatives of serving officers would be considered', thus reinforcing the already strong family links of service in the Excise. With the new streamlined organization and the improved salaries, if not conditions, the Excise service was well adapted to cope with the future changes in the new century.

From as early as 1700, Customs officers were expressly forbidden to 'use any influence in Parliamentary elections'. Numerous directives were issued strictly debarring them from either persuading or dissuading any elector from giving his vote to any candidate. In 1711 this ban had been extended to include Excise officers. In 1782 a Bill was introduced to debar all officers from voting at elections. Although the Bill was hotly contested at all stages, it was passed by a large majority. It had been calculated that revenue officers—which included not only the Customs and Excise, but also the Post Office, stamps and salt officials—formed nearly 20 per cent of the total electorate. It was argued that no less than seventy Borough elections depended solely on their votes, and that they could influence 140 votes in the House of Commons. Thus all revenue officers were debarred from all parliamentary activity. Even in the Reform Bill of 1832, a clause proposing to remove this disability was rejected. It was not until 1867 that they received the vote, despite the measure being opposed by both Gladstone and Disraeli (one of the rare occasions when these two politicians agreed on an issue). It was another eight years before they received complete freedom in parliamentary elections.

During the wars with France both services were involved with extra work, much of it accompanied by a good deal of danger for the officers. Perhaps the most exciting incident was on the occasion of the abortive landing of some 1,400 French troops at Fishguard on 21 February 1797—the last invasion of Great Britain. There were no regular troops stationed in the vicinity, or any naval establishment at Milford Haven. Lord Cawdor, the Lord-Lieutenant, assembled the few militia in the area, but the credit of the affair must go to the Customs personnel in the collections.

Captain Dobbin, the commander of the Custom cutter *Diligence* stationed at Milford, landed all his men and joined forces with Captain Hopkin, the commander of the Customs cutter *Speedwell*, which just happened to be patrolling off the coast. They mustered a force of 150 men, unshipped the guns of the *Speedwell*, and carried them 27 miles to engage the enemy. The Collector at Pembroke, John Adams, showed commendable foresight and intelligence in obtaining and communicating important information, before joining Lord Cawdor's yeomanry force as a private.

The French force, surprised by the sound of the revenue guns, believed that they were opposed by a much larger force, and surrendered to Lord Cawdor on Goodwick Sands. So impressed was his lordship with the actions of the Customs officers that he sent a very fulsome letter of commendation to the Customs Commissioners:

> to express the high sense, I entertain of all the alacrity and determination of all your officers and men, in the ports of Milford and Pembroke . . . do credit to the profession to which they belong.

The history of the Customs and Excise in Ireland is a rather confused story. An Irish Revenue Board had been established as far back as 1662. As in England and Wales, the duties were farmed, although in Ireland there was a total farm for the whole of the Customs and Excise duties. When the revenue was taken out of farm one single Revenue Board was set up. It comprised seven Customs Commissioners, five of whom were also appointed to control the Excise.

This system continued until 1789, when the number of Commissioners was increased to nine and the business of the Customs and Excise was divided. The respective Boards were directed to sit and act separately, although still partly composed of the same members. With the Act of Union with Ireland in 1801, which established the United Kingdom of Great Britain and Ireland, the division of work was made more complex under the directions of the Lord-Lieutenant. In 1806 a Board was set up to administer the 'Customs and Port' duties, and one to collect the 'Inland Excise and Taxes'. The difference between this system and the rest of Great Britain was that elsewhere the Excise still collected the port duties, and the assessment of taxes was the responsibility of a separate department in England and Wales.

The biggest headache for the Excise authorities in Scotland was the taxation of their national drink, usquebaugh or whisky. It was taxed in two forms, one on the malt used in the production of the spirit and the other on the spirit itself. We have already seen the considerable opposition to the malt duty in Scotland. The tax on the spirit itself was from 1707 to 1787 in the form of a presumptive charge based on the amount of low wines and spirits assumed to have been made from each hundred gallons of wash (liquid). This type of taxation favoured the Scottish distiller to the detriment of the

English distiller. As a result of continual pressure by the English distillers, the now famous Wash Act of 1784 was passed. This resulted in the Lowland distiller being charged a very much higher presumptive rate of duty, and the Highland distiller being charged duty according to the capacity of his still.

Despite these changes, the main problem remained unresolved—that of illicit distillation, which continued to thrive. The enormity of the task to suppress the smugglers—a term used not only for illegal importers but for illicit distillers also—was quite beyond the resources of the Excise. The officers had had a bad reputation in Scotland from the days of the Union, when they were described as 'thae blackguard loons o' excisemen and gaugers, that have come doun like locusts'. Furthermore, illicit distillation was part and parcel of rural life; virtually every farmer had his own still. In Glenlivet alone there were estimated to be over two hundred small stills making illicit spirits, which were considered the only whisky worth drinking.

In 1797 Scotland was divided into three districts for revenue purposes, Highland, Intermediate, and Lowland, each with a different set of regulations and rates of duty. The following year a committee was set up to examine the Scottish distilleries. It reported—as was fairly obvious to the Excise—that there was a vast amount of illicit distillation. According to evidence given to the inquiry, 'It [illicit distillation] is not confined to the great towns . . . but spreads itself over the whole face of the country and in every island from Orkney to Jura.'

The Committee recommended a system of very close Excise control on all the distilling operations and processes. This control ultimately became the pattern of Excise supervision almost up to the present day.

During the next twenty years various changes were made to both the laws and duties, the severity of which served to encourage the smugglers. They established a virtual monopoly in the Highlands, and were greatly aided and abetted by sympathetic magistrates. There were many famous and bloody battles fought between the Excisemen and smugglers. Perhaps the most successful Excise officer was Malcolm Gillespie, who had entered the Excise in 1799 and during his service seized over 20,000 gallons of spirit and over 400 stills. He came to a sorry end when he was convicted of forging Treasury bills, and was executed in 1827 for this crime. He was reputed to have had forty-two marks or wounds received at the hands of the smugglers.

It was the Duke of Gordon, the largest landowner in Scotland, speaking on the subject of Scottish distilleries, who stated that it was impossible to prevent the Highlander carrying on his illicit trade. However, if realistic legislation were passed, he and his fellow-landowners would do their best to suppress the smuggling on their estates, and ensure that their tenants licensed their stills. As a result of this lead an Act was passed in 1823, which virtually founded the modern whisky industry.

An annual licence fee of £10 was imposed, stills under 500 gallons capacity in the Highlands were prohibited and duty was charged at 2s. 3d. per proof gallon. The first licence was granted to George Smith of Glenlivet, a farmer and previously an illicit distiller. He and the other early licensed distillers encountered fierce opposition from the smugglers. Smith had one of his distilleries burnt down. Slowly others followed his example and 'became legal', and within ten years there were over 250 licensed distilleries. In one year alone the amount of duty-paid spirits doubled. Smuggling was still carried on, but to a much lesser degree, and slowly diminished as the Excise control was tightened.

One of the major factors in the introduction of a new duty on spirits based on the proof gallon was the development of an accurate instrument and method to test the spirits. There were a number of ways of determining the proof point, apart from some elementary hydrometers. One of these was known as gunpowder proof. Some spirit was poured on a little gunpowder and then ignited; if at the end of the combustion the powder went off with a little explosion the spirit was held to be proof or above proof, but if the powder failed to go off the spirit was taken to be below proof.

The testing of the strength of spirits by use of a hydrometer dates from the early part of the eighteenth century. The earliest official reference to hydrometers was in 1762, when such an instrument was required for taking stock of British spirits. This instrument was designed by Clarke, and had probably been in use in the Excise for about thirty years. By 1787 the inaccuracy of Clarke's hydrometer was recognized and the Excise Board engaged the Royal Society to find a more dependable instrument. No action appears to have been taken as a result of the Society's findings. In 1802 it was decided to hold a competition for the best and most accurate hydrometer, which would be used as the official Excise instrument. A committee chaired by Dr Woolaston of the Royal Society was set up to examine and test the various hydrometers submitted for trial. Nineteen instruments were tested, including an 'improved' Clarke's, then in use in the Excise Department.

The hydrometer selected by the Committee was designed by Bartholemew Sikes. Sikes had entered the Excise in 1754, and had risen to become Collector at Hertford. During his long service in the Excise he had been actively involved in the checking of both British and imported spirits, and his interest in hydrometry had started early in his Excise career. His instrument was selected not only for its accuracy, but also for its robust construction, while the unique set of tables he produced to calculate the proof strengths made its use fairly simple. Unfortunately, he did not live to see his success, dying in October 1803. His widow did, however, receive £2,000 for the rights of the hydrometer, and his son-in-law Richard Bate obtained the contract to manufacture the instruments for the Excise Department.

The new hydrometer and tables were authorized as the official instrument in 1816 as a temporary measure. In 1818 a new Bill was passed which not only established the hydrometer and the tables but for the first time laid down the legal definition of proof spirits, exactly as Sikes had defined in his papers. With some slight variations, the Sikes hydrometer has been in use in the department continually for over 160 years. However, in

Jamuary 1980 it became the victim of the Common Market, being replaced by a new alcohol hydrometer which tests spirit by volume and mass, with the introduction of the OIML system (International Organisation of Legal Metrology).

As early as 1661, Pepys reported in his diary that he had visited 'the new wet dock at Blackwell'. This dock, together with one built slightly later at Rotherhithe, is the first recorded wet dock; by 1800 London had not added to these small wet docks. The first floating dock with approved legal quays had been constructed in Liverpool, and by 1796 there were seven commercial docks in that port.

A committee was set up in 1796 to examine the state of trade and shipping in the Port of London. It was found that the legal quays and sufferance wharves were sadly inadequate to cope with the trade of the port. The river was constantly congested with shipping, and long delays were experienced in obtaining a place to discharge. Very great concern was expressed about the enormity of the theft and pilferage of cargoes on the quays and wharves. It was the considered opinion of several Customs witnesses giving evidence to the committee that much of the pilferage was due to 'lumpers' (the labourers unloading the vessels), who went on board with 'large Trowsers and Jackets to secrete the goods'. Whether the lumpers were solely to blame for the pilferages is doubtful. The now famous *Treatise on the Police in London* by Colquhoun, written in 1796, lists among the 'criminal classes':

> A class of inferior officers belonging to the Customs and Excise including what are called "Supernumaries" and "Glutmen", many of whom connive at pillage as well as frauds committed on the Revenue, and share in the plunder to a very considerable extent; principally from their inability to support themselves on the pittance allowed them in the name of salary.

As a result of the inquiry, plans were drawn up to construct large and enclosed docks in London. The West India Docks on the Isle of Dogs were the first to be opened in 1802, followed by the London Docks in 1805, and the East India Docks in 1806. These new floating docks were built with formidable high walls, which afforded far greater security for the goods. Twenty years after their opening the Customs were able to report 'the Dock system has entirely stopped large-scale pilfering'. The new enclosed dock system greatly assisted the Customs in their control over all aspects of shipping work. The Commissioners constrained the dock companies to segregate the import and export activities in separate docks, and they were also compelled to provide suitable accommodation for the Customs staff. Other ports around the country soon followed suit in erecting docks—e.g., Bristol Docks were opened in 1809. The next seventy years would show a feverish activity in the construction of new docks as the foreign trade prospered, while the advent of larger vessels and later steam vessels made the change from the small river wharves to the larger floating docks essential.

Early in 1821 the remaining Customs duties on tea, coffee and cocoa were transferred to the Excise. This change resulted in a number of Customs officers being made redundant, although some found posts with the Excise Port establishment. It was surprising to find, just four years later, that there was a massive reorganization of all the duties collected at the ports, with the result that there was a complete volte-face—the duties on coffee, cocoa, foreign spirits and wines were now transferred back to the Customs. The Excise were left with the control of the home consumption of these goods. The redundant officers were transferred to the Customs, no doubt among them staff who had been moved only four years earlier. At a stroke the collection of over £16 millions of revenue was passed over to the Customs. For the first time for nearly eighty years, the Customs collected a greater share of the revenue than did the Excise.

The Excise were left with a remnant of staff at the ports, controlled by port surveyors. Most of these remaining staff were permit writers, permits being the basic control over the movement of duty-paid excisable goods. They were also left with the import control of tea, but with the cessation of the East India Company's monopoly in tea in 1835 the control of tea passed to the Customs.

A further step was taken in 1823 to rationalize the administration of both services. The existing patents of the six separate Boards were revoked. A single Board of Customs and one Excise Board were set up in London, to have control over the whole of the United Kingdom. The new Customs Board comprised thirteen Commissioners, replacing the existing nineteen, and the Excise board also contained thirteen members.

For a short period 'subordinate Boards' were authorized for both Edinburgh and Dublin, to whom relatively minor and routine matters were delegated. (Both minor Boards functioned until 1829. From this date the United Kingdom administration has been controlled from London.) This move enabled a greater uniformity of practice throughout the three countries, and a more efficient use of resources. The staff of both departments were warned by General Letters that they could expect to be moved to any part of the United Kingdom.

Two surviving links with the distant past disappeared at this time. One of these went back to the very early days of the Customs—the Prisage and Butlerage of Wines, which in Charles II's days had been granted to the famous (or infamous) Barbara Villiers, Duchess of Cleveland. The various Committees of Public Accounts had recommended that these duties should be reverted to the Crown. In 1806 the majority were purchased by Parliament for an annuity of £6,870, the final outstanding prisage patent being bought in 1824 from the Duchy of Cornwall. Thus these very ancient duties passed into history.

The other historic link went back to the days of Elizabeth I—the Exchequer Port Books. Their compilation had been one of the duties of the patent customer at the ports. Even in the late eighteenth century only a few ports completed the returns, and now there were no patent officers in the port to complete them. Their demise was long overdue, as they had became an anachronism in a department with a long-established Statistical branch.

One of the most useful sources of shipping information was the Bill of Entry. The Bills were basically a digest of information concerning the arrivals and sailings of vessels, with details of cargoes. The information was extracted from Customs reports and entries, and published daily in the form of a newspaper for the benefit of merchants. They had first appeared in London in 1660, and the patent for publication had been granted to Andrew King, but by the middle of the eighteenth century the patent had passed into the hands of the Lewis family. In 1816, when the Customs Annuity and Benevolent Fund—or Customs Fund for short—was established to provide some help for the widows and orphans of members of the Customs service, it was suggested that one way of providing a source of income for the Fund would be to purchase the right to publish the Bills of Entry. The existing patent had only another six years to run, and the rights were obtained for £28,000. The Customs Fund published the Bills of Entry until they were taken over by the Customs Department in 1880.

As the trade of London Port had greatly increased, especially since the opening of the new docks, the existing accommodation at the Custom House had become grossly inadequate. In 1810 it was thought that the Long Room could be extended and an extra wing added to alleviate the overcrowding. However, it was soon realized that such alterations could not be undertaken without serious interruption to the public business. Furthermore, the state of the building did not warrant such a large expense. It was therefore decided that an entirely new building, situated near by, should be erected. The site acquired for the new building extended from west of the existing Custom House to just east of Billingsgate Dock. It was purchased in July 1813 for the sum of £41,700.

David Laing, the Departmental Surveyor of Buildings, was appointed architect. Because of the nature of the subsoil, which was a mixture of Thames mud and broken bricks and tiles, it was felt necessary to obtain the advice of an engineer as to the strength of the foundations. John Rennie, the famous engineer, was called in, and he recommended that the building should be constructed on piles that were 'drove in at least two feet into hard ground'. In the light of subsequent happenings, Rennie's advice was most pertinent. The contract with the builders was agreed at £165,000, and the foundation stone was laid in October 1813. By February 1814 the first signs of new building were appearing, although the work had been hampered by the very severe winter. One of the last 'Frost Fairs' had been held on the Thames earlier in the winter.

One of the essential features of the project was to transfer staff from the old building to the new building without any inconvenience to the public business. These plans were frustrated when on 12 February 1814, at 'about six in the morning, a most dreadful fire burst out from the west wing of the Custom House. A little after seven ten barrels of gunpowder exploded, which blew up and entirely shattered the east wing ... the explosion was tremendous. Burnt papers were carried as far as Dalston, Hackney and Highbury.' It was reported that 'the whole Custom House is now down except the front wall'. The following day, Sunday, the Commissioners met to decide how best to carry on public business. They eventually leased the Commercial Sale Rooms in Mincing Lane as a temporary Custom House at a rent of £12,000 per annum.

The contracted date of completion of the new building was February 1816. In the event it was not finally ready for occupation until March 1817, at a total cost of over a half a million pounds, almost double the original estimate of £140,000. During 1820 some cracks began to appear in the central portion of the building, and in January 1825—due, it was found afterwards, to a weakness in the foundations—the whole of the central portion collapsed. Laing was dismissed from his position, and legal proceedings were taken against the contractor, Mr Peto. A full investigation was carried out into the disastrous affair, and much of the debate was centred on the advice given by Rennie. Sir Robert Smirke was then called in to reconstruct the centre portion, including a fine new arched Long Room. He also added to the south front, that facing the river, three porticos of classical design, one to each wing and with a larger and more impressive one in the centre. Smirke repeated the experiment when he designed the British Museum, and the style has become known as the 'Museum' style. Other than the east wing, which was badly damaged during 1940, the present Custom House is substantially the same as when it was rebuilt in 1825-6.

Sadly, another fine old Custom House was destroyed in 1831. The Collector Bristol reported to the Board on 31 October:

> We are under the painful necessity of acquainting your Honours, that the Custom House here was burnt to the ground last night with the Mayor's Mansion House and the whole of the North and West side of Queen Square by a dreadful riot, which began on Saturday and still continues but few of our papers and books, which we have not been able to ascertain correctly, have been saved and we shall use our utmost endeavours to secure the Revenue at this juncture. We have not been able to find any house to hire as a temporary Custom House at present, all business is suspended in the Port.

This bare official report does not begin to describe the ferocity of the Bristol riots, caused, as were others around the country, by the Reform Bill. The Excise Office, which was situated on the corner of Queen Square, was also completely destroyed. One of the reports of the firing of the Custom House described some of the rioters being trapped in the upper apartments of the building and 'dropping into the flames and jumping out of the windows'. Nearly a hundred persons were killed, and many more injured in the riots. Charles Penney, the Mayor of Bristol, was charged with neglect of duty, but was found not guilty. The Customs business was conducted from a private house in St Augustine's Back, until a new building, again designed by Smirke, was erected in 1837.

The fifty years between 1790 and 1840 may be aptly sub-titled 'The Rise and Fall of the Excise Service'. From 1790 the number of duties it controlled, the amount of revenue it collected and the number of staff it employed grew steadily each year. By 1815 the Excise duties amounted to over £27 millions. They reached a peak in 1820, and from then onwards the work of the Excise drastically declined. The number of Excise duties dropped from twenty-seven to ten, and all the import work was lost to the Customs.

There is a fascinating record of the daily work of an Excise officer of about this period, when the main duties were on beer, candles, hops, malt, leather, paper, spirits, sugar, printed linens and salt. The writer Joseph Pacy had entered the Excise in 1827, and ultimately rose to the rank of collector. He was taken aback 'by the amount and variety of the work'. It was his custom to rise 'at an early hour every morning to go to unlock the utensils of the chandlers' (these were always kept under lock and seal when not in use). This he considered the 'most tiresome and trying part' of his duty, on account of the very long hours the chandlers worked, both summer and winter. The unlocking of the utensils and an early visit to the malt-houses would occupy him until breakfast. After 'a hasty meal', he visited the innkeepers to see which were brewing, with a further visit to the chandlers (he was compelled to visit them every four hours, while they were working). The rest of the time before dinner was spent at the tanners, check-weighing and stamping leather.

After dinner he was employed measuring and testing spirits and weighing tea and tobacco at the various dealers and retailers. 'After tea to bedtime' he laboured on 'indoor work'—making up his accounts, records and vouchers. He made his final visit of the day to the chandlers to weigh and take account of the candles made during the day, and to lock away the utensils. Frequently, he recalled, 'this would be as late as midnight'. Sunday was not a day of rest for him: he had visits to make, dressed in 'a capacious coat with large pockets to carry the malt sticks and account books, and with a gauging stick in one hand and in the other a large bunch of malt-house and chandler's keys, giving the appearance of a turnkey of a prison'. It was his considered opinion that the work was so onerous that it could only be achieved by 'incessant application' and life appeared 'all work and no play, with no intermissions'. It is not surprising that any reduction in the number of duties under their charge was favourably received by the Excise officers.

One of the main reasons for the decline of the Excise was a radical change in the taxation policy of the government. The main inspiration of the new views on taxation policy was Sir Henry Parnall, who had gained considerable experience chairing various finance committees. Parnall propounded his views in a *Treatise on Financial Reform*, which was published in 1830. He considered the Excise laws, and the close control imposed on the various trades, to be restrictive, and to hamper greatly the progress of manufacture. He also advocated the reduction of the high Excise duties on spirits, tobacco and wines, as a solution to the smuggling problem. In general Parnall advocated a reduction of Excise duties in favour of an increase in property and income taxes; the perennial choice between direct and indirect taxes.

His views found favour, and the first tax to disappear was salt. This 'odious tax', as it had been called, had fallen largely on the poorer members of society, and its abolition was long overdue. In 1830 the duties on beer, cider and leather (all dating from the earliest days of the Excise) were ended. For some time the duty on beer had been considered unfair, in that the Excise laws and regulations had greatly favoured the large brewers—who were now gaining a monopoly of the trade—to the detriment of the small brewers. Furthermore, as the duty stood, it was most unequal, since only beer for sale was dutiable, private brewing being exempt. Most large houses and farms had their own private brewhouse, and it was estimated that over a quarter of all beer brewed was private. Thus the duty fell largely on the poorer classes, who were unable to brew their own beer. Soon many illegal brewhouses flourished, selling cheap beer to the working classes. These 'lush shops', as they were called, caused many control problems for the Excise.

The Act which repealed the beer duty included a provision for establishing a virtual free trade in the sale of beer. Almost anybody, on payment of a two-guinea licence, could retail beer and cider. Within a short time over 31,000 of these beerhouses were opened, and were nicknamed 'Tom and Jerry' shops—from the two characters from Egan's *Life in London*, who became a byword for drunken rioting and roistering. (Disney had the same idea.) No justices' certificates were required for a beerhouse licence, only a statement of good character signed by six ratepayers. This statement was presented to the Excise officer for his approval, and the attempted control of these low beerhouses was then a matter for him. Over the next thirty years the numbers of these beerhouses so increased that in many towns and villages almost one house in three sold beer. This was the situation which, according to many Victorian reformers, accounted for the widespread drunkenness of the working classes.

Other duties to disappear were those on candles, printed cottons and silks. The repeal of the candle duty was 'hailed with delight by the officers', and was a 'great source of annoyance to the makers'. The cost of collection of the duty was very high, due to the very close control, and the duty collected barely covered the administration costs. By 1835 over £18 millions of Excise duties had either been repealed or transferred to the Customs. With such a large reduction of work, the Treasury had expected some commensurate savings in staff and the cost of management, but the reduction in number of officers was meagre, and the cost of the department increased rather than decreased. The Treasury continually called on the Excise board to reduce its numbers of staff, but all to no avail. In desperation, the Treasury appointed a committee to inquire into 'the work and management of the Excise Department'.

The committee of three was appointed in April 1833, and it was chaired by none other than Sir Henry Parnall, the taxation 'expert' and no great friend to the Excise. It worked in a most dedicated and systematic fashion, and did not complete its labours for more than three years. The members looked at every duty in very great detail, scrutinized the accounting procedure and inspected every branch of the Establishment. Their reports were issued at regular intervals from July 1833 to July 1836, and totalled twenty volumes of over 3,370 pages. Mr Disraeli considered them to be 'some of the most valuable documents in our Parliamentary Library'.

For all the vast amount of work and meticulous inquiry that was involved, the committee achieved few changes. Perhaps its most valuable recommendation was that the Excise laws should be consolidated, as the Customs laws had been some years earlier. There was some minor revision of penalties and some relaxations in Excise control, but overall little fault was found with the existing system. The Excise Commissioners had successfully defended their administration and management of the revenue. They also demonstrated why the cost of collection had increased. Most of the Excise duties they had lost had been those which were cheap and easy to collect—for example, import duties. They were now left with the relatively involved duties, such as those on spirits, malt, paper and soap, and these all required frequent visits to the traders, that were costly in both staff wear-and-tear and time. They also pointed out that the largely rural areas of Scotland and Ireland were now under their control, and these areas required a yet greater number of officers to collect a relatively small amount of duty. The Excise inquiry was the most exhaustive examination ever conducted into any government department, and despite the few adverse comments, it had demonstrated the very high standard of management and the general efficiency of the Excise service.

Since its inception the Customs had virtually no system of promotion within the service. Normally officers appointed to a post not only stayed in that grade for the rest of their working life, but also invariably remained in the same port. For a number of years the Customs Board had been deliberating on a promotion scheme, which would also promote greater staff mobility.

A new scheme was introduced on 1 December 1827, and was based on the classification of the ports. Six classes were established, from the very small port with very little foreign trade to ports on the scale of Liverpool. There was a graduated scale of salaries for all the staff, from collector down to landing waiter, according to the class of the port. Strict rules were introduced for promotion within the grades. The Board felt 'the scheme would give encouragement to superior talent and meritorous officers to advance through the Department, but it is not a regular graduation on senority but solely based on merit'. Conversely, it proved useful as a disciplinary measure enabling the Board to move an offender to a lower-class port (and thus a lower salary) without any difficulty.

London was the only port not included in the scheme: there had always been a sufficiently large number of staff for it to have its own built-in promotion scheme. There were only three first-class English ports—Liverpool, Bristol and Hull; three Irish—Dublin, Cork and Belfast; and two in Scotland—Leith and Greenock. One of the features of the system, during the seventy or so years it was in operation, was the frequent reclassification of the ports as their trade prospered or diminished. The moves up and down the league ladder were watched with great interest, not only by members of the department, but also by those in the mercantile and shipping circles of the port. A promotion in classification was treated as a great success, not only for the port but for the town as well. The scheme proved so flexible in operation, and popular with the staff, that the Excise Board adopted it to classify their collections.

The last sixty years had seen considerable improvements in the structure of both departments. The greater changes had occurred in the Customs, mainly because its rather antiquated system had demanded more radical reforms. The Excise had lost much ground and status, but it evolved as a smaller and more cohesive service, efficient and expert in a reduced field of operation. Many of the changes to both departments in the remainder of the century would be occasioned by outside influences, rather than reforms from within. The growth of a co-ordinated Civil Service with more centralized government, along with rapid changes in all forms of communications, would play its part in the further development of both services.

CHAPTER SIX

At War with the Smugglers

There was a perceptible decline in smuggling for a short period from 1750 to the outbreak of the Seven Years War in 1756. This can be largely attributed to a reduction in the tea duty, making the trade far less profitable for the smugglers. In fact, during this period the sales of legal tea increased considerably. Another factor to be borne in mind was the comparatively successful use of dragoons in the capture of smugglers. With the advent of war, not only did the duties on goods increase, but there were far less dragoons available for assistance, with the result that the smuggling trade increased, and by the end of the eighteenth century had reached an unprecedented level.

This period of intense smuggling activity has rightly been called the heyday of smuggling, and it brought out two new features of the trade. For the first time there was a noticeable increase in smuggling via the packet boats. At Falmouth the postal packet vessels were estimated to carry goods worth over £4 million per year, the majority being smuggled ashore by the passengers. This trade was considered to be the best support of the shopkeepers in Falmouth: 'Any item of goods were available in the shops, inns and taverns of the area, and pedlars carried the smuggled goods into every town and village in Cornwall and Devon.' Falmouth was considered 'a veritable store-house of merchandise'.

The passenger packet boats at both Dover and Harwich saw a large increase in smuggling by passengers. Seizures were frequently made from government messengers, carrying goods in their official letter-bags. The coaches en route to London were often stopped and searched by Excise officers, and trunks containing silks and lace were seized. In March 1752 a lady passenger arriving at Harwich on the packet boat from Holland complained bitterly to the Customs Commissioners of the 'indecent treatment received from the Customs officers at the port'. The Collector's report of the incident is quite amusing, and gives an insight into passenger clearance in those times:

When we enquired of the officers, we found no indecancys asked but by herself, for whom the tydesurveyor found she had something concealed in her stays, she took him round the neck and held him and kissed him a considerable time in the presence of several people. And when Mr Orlibar and Mr Pelham went to her in the Publick House and acquainted her that they had some information that she had some prohibited goods concealed about her, she immediately lifted up her petticoats up to her waist, so that her whole behaviour, while there was very like a common strumpet. We are therefore humbly of the opinion that the officers were not guilty of any indecency towards her.

The other dominant feature of this period was the use of both revenue and naval vessels in a vain attempt to suppress smuggling. Prior to this time most of the battles with smugglers, and the majority of seizures of smuggled goods, were on land. In fact, in some instances Customs vessels were removed from the ports in favour of extra riding officers. Henceforth the number of revenue vessels employed would greatly increase, and many of the most successful seizures during the next fifty years would be made by the cutters of both the Customs and the Excise services. They became the first line of defence in the war with the smugglers, and were the most essential and important of the many services employed for the suppression of smuggling.

Despite the disappearance of some of the more notorious gangs, the violence of the smugglers did not abate. In 1755 the Collector at Exeter reported the death of a riding officer at Branscombe, where the blame was laid on the smugglers' wives. John Hurley, the riding officer, was on the look-out at White Clift, Seaton, 'in expectation of a smuggling boat, which afterwards ran its cargo into Beere. Present on the cliffs were a great number of women (smuggler's wives) making fires on the edge of the clift as a signal to the boat expected in, it was suspected that he was thrown over the clift by them.' The coroner brought in a verdict of accidental death, based on the women's oaths that the officer accidentally fell over in running from one fire to another in order to put them out. The report concluded by saying, 'Mr Boots, the Riding Officer at Beere says that there is still reason to fear he was pushed over and therefore we will spare no pains to come to the real truth.'

These women were no doubt married to members of the Beere gang, which was one of the most noted and vicious gangs operating in Devon. They mainly worked around the port of Dartmouth, and gathered in such numbers as to preclude any opposition from the officers. On one occasion in 1766 some Customs officers 'fell in with a body of smugglers of upwards of forty in number, with about fifty horses loaded with tea'. The Customs men decided that retreat was the best policy; however, one of their number, William Hunt, was on 'an indifferent horse' and was caught by the gang. He was 'beaten unmercifully and so wounded that his life was in great danger'. When the surgeon attended him he was found to have a dislocated shoulder. This was wrongly reset, and three weeks later the 'shoulder was re-broken with the use of an apple machine' (cider press) and reset properly. Within a week or so Hunt was back on duty once again. Farther west at Falmouth, almost two years later, William Odgers, a Customs officer, attempted to prevent the landing of tea and brandy by a party of twenty smugglers; he was so badly assaulted that he died before help could be summoned. Three of the smugglers known to be involved in the murder disappeared to Guernsey until it was safe to return. The smuggling activities around Dorset, and especially Poole, had greatly increased; the goods run were tea, coffee, brandy, rum, geneva, currants, and a variety of 'East India goods'. In 1770 a Customs boat was stationed at Brownsea Island in the centre of Poole Harbour to prevent the 'pernicious practice'. The Collector complained that the rent charged for the boathouse was £3 per annum—'more than the island in all is worth'. (In later and more peaceful days the island was the site chosen by Lord Baden-Powell for the first Boy Scouts camp.)

Perhaps the most vicious gang operating at this time was the Ruxley gang, based at Hastings. In 1768 they boarded a Dutch vessel named the *Three Sisters* in the Downs on the pretence of trading for smuggled goods. In an argument with the master over the sale of the goods they killed him and most of the crew, by cutting them from the back of the head to the base of the spine with their swords. It was from this savage outrage that all Hastings fishermen became known as chopbacks. When they returned to Hastings they bragged about the dreadful murder, and 200 Inniskilling Dragoons were sent to Hastings to arrest the criminals. A pitched battle which lasted all day ensued, until the majority of the gang were captured. An eye-witness at the subsequent trial reported, 'Of all the monstrous wickedness with which this age abounds, nothing I will be bound to say, can parallel the senses of villainy that were laid bare . . . the judges, themselves declared, that in all their reading, they never met with such a combined sense of barbarity, so deliberately carried on and so cruelly executed.'!

By 1770 the smuggling trade had increased to such an extent, and become so organized, that payments for the goods to be smuggled were being made by banker's draft and cheque, rather than as previously by hard cash. The smugglers were now able to supply regular orders for goods, and many large estates and houses were receiving their wines and spirits on a regular basis from them, as they would have done from a merchant. The perennial problem of East India vessels trading with smuggling vessels in the Channel is highlighted by a report by William Hickey (he was even going then!) on his return from India in 1770. He witnessed a smuggling vessel meet his ship on entry into the English Channel, and take delivery of tea, silks, and other goods, in full view of a Customs vessel—which was powerless to act, as this took place in international waters. Payment for the goods was made by a cheque for £1,800 drawn on a London bank.

Special distilleries had been established in Dunkirk and other Channel ports for the manufacture of geneva exclusively for the smuggling trade. In an attempt to control that 'den of smugglers' the Channel Islands, where everybody was actively engaged in the trade, Customs officers were stationed on both Jersey and Guernsey in 1767. It would, however, be another forty years before a Custom House was built at St Helier, and some semblance of control exercised. Some of the smugglers were nevertheless forced out of Guernsey by the attentions of the Customs officers; but they immediately transferred their activities to ports like St Malo and Roscoff on the Brittany coast. Within a short space of time these ports were flourishing, with special warehouses to supply the illegal trade. The Channel Islands continued their profitable trade in the manufacture of small kegs for smuggled spirits, only now they exported them to France.

Smuggling extended to virtually every part of the coast, from Carlisle in the north-west right round to Newcastle in the north-east. The goods reached every inland town, normally being carried and sold by the hawkers and pedlars. There are frequent examples of goods being seized by Excise officers many miles inland. The north-east coast of England was very active in smuggling; ports like Stockton, Redcar, Whitby, Scarborough, Staithes and Saltburn were in the virtual control of the smugglers. The coal vessels were very involved in the trade, taking coals to many English ports and meeting trading vessels at sea to collect their smuggled goods. In 1768 John Smith, an Excise officer, was murdered while trying to seize a quantity of smuggled goods at Scarborough. A year later William Deighton, an Excise supervisor at Halifax, was murdered a short distance from his home. This murder was ascribed to a large gang of counterfeit coiners, which was operating in Yorkshire. Deighton had been collecting evidence about the gang, and was on his way to meet an informer when he was murdered. In 1772 a gang of smugglers at Southampton attacked a party of Customs officers with large clubs and loaded whips, so violently that the officers 'were obliged to retreat'. One of their number 'was rendered senseless by two dangerous wounds on each side of his head'— two days later the officer died. At Bexhill a year later James Leverau, a Customs officer, was beaten and thrown in the sea by a party of smugglers, and 'was struck in the water with handspikes or long staves upon which Leverau begged that they would forbear such barbarous usage'.

Smuggled goods were bought by all levels of society. A gentleman having a large estate at Childwell, near Liverpool, was obviously greatly involved in the trade, for in 1765, 656 pounds of tea was discovered in his summer-house. Parson Woodforde wrote in his diary, 'March 29 1777 Andrews, the smuggler brought me this night about 11 o'clock a bagg of Hyson tea 6 Pd weight. He frightened us a little by whistling under the Parlour window just as we were going to bed. I gave him some Geneva and paid him for the tea at 10/6d per Pd. [The proper cost was perhaps 14–15s.]'. Subsequent entries show that his propensity for smuggled tea extended also to brandy and gin. In fact, in 1783 he complained that his tub of gin when bottled was deficient by two bottles.

One of the few prominent persons who was not prepared to condone smuggling was the evangelist John Wesley. During his preaching tours he constantly exclaimed against 'the accursed thing, smuggling'. His hatred of the trade led him to refrain from drinking tea, and he published a pamphlet against it, in which he says 'every smuggler is a thief general, who picks the pockets, both of the King and all his fellow subjects. He wrongs them all.' However, his words went largely unheeded, especially in an area like Rye, where they would not part with the 'accursed thing. So I fear, with these, our labour will be in vain.' Even Adam Smith, Customs Commissioner in Scotland, did not directly condemn the smuggler and considered him 'as a person who, no doubt blameable for violating the laws of his country, is frequently incapable of violating those of natural justice and would have been in every respect an excellent citizen had not the laws of his country made that a crime that nature never meant to be so.'

The American wars, which had caused further increases in the duties and had resulted in a depletion of the number of dragoons to assist the revenue officers, naturally led to a vast increase of smuggling. The numbers of smugglers working the coasts increased threefold, and they met virtually no serious opposition, either on land or by sea. They reigned supreme; the revenue officers could not combat the virtual private armies around the coast. Without the aid of a very large military force, the situation was completely out of hand: in Deal it was considered that a whole regiment would be needed to have any effect. In Hampshire and Dorset bands of over two hundred men landed tea and brandy unmolested by the handful of Customs officers. Even the tide-waiters in the Thames were armed with cutlasses to prevent 'the frequent and daring attempts of the plunderers and smugglers which infest the river'.

In 1779 a new smuggling Act was passed, which greatly strengthened the earlier legislation. In the following year the government issued a pamphlet entitled *Advice to the Unwary*, which explained that the new legislation had been 'occasioned by the gangs of daring and dissolute persons armed with offensive weapons.' The pamphlet maintained that smuggling now pervaded every city, town and village, and brought universal distress to the fair trader. It further asserted that 3,870,000 gallons of geneva were being smuggled into England and Wales, and 5 to 6 million pounds of tea entered the country without payment of duty. The new Act made ships under 200 tons, carrying goods in illegal packages, forfeit to the Crown; boats with more than four oars were forbidden, and gaolers allowing smugglers to escape were liable to heavy penalties. Smugglers might now be pressed into the Army as well as the Navy. However, the severe smuggling laws in operation did little to abate the trade, which had reached such proportions that Lord Pembroke asked in 1781, 'Will Washington take America; or the smugglers England first?, the bet would be a fair, even one.'

The situation had become so desperate that Lord North called for a detailed report on smuggling from the Customs Board. They estimated that within the last three years (1780-3) smuggling had increased threefold; the illegal trade in tea was thought to be close to £7 million per year. They reported, 'The smugglers carry on a system of business, which set all the laws at defiance.' Concern was expressed with the quality of the riding officers; many were too old and 'not resolute enough' to provide any serious obstacle to the smugglers, who in some instances were even related to them. They were not sufficiently numerous, yet 'they could not be increased so as to render effectual service, unless one half of the inhabitants could be hired to watch the other.' The military too were frequently in league with the smugglers, and on occasions had actively assisted the gangs against the revenue officers. When the military did intervene they became involved in 'the most dangerous of all warfare'. In the light of such an alarming report—with large areas of the country in a state of virtual anarchy— desperate and drastic measures were needed.

It fell to the new incoming Minister, William Pitt, to take the necessary action. One of his first steps was the reduction of tea duty from an equivalent of 125 per cent to $12\frac{1}{2}$ per cent. With this one stroke he made tea smuggling virtually unprofitable. The success of this change could be seen in the very first year, when the sales of legal tea increased almost threefold. The existing laws on smuggling were strengthened, although what was required in preference to new laws was the better implementation of the ample existing legislation. Pitt's determination to tackle the problem can be seen from his actions in January 1785.

On being informed that because of the severity of the winter most of the smuggling boats in Deal were laid up on the beach Pitt quickly realized that this was an unique opportunity to strike a blow against the 'smugglers of this infernal town'. He ordered a large detachment of soldiers to march on Deal, with instructions to destroy as many vessels as possible. Despite token resistance from the inhabitants, for once the smugglers were outnumbered: the military force set fire to all the vessels on the beach, while the townspeople looked on helpless. This was the first example of a positive act of retaliation against any smugglers. The success was, however, short-lived; the Deal smugglers were back in business within a few seasons.

By 1785 the most important, and in many ways the most successful, means for the suppression of smuggling was the revenue vessels. As we have already seen, Custom House smacks were in operation as early as 1660, although these were small vessels, used mainly for visiting vessels in the rivers and estuaries. Certainly by 1698 there was a proposal for 'surrounding the coasts with smacks', but this suggestion was not pursued, and vessels were only established at the main ports in East Anglia, Kent and Sussex, and the mouth of the Thames. However, by 1724 the Treasury approved the 'construction of seven sloops for the coasts of Scotland'. Although these sloops were used privately in the protection of the revenue, they were mobilized from time to time for coast defence. For example, on the outbreak of war with Spain in 1745 they were placed under the direction of the Admiralty.

These Customs vessels were allowed by the Admiralty to 'wear colours but no pendant'. The colours were 'a Jack and red ensign with the seal of office thereon, the mark of the ensign being twice as large as that in the Jack'. The seal of office at that time was a 'castellated portcullis'. The Excise Department also had their own vessels, and their flag had a Jack with a star with the letters EX emblazoned in its centre.

The vessels were employed under two systems. Some were on the direct establishment, the vessel being the property of the Crown. All the expenses, such as repairs, wages and victualling, were paid by the collector of the port where the vessel was stationed. The money for the upkeep of the vessel was normally paid out of the seizure money. The other system was by way of contract. The contractor provided a vessel for a charge of 4s. 6d. per ton per lunar month, and the upkeep of the vessel was paid by the contractor. Any seizures made by these contracted vessels were shared equally between the Crown and the contractor.

The crews of both types of vessels were under the control of the Commissioners, although those serving on the contract vessels were recommended for their appointments by the contractor. The crew's pay was not large: the commander or master received £50 per annum, the mate £35 and the general seamen—or mariners, as they were called—£15 per year. The reason for the low wages for a situation which was to say the least hazardous was that the low wages acted as an incentive and encouragement to the commander and crew to make as many seizures as possible to augment the meagre salaries. Each vessel was stationed at a port, and came under the direct control of the collector. The commanders were given a set area of the coast to patrol, but frequently they exceeded their limits, much to the annoyance of other vessels in the area.

During the period from 1776 to 1779 there was considerable activity in the construction of new vessels. In addition to these new vessels, smuggling vessels which had been seized by the Crown were brought into service if they were suitable. In April 1775 Mr James Major was appointed to the command of a 'seized shallop, to be renamed Ferret'. Unfortunately, this vessel did not survive very long, as it sunk two years later. Contrary to popular belief, the various Customs officers of the eighteenth century did not wear any uniform. The first Customs officials to have uniform approved by the Board were the commanders and mates of the revenue vessels. In 1777 the Customs Board recommended a naval-type uniform and provided 'the first set of silver buttons free'. The approved uniform closely resembled the naval officer's uniform of the time. In fact in 1804 the commanders asked the Board to supply silver epaulettes, but this request was refused on the grounds that their officers would be confused with naval officers.

From very early days vessels of the Royal Navy were issued with commissions or deputations to make seizures. In 1698 four naval vessels were appointed 'to cruise against the owlers', and by 1757 a Treasury warrant was issued directing that two-thirds of all seizures made by men of war were to be paid to the officers concerned. The commissions issued to the naval vessels were not always put to good use. In March 1785 the master of H.M. sloop *Pylades* was convicted of protecting smugglers and discharged from the Navy. Frequently Customs officers detected both officers and crews of naval ships smuggling tobacco and spirits ashore. In 1786 an important extension to the powers of naval officers was made when it became lawful for any naval vessel to make seizures without requiring a special commission. However, the naval vessels did not play a large and active part in the war against smuggling until the end of the Napoleonic wars.

There were forty-four revenue vessels in operation in 1784, and they covered the coast from Newcastle around to Milford Haven. The total cost of this fleet was £44,000; of these, twenty were on the Customs establishment, and the rest under contract—sixteen of these contract vessels belonged to the collectors at the ports where they were stationed. A Committee of Public Accounts was appointed in 1786 to examine the whole system of revenue vessels and the efficiency of their management. The Committee was not satisfied with the contract system, and recommended that it should be abolished, with all vessels being placed directly on the Customs establishment. This suggestion was approved by the Treasury, and with effect from 1 June 1787 the contract system was discontinued. Nineteen vessels were removed, and all the other five vessels were transferred to the Customs service.

The most famous collector to contract a revenue vessel was William Arnold, the Collector of Cowes in the Isle of Wight, where he served from 1777 until his death in 1800. He is perhaps more famous as the father of Thomas Arnold, the headmaster of Rugby School. William Arnold during his time as Collector fought a long and bitter battle to clear the smugglers from the coasts around the Isle of Wight. He was a most able administrator, a conscientious and dedicated officer, who succeeded despite seemingly insuperable odds in bringing the widespread smuggling under control. If there had been more collectors of his calibre the story of smuggling would have been vastly different. The only other collector to equal him was Samuel Pellew, Collector at Falmouth, who like Arnold contracted a vessel and largely put a stop to wholesale smuggling in his area. Both Arnold and Pellew fought a losing battle, for although they cleared their own ports and coasts, the smugglers only moved elsewhere—there were all too many other places where the collector and his officers were not so diligent.

William Arnold's first venture into the contract business was a disaster. He had purchased a vessel called the *Swan*, and appointed George Sarmon as commander. George's brother James was the commander of an Excise vessel. On its first venture near Hurst Castle the *Swan* was driven on to rocks near the Needles and battered to pieces. Undeterred by this failure, Arnold contracted another vessel, *Swan II*, and appointed yet another Sarmon brother, Francis, as commander. This vessel was brought on to the establishment of the port when the contract system was abolished. Sarmon and *Swan II* achieved considerable success, until in 1792, when chasing a cutter near Shoreham, it ran aground in bad weather. The replacement

Swan III was captured by the French in the Channel, and Sarmon and the crew were detained in a French prison. After several months they were released in time for Sarmon to command *Swan IV*, but after many notable seizures this vessel too was captured by the French, and this time in the battle Sarmon was killed. Arnold petitioned the Board to supply a new cutter of not less than 150 tons, and recommended John Gely, a boat-builder of Cowes. Gely became the most prolific builder of revenue cutters in the next twenty years.

The revenue cutters of this time were 'clinker built' (with lapped planking), and were of a very sturdy construction, with a strong and heavy mast and with a great sail area for their size. The main feature of all revenue vessels was the bowsprit, which was almost as long as the hull, being designed to give the vessels extra speed. The long bowsprit was in fact unique, for under an Act of 1787 it was illegal for any vessel to carry a bowsprit more than two-thirds the length of the hull. Any vessels found with such long bowsprits were automatically seized, irrespective of whether or not they were engaged in the smuggling trade.

The revenue cutters were normally armed with twelve carriage guns as well as swivel guns, and the crew (who numbered about twenty-five) were armed with pistols, muskets and cutlasses. The life on board these vessels, though particularly arduous and hazardous, was no doubt much easier than service in the Navy, which perhaps accounts for the ample number of volunteers applying for service on the cutters. The crew also received certificates exempting them from impressment. The cutters went out in all weathers, and often found themselves engaging smuggling vessels far heavier armed than themselves, while they were in most cases sadly outnumbered. They were frequently injured—one of the mariners on the *Ranger* in 1788 was so badly beaten around the head that 'his skull was bare in several places'.

In several instances members of the crew were killed; in 1783 Captain Haddock of the Deal vessel was shot while attempting to board a vessel, and he died shortly afterwards from his wounds. In 1799 Humphrey Glynn, a boatman at Cawsand, was shot and killed by smugglers from a vessel called the *Lottery*. During the French wars there was the added danger of capture by the French and a long spell in a French prison. In one case the crew of the *Surprise* from Newhaven landed on the beach in France in pursuit of smugglers, only to be captured themselves and accused of being spies! Frequently they faced 'indignities at the hands of the smugglers', being captured, beaten and tied up and forced to witness the latter unloading their cargo at their leisure. This happened to Sarmon and his crew, and he considered it 'most insolent'.

The men of the cutters were left in no doubt as to the smugglers' opinion of them. Captain Brisac of the *Speedwell* cutter at Poole found this in his mail:

Damn thee and God damn thy two Purblind Eyes thou Bugar and thou Death looking son of a Bitch O that I had bin there (with my company) for thy sake

when thou tookes them men of mine on Board the Speedwell Cutter on
Monday e/y 14 Decr I would cross thee and thy gang to Hell wher thou belongest
thou Devil Incarnet. Go Down thou Hell Hound into thy Kennell below &
Bathe thy Self in that Sulpherous Lake that has bin so long Prepared for such as
thee for it is time the World was rid of such a Monster thou art no Man but a
Devil thou fiend O Lucifer I hope thou will soon fall into Hell like a star from
the Sky; there to lie (unpitied) & unrelented of any for Ever & Ever Which
God Grant of his Infinite Mercy   Amen

J. Spurier
Fordingbridge Jany 32 1700 & fast asleep

By 1797 there were thirty-seven Customs vessels patrolling the coasts of
England and Wales, as well as seven Excise cutters. Scotland had its own
fleet, both Customs and Excise. Some of the names selected for the vessels
seemed to have been chosen to instill enthusiasm into those who manned
them, and fear into those who were being chased. Names such as *Active*, *Alert*,
Alarm, *Falcon*, *Fox*, *Hound*, *Hunter*, *Success*, *Viper*, *Valiant*, and *Vigilant* were
used continually, and some have been perpetuated in the modern Customs
cutter service.

The state of smuggling at this time is best described by William Arnold in
a report to the Commissioners:

> Illicit trade is principally carried on in large armed cutters and luggers from
> two to three hundred tons, with which the Revenue vessels are not able to cope.
> It is no unusual thing for them to land their goods in open day under the
> protections of their guns, sometimes in sight of the Revenue vessels, who they
> will not suffer to come near or board them. The large vessels frequently convey
> over other smaller vessels. They keep off until the night, when they run in and
> land their cargoes at places where gangs of smugglers to the number of
> 200—300 meet them. To such a regular science is smuggling now reduced that
> we are informed the smugglers have stated prices for their goods in proportion
> to the distances they bring them. If they sell at sea, the price of a four gallon
> cask is about half a guinea; if landed on shore 14s. to 15s. a cask, and if brought
> into town one guinea.

The Customs Board received very similar reports from the collectors at
almost every port; no part of the coast was immune from the trade. In the
West Country, 'Salcombe people gather in numbers of 50 to 100 with loaded
whips and pistols', and at Polperro 'all joined in—women and children
turned out to assist in the unlawful trade'. In Cornwall the notorious Carter
gang had taken over a cove, where they had erected a battery of cannons to
prevent the revenue vessels from landing. At Caernarvon the Collector
maintained that the town was full of smugglers; not an honest trader could
be found. The Collector at Dover reported that not only were fires lit as
warnings of the presence of the revenue vessels, but special light rowing-
boats called scout boats were being used to carry information as to their
whereabouts. The *Prince of Wales*, a packet-boat at Harwich, was seized by
the Excise cutter *Fly*, because geneva, tea, coffee and tobacco was found

concealed in the ballast. The commander of the *Fly* maintained that the packet boats were regular smugglers, and that seizing the vessel was 'the only way to stop the business'.

It was now estimated that there were over 300 vessels permanently engaged in the smuggling trade, and at a conservative estimate over 20,000 people gained their living from full-time smuggling. With the trade reaching such heights, and being so widespread throughout the country, it is not surprising that among the professional smugglers certain persons achieved considerable notoriety or fame (depending on one's viewpoint). Each area of the coast boasted its own famous smuggler, whose exploits at the expense of the revenue became greatly embellished and exaggerated, before passing into folk-lore. Few of these names appear in the Customs records of the period, but perhaps the explanation is that they were successful enough to escape capture.

In the north-west Jack Yawkins of the *Hawke* cutter caused considerable problems for the various collectors whose ports bordered on the Irish Sea. In 1787 he was captured by the Admiralty cruiser *Pilote*. Despite the reputation of his vessel, it was not considered a good enough sailor to be of use to the revenue service, and was accordingly broken up. Yawkins was used as the model for Dick Hatterick in Sir Walter Scott's novel *Guy Mannering*.

The Carter gang in Cornwall, a family of eight brothers and two sisters, all smugglers, was very well known to the Customs in the area. The leader of the gang was Henry Carter, nicknamed 'The King of Prussia'. They operated from a small cove near Mounts Bay, which was named after them Prussia Cove. Henry was eventually converted to Methodism and retired from the trade to become a respectable farmer, while his brothers continued in the trade, but with less success, without the guidance of Henry. Much of Carter's fame was attributed to his published life-story, *The Autobiography of a Cornish Smuggler*. This story was greatly embellished, and in places reads more like a religious tract than a factual account of smuggling.

Another smuggler to gain much of his reputation by writing his history was Jack Rattenbury of Beer in Devon, who was also known as 'the Rob Roy of the West'. His memoirs, which appeared in 1837, tell of an exciting life, evading the various revenue vessels and rarely being caught, although he did spend some time in a French prison. It would appear that he was not very successful financially, because when he had 'retired' from the trade he was granted a pension of one shilling per week by a Lord Rolle.

Perhaps the most successful of all was Isaac Gulliver, who operated around the Hampshire and Dorset coasts. His centre of operations was a farm about four miles from Poole, in an area that is now called Lilliput, most likely from its connection with Isaac, and with reference to Lemuel, his famous fictitious namesake. In 1788 the Collector of Poole was asked to report on Gulliver's whereabouts, as he 'was the greatest and most notorious smuggler in the West Country in the tea and spirits trade'. The Collector thought that Gulliver was now in the wine trade 'to the west of the port'. It was rumoured that he constantly undersold the regular traders—no doubt by using smuggled goods—although 'it had been heard that he had stopped'. It was the Collector's opinion that Gulliver was 'a person of great speculating genius, has many other businesses besides smuggling and lives now in a farm in the country—a considerable estate'. Gulliver had in fact been one of the many smugglers who had taken advantage of the general pardon of 1782. This offered smugglers a free pardon if they were willing to serve the Navy, or were able to find a suitably qualified substitute to serve on their behalf. For someone of Gulliver's influence and wealth the right person could easily be found for a reasonable sum of money. He was now legally free to live the life of a landed gentleman, while no doubt still financing most of the smuggling runs in the area. He finally settled in a large estate in Wimborne in Dorset, and died in 1822 at the age of seventy-seven, being buried in the Minster church, with his tomb inscribed 'Isaac Gulliver Esquire'.

The most fascinating and colourful character of this smuggling era was 'Captain' Thomas Johnston, the 'famous Hampshire smuggler' (although he seemed to operate mainly from the Sussex coast). In 1798 he was caught and sent to the New Prison in the borough, but managed to escape with the judicious help of a warder. Some idea of his importance can be gathered from the £500 reward offered for his capture—the highest amount ever offered for a smuggler. Johnston soon was back at his old trade, and became involved in smuggling guineas out of England to France. After offering his services to pilot the British expedition to Holland, he received a free pardon. After some time in a French prison, he again managed to make his escape, and landed up in America, where he went back to his old trade. The next appearance in Europe found him assisting a naval squadron at Brest, for which he received £100 pension. In 1807 he was offered the command of a new revenue cutter called *Fox*, which was based at Plymouth. Presumably this offer was based on the principle of 'set a thief to catch a thief'. It is highly likely that he mixed duty with smuggling, although he did manage to seize two vessels. After about two years' service he resigned, and devoted the rest of his life to designing a submarine. He died in 1829 at the age of sixty-seven in a house in the Vauxhall Bridge Road, a far cry from the violence and excitement of his earlier life.

William Pitt, who according to a colleague 'laboured harder than any man to prevent the fair trader from being hurt by the smugglers', had directed his attention to the tobacco trade. Tobacco could be purchased for 3*d.* per pound on the Continent, and then sold to the English manufacturers for 1*s.* 7*d.* per pound. Strangely enough, a tobacco factory had been allowed to operate very close to the shore at Sandgate near Folkestone, and according to the Collector, it received all its tobacco illegally. During 1789 there had been a battle between the officers and the smugglers, when the Customs men had attempted to search the premises. They were beaten back 'by a large company of armed men, greatly encouraged by the proprietors of the factory'.

The simplest way to import tobacco illegally was through the main ports, using fake permits or by collusion with the land-waiters. Pitt was unable to follow the dictum of Adam Smith, that the surest way to control smuggling was greatly to reduce the duty. Instead he brought in a series of measures—already described in the last chapter—which although they did not halt the illegal trade, did at least make smuggling much more difficult. These efforts were largely frustrated by the large increase in duty occasioned by the various war budgets.

With the advent of the long war with France all duties increased greatly; by 1815 tobacco duty was at the very high figure of 3s. 2d. per pound, almost three times as much as at the beginning of the war. The duty on tea mounted steadily during the war years, until it was equivalent to a 96 per cent tax. All trade with France was totally prohibited, although there was no shortage of French brandy—it was still being drunk by the upper classes of society, including members of the Government! Such high duties and near-siege conditions were ideal for an increase in smuggling. The chances of capture now, moreover, were even less than before, with most of the naval vessels being fully occupied elsewhere, and many of the revenue vessels in service with the Admiralty as fleet auxiliaries. In addition, there were few dragoons left to assist the revenue, and so large areas of coastline were left unguarded save for a handful of riding officers and the odd preventive boat. Along the South Coast a system of 'sea fencibles' had been established; these were specially licensed fishing-boats, whose crews were issued with arms, especially to guard against invasion. They formed a kind of floating Home Guard. Unfortunately for the revenue, they were—according to the Collector Cowes—'all in the smuggling trade and consider they have now been given a licence to conduct their illegal trade'.

The French government actively encouraged smuggling. Despite the war, the English smugglers were given free access to all the Channel ports, and in Dunkirk a part of the port was set aside for the smugglers. The French government urgently required English gold coins, especially sovereigns and guineas. After the financial crisis of 1789 gold was at a premium in France, and it is doubtful whether they could have paid their troops without the influx of English gold. (It is estimated that about £10,000 in gold coins was being smuggled out of England each week.) There was such a demand for the coins that a special boat was designed to smuggle the gold across the Channel. These 'guinea-boats', as they were known, were built in Calais, and were very long rowing-boats, sometimes up to forty foot and manned by about thirty-six oarsmen. They were able to make about 9 knots, and were very difficult to catch.

Equally important to the French was the information about defences and movements of vessels that the smugglers brought with them. Many of the smugglers saw this sale of intelligence as a profitable extra bonus. The 'letters for a spy' carried by Kipling's smugglers was very close to the truth. How important were these treasonable activities of the smugglers to the

French government? Napoleon commented on their activities during his exile, asserting:

> During the war, all the intelligence I received from England came through the smugglers. They are likeable people and have courage and ability to do anything for money. I had every information I wanted from them. They brought over newspapers and despatches from the spies we had in London, landed them and hid them in their houses. They are *genti terribili*.

Not all the smugglers acted in such a treacherous manner, and many played the part of double agent, bringing back equally valuable information about the French plans. Some served with distinction in the Navy, often acting as pilots to various naval expeditions. Those who were caught and forced to serve in naval vessels were considered some of the finest sailing and fighting men in the Navy. During the war, in fact, the Admiralty offered a prize to the revenue vessel transferring the greatest number of smugglers to the Navy. In 1810 a Captain Gunthorpe of the Excise cutter *Viper* won with a total of thirty men transferred in one year, and pocketed the first prize of £500.

Most of the battles between the smugglers and the Customs during the war took place afloat. In 1801 the Customs vessel *Tartar* and an Excise cutter *Lively* managed to intercept a smuggling vessel off Deal. After considerable fighting the revenue men boarded the vessel and drove the crew ashore. While they were attempting to off-load the smuggled goods the boat's crew of the *Lively* were attacked by a crowd of people who had gathered on the beach. The musket fire from the townspeople was so accurate that the Excise men had to retreat, with only a small part of the smuggled goods secured. One officer had been killed and several badly injured. The officers called for the assistance of the Lancashire Militia, but by the time they had arrived the smuggled goods had been distributed and hidden away. Battles such as these were commonplace around the coasts. It was reported in Pwlheli in North Wales that 'the smugglers paraded through the town with their contraband while the Customs sat tight'. No revenue man in those parts would attempt seizures unless they could muster forces as strong as those of the smugglers.

With the victory at Trafalgar many of the revenue vessels which had been acting under Admiralty orders were returned to revenue duties. By 1806 there were forty-six cutters and cruisers stationed at the main ports around the coast, although two-thirds of these vessels operated from London to St Ives. The smaller ports had six-oared rowing-boats, and these were backed up and supported by the very thin line of riding officers. The standard and efficiency of the riding officers had been a continual cause of concern to the Customs Board.

Sir William Musgrave, a Customs Commissioner, had commented:

> They never ride out except on their own private business and they fabricate their journals. Some of them are agents and collectors for the smugglers and they are not resolute enough to prove any serious obstacle to large bodies of smugglers.

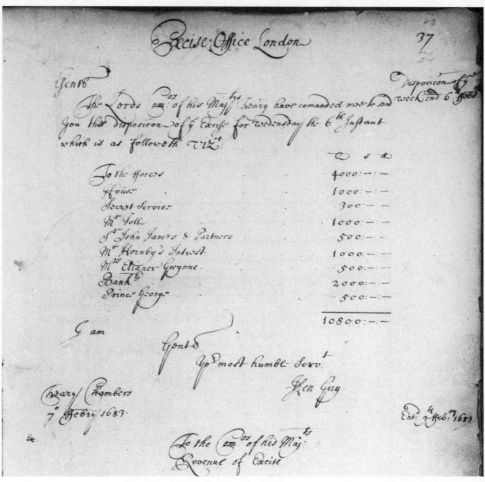

Nell Gwynn's payment out of the Excise (p. 25)   *HMSO*

Literary personalities of the Customs and Excise   *HMSO*

England.

The Imports and Exports compared with the Excess in each Country, from Christmas 1698 to Christmas 1699

Countrys	Imports £	s	D	Exports £	s	D	Imports Excess £	s	D	Exports Excess £	s	D
Africa	19225	18	7½	96295	5	8¾				77069	7	1¼
Canaries	84278	11	8¼	35973	7	10	48305	3	10¼			
Denmark & Norway	86744	11	9	37606	6	10½	49138	4	10½			
East Country	224546	6	5	165731	9	3¼	58814	17	1¾			
East India	717695	4	5½	156908	13	11½	560786	10	6			
Flanders	79518	16	9½	256475	16	4¾				176956	19	7¼
France	76712	14	4½	103259	1	3½				26546	6	11
Germany	818191	–	1	700834	12	1	117356	8	–			
Greenland	273	17	6				273	17	6			
Holland	512599	4	8½	1452940	16	2¼				940341	11	5¾
Ireland	417475	5	6	269475	19	8	147999	5	10			
Italy	329188	16	2	100549	7	4	228639	8	10			
Madeiras	2298	–	4	7741	1	4¾				5443	1	–¾
Newfoundland	18402	6	1¼	17661	8	5¼	740	17	8			
Portugal	164539	7	1½	337600	14	7¾				173061	7	6¼
Russia	99845	5	5	58118	5	–	41727	–	5			
Scotland	86309	19	1	66303	15	8	20006	3	5			
Spain	469903	3	3¼	574628	11	11½				104725	8	8¼
Streights				408163	12	2¾				408163	12	2¾
Sweden	245802	5	5¼	57166	12	10¼	188635	12	7			
Turkey	255904	–	5¼	223403	14	1¾	32500	6	3½			
Venice	50051	12	9	34034	10	7	16017	2	2			
Isles: Alderney	180	8	3	340	18	2¼				160	9	11¼
Isles: Guernsey	10199	9	11¾	15910	14	7½				5711	4	7¾
Isles: Jersey	15605	16	9½	12696	19	7	2908	17	2½			
British Plantations: Antigua	109440	15	2¾	30226	18	9¾	79213	16	5			
British Plantations: Barbadoes	273947	15	5	150532	7	5¼	123415	7	11¼			
British Plantations: Bermudas	300	10	–½	1439	13	11				1139	3	10½
British Plantations: Carolina	12327	1	9¾	11401	18	5½	925	3	4¼			
British Plantations: Hudsons Bay	4235	5	–¼	943	15	7¼	3291	9	5			
British Plantations: Jamaica	174845	–	8¼	136733	6	1	38111	14	7¼			
British Plantations: Mountserrat	23163	9	6	7162	14	2¼	16000	15	3¾			
British Plantations: Nevis	74857	13	6¼	16480	6	4¾	58337	7	1½			
British Plantations: New England	26660	16	8	127279	19	2½				100619	2	6½
British Plantations: New Providence				305	4	–				305	4	–
British Plantations: New York	16818	18	10½	42792	1	1				25973	2	2½
British Plantations: Pensylvania	1477	15	6	17064	1	7¾				15586	6	1¾
British Plantations: Virginia & Maryland	198115	16	10	205078	–	2½				6962	3	4½
Prize Goods	5986	9	6½				5986	9	6½			
Foreign Coin & Bullion				850904	14	6				850904	14	6
	£5707669	11	9¾	6788166	17	6¼	1839172	–	1	2919669	5	10
The Exports Exceed the Imports										£1080497	5	9

The ROASTED EXCISEMAN
or
The JACK BOOT'S EXIT.

Left: the first 'Balance of Payments' account, 1698–9 (p. 30)   *HMSO*

Above: a cartoon at the time of the 'Cider riots', 1763 (p. 66)   *Miss G. Bulmer*

Below left: an Excise officer in the eighteenth century   *HMSO*

Below right: 'the Exciseman' in the nineteenth century   *British Library*

Riding officers on the Dover Road, November 1813   *HMSO*

Four romantic views of smugglers   *HMSO*

It was no doubt easy to express such sentiments from the comfort of the Board Room of the London Custom House, but it was quite a different matter to face the violence of the smugglers on a dark night on some lonely coast, with little hope of any assistance.

The *Journal* of Abraham Darby, Supervisor of the Riding Officers around Bournemouth during the beginning of the nineteenth century, vividly shows how difficult, dangerous and utterly frustrating the actual work was. Invariably he and his officers were out on patrol for long hours, only to find that a successful run had been made on another part of the coast. They were continually one step behind the smugglers, and even when they received information of a run and managed to arrive in time they were vastly outnumbered, and suffered defeat as a result. Much of their time was taken up by searching for the hidden goods after they had received information of their landing. The work was obviously physically demanding, and many riding officers were well over sixty years old, and therefore not fit enough for the dangers and rigours of such an arduous life. (At Rochester in 1805, though, one of the riding officers was Sir Thomas Wiseman, Bart., and it is unlikely that he ventured out in all weathers for the meagre salary of £60 per year!)

Certainly there were instances of riding officers being dismissed the service for collusion with the smugglers. In May 1806 a Customs officer at Folkestone co-operated with the boat-crew of the *Nimble*, a revenue vessel from Deal, in their own smuggling; two riding officers who helped in the landing of the goods were also dismissed. Although the Customs Board was becoming more strict in disciplinary matters, they were nevertheless very paternalistic towards officers injured on duty, and to the families of those killed. In 1808 they introduced a schedule of payments to widows of revenue officers, and also a scale of payments for various injuries. The widow of a riding officer received £15 per annum, plus £5 for every child under the age of fifteen. The loss of a limb was valued at a pension of £15. Before these scales had been introduced similar pensions had been granted only on the special application of the collector. For example, Anne Sarmon, widow of the commander of the *Swan* cutter, received £45 per year for herself and her three children. The son of Humphrey Glynn, a boatman who had been murdered in 1799, had been placed at a 'special school at St Germains' at the request of the collector, the Board agreeing to pay the annual fees of £20.

In an attempt to strengthen the defence of the coast against the 'new insolence of the smugglers', a new revenue force was established in 1809, called the Preventive Waterguard. This body of men was intended to link up with the existing services—the cruisers and riding officers. The coast was divided into three districts, each placed under the control of an Inspecting Commander. From London to Land's End, there were twenty-three cruisers and forty-two 'preventive' boats, to Carlisle ten cruisers and thirteen boats; and from Berwick to London four cruisers and thirteen boats. The duties of the new Waterguard were to operate in coastal waters and to tackle the smugglers who had managed to evade the Customs cruisers, which operated farther out to sea. When the weather was too rough to take out the small rowing-boats they were expected to patrol the coast on foot, watching for likely landing places, and also to give assistance to the riding officers.

The first Comptroller-General was Captain Henchett of the Royal Navy, who selected the recruits to his new force largely from the demobilized sailors. They were normally stationed in areas away from their homes, to avoid any collusion with either friends or relations, who might be involved in the smuggling trade. The pay was not high; the boatmen received £5 per year and 3s. a day when employed, and the chief boatman or 'sitter' received £15 and 4s. a day. Because they were moved from their own neighbour-hoods—frequently to some distance, the Cardiff boat being manned with men from Shoreham—accommodation had to be found for the crews at their new station. This proved to be a most difficult problem: because of the hostility and opposition of the local people, the collectors were unable to find suitable lodgings for the local men. The solution to the problem was to combine living quarters with the watch-houses that were being erected in suitable places overlooking the coast. Already, because of the reluctance of local landowners to part with their land, the Board had to seek compulsory purchase powers to obtain the desired sites. Until the new watch-houses were built many of the boat-crews were forced to live in tents, under most miserable conditions.

The supervision of the riding officers was greatly increased; six Inspecting-Generals were appointed to control closely the activities of the officers in their areas, and provide greater co-operation with the Waterguard. In 1811 the Board issued a general amnesty to past offenders:

> The Commissioners wish to forget and forgive all those who have been misled and tempted into improper acts and connections with persons connected with the illicit trade . . . and any of those who have erred or transgressed, will under this lenient measure be prompted to diligent, faithful and active exertion in future, and by doing so, have the conscious satisfaction of atoning for their former deviation and misconduct.

The end of the war brought fresh problems for the revenue service; over 250,000 soldiers and seamen were discharged, all well trained in the arts of battle, and with little inclination for a quiet and peaceful life. Although many of these men went to America to seek their fortune, a large number returned to their home towns, with little hope of gainful and honest employment. The Treasury had recognized the problem:

> after so long a period of war in every part of Europe, many of the most daring professional men discharged from their occupation and adverse to the daily labour of agriculture or mechanical employment, will be the ready instruments of those desperate persons, who have a little capital and are hardy enough to engage in the trade of smuggling.

It was therefore decided, in order to combat the expected rise in smuggling, to increase the number of preventive boats. The conditions of qualifications for entry into the Waterguard were regularized. In future all boatmen were required to be between the ages of twenty and thirty-five, and with at least six years experience at sea, or with a seven-year apprenticeship as a fisherman. It was also felt that a greater degree of efficiency could be obtained if the control of the force was passed to the Treasury. In the same year, 1816, the control of the revenue vessels was handed over to the Admiralty. Also, because there were so many naval vessels at the end of the war, they were utilized to provide the revenue with protection, and many of the latter's cutters were paid off, their crews being transferred to the enlarged Waterguard service. The Customs were now left only with the riding officers and two vessels, *Vigilant* and *Fly*.

A further way in which the surfeit of naval personnel were found useful employment was embodied in a plan put forward by the Admiralty. This was to set up a total 'coast blockade' of the area between North Foreland and Dungeness. The new force would set up a series of shore patrols of seamen, operating from a number of blockade stations, each under the control of a naval lieutenant. The idea had been proposed by Captain Joseph McCulloch of HMS *Gannymede*, who during his naval service off the Kent coast became convinced that such a blockade was the only answer to the smugglers. The Treasury readily agreed to the proposal and in 1817 the coast blockade service was established, with Captain McCulloch as its commander. The latter set up his headquarters in a vessel stationed offshore in the Downs, with a further man of war off Newhaven. Most of the patrols were based on shore and were housed in the many Martello towers along the coast, which had been originally built to repel a rather different kind of invasion!

After just one year of operation the coast blockade was extended to Seaford in Sussex, and the Preventive Waterguard was removed from the entire coast of Kent and Sussex. McCulloch now had complete control of the revenue forces in the two counties, much to his delight. In common with many other naval officers, he considered the Waterguard to be an undisciplined and inefficient force, frequently in league with the smugglers. McCulloch was a strict disciplinarian, and was known within the Navy as 'Flogging Joey'. The harsh discipline, uncongenial living conditions and hazardous nature of the work made it difficult to recruit the right type of seamen, a factor which ultimately undermined the general effectiveness of the blockade.

The presence of such a strongly armed force in the area caused the smugglers to resort to even greater violence in an attempt to carry on their trade. Now they all, without exception, carried some form of firearms, and the degree of physical force and brutality exceeded that of the days of the Hawkhurst Gang. One of the most desperate gangs operating in the area was called 'The Blues'. In February 1821 around two hundred and fifty smugglers were gathered on a beach at Comber, near Rye, to unload a cargo of spirits. A party of the blockade service led by three midshipmen rushed to the spot, and a long and desperate battle broke out. The smugglers managed to land the goods and carry them off inland, where they waited to ambush the following blockaders (or 'warriors', as they were nicknamed). Another furious and brutal fight took place, in which four smugglers were killed and sixteen seriously injured, whereas one midshipman was killed and four seamen badly injured. This 'Battle of Brookland', as it later became known, marked the start of an all-out civil war between the smugglers and 'the Warriors'.

Several weeks later another midshipman was killed near Herne Bay, shot in the back by a gang unloading tubs of spirits. On a number of occasions the smugglers had sufficient confidence and numbers to take the offensive; they attacked the watch-houses of the blockade, to divert attention, while other members of the gang unloaded the cargoes undisturbed. In one instance a gang of 'upwards to fifty strongly armed smugglers attacked a Martello Tower'; this was a revenge raid against the patrol that had captured four of their gang a few nights earlier. In another affray near Worthing six men of the blockade service faced over three hundred smugglers, and kept them engaged until reinforcements arrived. At the end of .this battle all the blockade men were injured in some way; one seaman had 'his arm broken in two places, his ear cut open and his head much bruised'. None of the smugglers were detained, but two of their number were killed. Even when smugglers were caught and brought to trial they were often acquitted. As a Treasury solicitor explained, there was no way of identifying the men—'they all dressed in white smocks, like farm labourers, with faces blackened and their feet muffled by worsted stockings over their shoes'.

Without doubt the various preventive measures in operation—the Waterguard, riding officers, the cruisers and the coast blockade—were at long last achieving some moderate success, but it was at a great financial cost. There were now nearly 6,700 persons employed in the four services, at an annual expenditure of over half a million pounds. In 1821 a committee was set up by the Treasury to examine in detail all the various services involved in the prevention of smuggling. It found:

> The difficulty of protecting the Revenue has been unquestionably very great; the attempts of the smugglers have been carried to a most flagrant degree of audacity and violence. They have, indeed, suffered severe losses in goods, conveyances and men (the capture of the latter being the most effective mode of repressing these practices); but we have found that they have succeeded in introducing considerable quantities of spirits and tobacco from the opposite coasts. In the article of tea, it does not appear that they have attempted much; and although the principal towns on the southern coast, and even the metropolis, have largely been supplied with prohibited and high duty goods, such as silks, gloves, laces etc. We have reason to believe, that these have for the most part been brought in clandestinely by individuals arriving in the packets, or in trading vessels.

The Committee had grave misgivings at the lack of central control of all the preventive services, which in their opinion gave 'a lack of unity to the whole arrangements'. They therefore recommended that the Preventive Waterguard should be returned to the control of the Customs Board. However, because 'of the change in the nature of its duties since its introduction, the term 'Coast Guard' would be a more appropriate distinction'. The force of the riding officers were reduced by over one half to just fifty men, and the much reduced number of small revenue vessels returned once again to Customs control. The larger vessels stayed under the Admiralty control.

The Treasury approved the report, and with effect from 15 January 1822 the new preventive establishment renamed the Coast Guard came into being. The Customs Commissioners once more had the control of virtually all the services involved in the prevention of smuggling. The first Comptroller-General of the new force was Captain William Bowles RN, who replaced Henchett. Although Bowles was was under the direction of the Customs Commissioners, all the officers and men appointed to the Coast Guard were nominated by the Admiralty, thus establishing the now long naval tradition of the Coast Guard (the two words of whose name were separate for a number of years).

Despite expressing certain misgivings about the efficiency (and suspicions about the loyalty and integrity) of the coast blockade service, the committee felt that they could not warrant or justify 'the removal of this service at the present time, when the smuggler is exerting himself in a peculiar manner to defeat its vigilance, the dangers of any alteration under such circumstances are sufficiently obvious'. Thus the coast blockade was retained under the control of the Admiralty, and continued to fight many a battle before it was disbanded in 1831.

The final paragraph of the report summarizes the new attitudes to smuggling and makes a fitting epitaph to this period of bitter and brutal warfare waged against the illegal trader:

> We think, indeed, that from the moment when a disposition has been manifested by the body of smugglers to offer an organized and armed resistance to the military and civil functions of the public, the force directed against them should be such as to leave them neither chances nor hopes of success. Every principle of policy and every consideration of humanity forbid, that the means employed against those deluded persons should be either really or apparently, so nearly balanced with their own strength, as to give any degree of encouragement to men stimulated as they are, by the prospect of great gain, to undertake, or to protract so pernicious a contest.

CHAPTER SEVEN

The Age of Reform

For the last century and a half both services had grown and developed in the wake of continual increases in taxation, which brought new and fresh responsibilities to each department. From 1840 onwards the position was drastically reversed. This was now the era of free trade, the abolition of restrictive Excise duties, which were thought to hinder the development of manufacturing industries, and last but not least, the general reforms of the Civil Service. All these improvements were undertaken in the flush of Victorian liberalism. Faced with these changes, both services were forced to contract, and concentrate their resources on the few remaining but nevertheless major duties. These were the 'traditional Revenue duties', such as spirits, beer, wines and tobacco, which even today account for a large part of the revenue of the Customs and Excise.

The repeal of many of the Excise duties over a period of ten years had set a pattern, which was now to be repeated in the Customs. It was William Huskisson, as President of the Board of Trade, who introduced the first preferences for goods from the Colonies. He was the leading proponent of free trade, and but for his sad and early death (he was killed in one of the first railway accidents), he would have been in the forefront of the attack on restrictive tariffs. However, he left an able disciple, Sir Robert Peel, who was also an avowed free-trader, and who carried out a policy of tariff reform which culminated in the repeal of the Corn Laws.

Peel had a very poor opinion of the Customs department. In 1843 he remarked, 'I confess I distrust everything about the Customs, so far as to feel assured that a vast many have been dishonest and none have been vigilant.' Whether this opinion influenced his views on free trade is doubtful; he was nevertheless responsible for a vast reduction in Customs duties.

The first revision of the tariff was carried out in 1842, the second in 1845 and the third a year later. Within a short period of time over 1,200 dutiable articles had been freed from duty. Now no single duty exceeded 10 per cent, and all export duties had been abolished. A total of over £7 millions of Customs duties had been repealed. In 1853 Gladstone continued the policy, again lowering the existing duties and freeing a further 140 articles. Greater changes resulted from the treaty with France; the duties on French wines and brandy were reduced, and a wide range of French-manufactured goods became duty-free.

By now Great Britain was essentially a free-trade country; only forty-eight articles remained on the tariff, and of these only sugar, tobacco, tea, wines, coffee, timber, and rice brought in any appreciable revenue. Despite all the reductions, the Customs revenue still amounted to almost £25 millions, an increase on the 1840 figure. This increase was solely due to the vast increase in trade; both imports and exports had virtually doubled in the last twenty years. Many of the redundancies of officers caused by the free-trade policy were taken up to cope with the boom in trade.

The reduction of the Excise Department continued in the 1840s. The duty on glass was repealed in 1845, and three years later considerable savings in staff were made by the abolition of survey visits to spirit dealers and retailers. As a result of the Parnall Committee report, the separate 'Town' and 'Country' establishments were abolished. These had been set up in the early days of the Excise, when the 'Town' Excise had consisted of a number of specialized districts controlling the brewers, distillers and other Excise traders in the whole of London, and housed at the head office. Now London was arranged on a collection scheme like the 'Country' Excise, and the new establishment totalled sixty-one collections.

With the reductions in the range of Excise, it is not surprising to find that the Treasury were considering some form of rationalization in the revenue departments. Already in 1833 the stamp department had merged with the taxes, and the formation of one large revenue department was now being mooted. All the initial correspondence relating to the merger of the Excise with the other services referred to the new department as the 'Internal Revenue', but when the Bill was presented to Parliament in 1848 the name had been changed to that of the 'Inland Revenue'. It was anticipated that the proposals would achieve savings of between £70,000 and £80,000; but it turned out that this figure had been grossly exaggerated, and the total economy was closer to £20,000.

The patent for the new Board of Inland Revenue was granted on 5 January 1849. The Board comprised a Chairman and Deputy, with five junior Commissioners. Mr John Wood, the Excise Chairman, was appointed head of the new Board, with Mr Charles Pressley of the Stamps and Taxes as his Deputy. The 'junior' Commissioners were required to attend 'at least between 10 am and 4 pm, and later if required and their vacation was limited to two months'!

Although the three departments were now under one Board, each operated quite separately from one another; each had their own secretaries, accounts, solicitors and surveying staff. This system prevailed, with only a few minor alterations, for the next sixty years. However, it was actually amalgamation in name only, for the Excise still continued to use their office in Broad Street until 1852, when the building was sold for £132,000. They then moved to Somerset to join the Stamps and Taxes, where a new wing was added in 1856 to accommodate the extra staff.

The policy of repealing further 'restrictive' Excise duties was continued. During the years between 1850–61 the duties on bricks, soap and paper were abolished. The paper duty had been in existence since 1712, and in its latter days had caused an inordinate amount of work for the relatively small amount of duty collected. Much of this extra work was due to the rapid growth of the manufacture of envelopes with the introduction of the penny post system. Although there were some staff savings by this abolition, these were amply compensated for by the work arising from other duties trans-ferred to Excise control, with the result that the size of the department stayed fairly constant for a number of years.

One of the most unusual duties passed to the Excise was railway passenger duty. This had been introduced initially in 1832, only two years after the opening of the first passenger railway, which ran between Liverpool and Manchester. The duty was administered at first by the Commissioners of Stamps, and control passed to the Excise in 1847. By then the original duty charge had been changed by an Act which was to have a decisive effect on the development of railway operations in this country.

With due Victorian philanthropy, it was considered essential to ensure that the poorer classes of passengers were given the opportunity of rail travel at moderate, if not cheap, fares. The method chosen to achieve this aim was by financial legislation. As President of the Board of Trade, William Gladstone introduced a Bill in 1844 which created what were called 'Parliamentary' trains. These were passenger trains which were compelled to provide third-class carriages (duly protected from the weather) at a fare of not more than 1d. per mile. The trains were further required to stop at every station and every halt on the line, and to travel at an average speed of not less than 12 m.p.h. If all these conditions were fulfilled all fares on such trains (including both first and second class) were exempted from the 5 per cent duty on fares. The railway companies quickly realized the potential of these cheap trains, and soon receipts from 'excursion' trains exceeded those from the other two classes, with a large resultant loss to the revenue.

Various amendments were made to the Act in an attempt to redress the balance, and so to improve the amount of duty collected. Several committees examined the problem and recommended a variety of changes, but the end-result was an unwieldy mass of complicated orders and exemptions. The control of the duty was fraught with difficulties, and involved the Excise in endless litigation with various railway companies on questions of detail. It was not until 1883, with the passing of a new Act, that many of the problems were resolved, although the new Act itself brought headaches, with exemptions for workmen's fares and reduced rates of duty for travel on suburban lines (an early example of subsidies for commuter travel?). At its height the duty only amounted to £800,000, but after all the changes in 1883 it fell to a steady £300,000, until its repeal altogether in the next century.

For some time rumours had abounded in the shipping circles in London about widespread frauds in the department of land waiters in London Port. By 1842 reports were circulating freely in the City as to the immensity of the frauds and the amount of collusion in the port. The situation became so serious that in October three commissioners formed a special committee of inquiry to investigate the allegations. The facts unearthed were so serious that the Board felt they had no option but to report the whole sorry matter to the Treasury. Their report was an admission of their gross mismanagement: 'It is with deep regret that we have to perform the painful duty of calling your Lordships' attentions to the subject of various frauds and malpractices affecting the Revenue under our control.'

The Treasury for its part appointed its own committee to investigate. This inquiry disclosed an amazing system of long-standing frauds in the port, which involved over 200 officers and some of the most respectable merchants in the City. In all 42 officers were prosecuted and over 100 were demoted, but some of the worst offenders had escaped to the Continent. *The Times* published two very damaging articles, hinting at even greater mismanagement than had been discovered. The Chairman of the Customs Board engaged the Editor in a lengthy and acrimonious correspondence in an attempt to obtain some retraction and apology—but without success. This prolonged public debate in the columns of the newspaper was a sad error of judgment, because the Customs took many years to live down the opprobrium.

As a result of the inquiry the Commissioners were issued with a volume of instructions for their own conduct. The work of the department was put into divisions, with a Commissioner directly responsible for the work and conduct of the staff within that division. Tours of inspection to the out-ports were in future to be made on a systematic basis. Perhaps one of the most unfortunate aspects of the whole unhappy business was that one of the members of the Treasury Committee was a young Member of Parliament named William Gladstone. The unsavoury details of the frauds gave him a lifelong dislike and mistrust of the Customs, and this antipathy coloured his future decisions on the department through his long and distinguished career.

In 1846 there was a departure from a practice which had existed since the days of Elizabeth and earlier. Since those times the Court of Exchequer had laid down the limits and legal quays of the ports. This rather cumbersome method was now abolished, and a more simple procedure by way of Treasury Warrant was substituted. The Treasury were authorized to appoint ports and legal quays, and to alter them as the need and occasion arose.

Only six years after the disclosure of the frauds in the Customs in London

Port, the department thought that they had uncovered serious frauds in the London docks. They were under the impression that large amounts of sugar, tea and coffee were leaving the warehouses without payment of duty. In December 1849 a large number of Customs officers descended on St Katharine's and London Docks to examine all the stock accounts and to check all deliveries. As a result over fifty informations were laid against the various dock companies, which if proved would result in very large penalties.

The excitement in the City was tremendous. A group of London merchants made their own investigations into the so-called frauds, and a Select Committee of the House of Commons was formed to look into the matter. It published eight volumes of reports, which with the evidence and appendices comprised over 4,300 pages. Considering the size of the report, very little was discovered amiss. The trouble had arisen over the repacking of bulk goods and the floor sweepings of tea and sugar. These had been sold to contractors as rubbish, but they found their way to inferior tea-blenders and the manufacturers of cheap sweets. Once again the Commissioners were strongly criticized for their mishandling of the affair. The newspapers called for the resignation of the Board, and suggested that the Custom House required sweeping out rather than the warehouses. The prosecutions were withdrawn on payment of a token sum of £100 by each dock company. The immediate interest died down, but it took far longer for the Customs to live down their inefficient image.

Partly as a result of the report, there was a change in procedure in the control of vessels in the docks. For centuries when a vessel arrived at the boarding station, a tide waiter was placed on board, and stayed there until all the cargo had been discharged. (Up until twenty years before, they had been allowed to be accompanied by their wives!) With the new enclosed docks, this system was both unnecessary and expensive. In its place a shore patrol system was introduced, which policed the quays and warehouses by day and night. The success of the system in London and Liverpool led to its extension to other ports. The new system was very unpopular with the staff; many of the old-timers regretted the passing of the old tradition. One collector was moved to comment, 'Their opposition to the patrol, is their aversion to work and closer control by the Surveyor, and I suspect less opportunity for drinking'!

Because of the steady introduction of free trade, and more especially the new treaty agreement with France—and perhaps as reaction to their recent bad publicity—the Board were now well aware that they were expected to make considerable savings in staff. A tour of inspection of over a hundred ports was undertaken by two Commissioners and the Surveyor-General, and was accomplished in just two months, which shows a remarkable sense of urgency. By April 1861 the proposals for the reorganizing of the service were complete, and were laid before the Treasury. Within one week they were agreed.

The main feature of the new scheme was the amalgamation of the

Landing and Waterguard departments. As was pointed out, the duties of the landing officers were now greatly simplified, and it seemed reasonable and economical to place all Customs work under one set of officers. The reductions achieved were 552, which was almost 10 per cent of the total staff. The majority of the redundancies were in the larger ports, especially London and Liverpool; although one Commissioner and two Surveyor-Generals were 'voluntarily retired early'. The whole exercise was estimated to save £85,000.

From an historical point of view, the reorganization saw the disappearance of the old title of 'waiter'. The tide waiters now became 'outdoor officers', and were occupied in both Landing and Waterguard duties of a minor nature. The landing waiters were now called 'examining officers'; their work largely concerned the examination of imported goods. The only grade to retain its old name was the import gaugers, and they operated only in the few large ports.

Although there had been many changes in the control of spirit duty, the Excise still found that this was the one to cause them the most trouble. One of the problems was the border between England and Scotland. As there was a lower rate of duty on spirits in Scotland— 4s. 2d. per gallon less—smuggling across the border became a very profitable trade. Over sixty Excise riding officers were stationed along the border from Carlisle to Berwick, and a preventive boat was based at Carlisle to cover any smuggling across the Solway Firth.

Special instructions were issued to the Border staff. They were ordered to 'employ themselves at least three nights in every week, in traversing and watching the roads by which the smugglers travel'. Each officer while on duty was required to be armed and mounted, and must 'abstain from drinking to excess'. With the completion of the railway between Edinburgh and Newcastle in 1846, and the west route a year or so later, new problems were posed for the control of the rail traffic. It was decided to establish a border control at both Berwick and Carlisle stations. Excise officers were detailed to attend to examine the rail passengers' baggage for smuggled spirits. This form of control was certainly novel to this country, and caused considerable public interest. A letter to *The Times* even suggested that the country was becoming 'like a mere European principality with petty and annoying restrictions to law abiding passengers'.

Such restrictions, however, were not to last long; in 1855 the duty on spirits was equalized between the two countries, so the need for the border service ceased. By now too much of the illicit distillation in Scotland had been suppressed; in 1856 there were only 48 detections. (Strangely, there were more than 300 detections in England.) Unlike Scotland and Ireland, where the trade was predominantly rural, much of the illicit spirit in England was produced in the large towns, and in an attempt to suppress the trade Excise officers worked very closely with the police. Special commissions were issued to the latter, investing them with the wide powers of the Excise. Slowly the combined efforts of both brought the illicit trade under control.

Unfortunately, the same could not be said for the situation in Ireland. Even more than in Scotland, illegal distilling was a peasant industry. The poverty and wretchedness of the living conditions made private distillation the only way to pay the rent. It was estimated that in 1823 *poitín* or pegeen (the illegal spirit) accounted for nearly two-thirds of all spirits sales in Ireland. As in Scotland, 'poitin' or 'poteen' was considered a far superior whiskey to the legal 'Parliamentary brandy'. The poor roads and lack of transportation vastly assisted the illegal trade, by greatly hampering the Excise in their attempts to control it.

The Excise control was based on a revenue police force, whose sole purpose was the suppression of illicit distillation. The force had been set up as early as 1787 in Leitrim; however, it was not until 1818 that parties of police were formed in other counties. By 1833 there was a force of over 900 strong, costing £35,000. They were on a daily rate of pay, but were allowed rewards for the arrest and convictions of smugglers and the seizures of illegal stills. The abolition of this force was recommended by the Parnall Committee, but it survived until 1857, when it was disbanded, and the control passed to the Irish Constabulary. Neither force were particularly successful in combating the trade. The decrease in the production of poitin can be attributed more to poor harvests, famine, and the enforced migration, rather than to the efforts of the Excise and the police. However, throughout the country, and certainly up to the First World War, the illicit trade flourished, especially in the more remote western counties.

Much of the illicit spirit produced in England—and to a lesser extent in Scotland—was supplied to the manufacturers of polish, varnish and other chemical products. In 1855, after numerous experiments, it was considered that the addition of crude wood naphtha to spirits would make them so unpalatable as to render them undrinkable. Spirits treated in this manner were therefore allowed to be used duty-free in certain approved manufactures; they were called methylated spirits. The treated spirits were not only a great benefit to industry generally but were a major factor in the marked decrease of illicit distillation.

The successful introduction of the new system owed much to the work of George Phillips, Surveying-General Examiner of the Excise. Phillips had entered the Excise in 1826, and very soon became interested in the problems associated with the adulteration of tobacco. It was estimated that there was as much as 70 per cent foreign matter mixed with tobacco products, with a consequential large revenue loss. Phillips worked on a detailed analysis of the products, and, certain that he had an answer to the problem, offered his services to the Excise Board. In 1842 a laboratory was set up in Broad Street, where he carried on his research in an official capacity.

The Excise Board decided to make the laboratory a permanent part of Headquarters. Phillips and seven other officers were directed to attend

London University to study chemistry. This was a very unusual and revolutionary move, as it was well before the University Act of 1854, which opened the doors to persons of poorer means. From tobacco products the laboratory extended its research into the materials used in brewing and distilling. When it was moved to specially constructed accommodation in Somerset House in 1858 Phillips was made its first principal. Assistants were now trained at the laboratory, rather than at university.

The Customs Department was later in establishing its laboratory. Its foundation was due largely to a change in the method of charging wine duty. One of the results of the treaty with France in 1861 was that wine became liable to duty according to its alcoholic strength. From 1861 wine-testing stations were set up in the London Docks, and later in the out-ports approved for the import of wine. In 1875 the Sale of Food and Drugs Act involved the Customs in ascertaining the purity of imported tea. The wine laboratory was centralized in the Custom House, London, under a principal, and its work was extended to the testing of other foodstuffs, notably butter and margarine.

Although the departments were still separate, the two laboratories were combined in 1897 to form the 'Government Laboratory', and remained under the control of the department until 1911, when it became a department in its own right. For a number of years, however, officers of Customs and Excise were detailed to serve in the laboratory—Richard Church, novelist and poet, started his official life in the Government Chemist's at the Custom House.

Another example of the introduction of special sections in the service was the formation in 1855 by the Excise of a detective force. This comprised one supervisor, six officers and some preventive men. Their main duties were the investigation of all revenue frauds throughout London. Once again the Customs were tardy in setting up a similar force; it was not until 1890 that officers were invited to volunteer for this duty. Its main purpose was the detection of smuggling, and officers were liable to be sent to any part of the coast. For this inconvenience they received a daily allowance of 24s. Both forces can claim to be forerunners of the present Investigation Division.

Largely as a result of the railway boom, the mid-century saw a vast increase in the number of passengers travelling abroad. The examination of baggage has been a subject of complaint, no less today than it was a hundred years ago. A report in the early part of the nineteenth century complained of 'long delays in a draughty warehouse waiting for the baggage to be unloaded and cleared'. (The officers of the port in question, Southampton, commented, 'Lady passengers are dressing themselves in valuable dresses and jewels, more calculated for their entry into a drawing room, than merely to come ashore. They are all items newly acquired abroad.') At this time there were no 'passenger concessions' as there are today. Duty was paid on all goods, and it was not until 1850 that an allowance of $\frac{1}{2}$ lb of tobacco was granted duty-free, and extended to include one pint of spirits in 1875.

By 1850 London had become an important passenger port, with passengers landing at Gravesend or coming up the river to the packet berth situated near the Tower. In fact as early as 1826 it was found necessary to appoint temporary women searchers, normally the wives of tide waiters, to deal with the female passengers. These women searchers, as they were called, became the first women to be employed in the Civil Service.

There was a great increase in passengers in the 1850s. Southampton reported over 400,000 passengers landing each year. Each vessel had to produce a passenger list, and when the passengers landed they were shown to a waiting-room and were called forward individually to clear their baggage—a vast change from the scenes at a port or airport today. With the opening of the various London railway termini, officers were established at the stations to clear passengers from the Continent. The first such clearance was undertaken at London Bridge in 1853, followed by Charing Cross in 1864, Victoria a year later, and Holborn and Liverpool Street towards the end of the century. Victoria was the last station to have Customs staff, these being dispensed with only in the last fifteen years. Contrary to public belief, the question 'Have you anything to declare?' was not used; officers were instructed to ask, 'Have you anything in your possession liable to duty, such as tobacco, cigars, spirits or perfumery?'

The term Civil Service did not come into general use until after 1855. Some time earlier Sir Robert Peel had referred to 'civil servants' in order to differentiate between political and Ministerial servants. In the 1851 census 53,000 persons were shown as employed in the 'public service', and of this figure over a fifth were employed in the two revenue departments. However, the inferior grades of the Civil Service were not then considered civil servants in the accepted sense. They were dismissed as unimportant, because 'they only require arms, legs, health and strength, little education but frequently some degree of worthiness!'

In 1853 a report was submitted by Sir Charles Trevelyan, Permanent Secretary at the Treasury, and Sir Stafford Northcote, on the administration of the Civil Service. It recommended a proper system of examination controlled by a central body. Proper inquiries were to be made into age, health and character, a period of probation for all grades, promotion by merit, and salary increments based on a system of 'satisfaction certificates'. Perhaps the most important and far-reaching recommendation was the separation of 'intellectual' and 'mechanical' work. The report was accepted, and by an Order in Council dated 21 May 1855 the Civil Service Commission came into being, and with it the modern Civil Service.

The Civil Service Commission examined the candidates for all junior situations in the various departments and issued what became known as 'C of Q's—certificates of qualifications, which were the authority for entry into the Civil Service. Most departments already had some form of examination, the Customs being one of the exceptions. Almost immediately the Customs Commissioners introduced an examination system for clerks and landing waiters under the aegis of the Commission. The examination covered handwriting, English composition, arithmetic, geography and history, and for the lower ranks just writing and the four rules of arithmetic. Minimum and maximum ages of entry were laid down, as well as a system of references and health certificates. Strict rules on probation were brought in, and a more formal method of training replaced the hitherto rather haphazard system.

The Inland Revenue reported that the Civil Service Commission were satisfied with their existing system of examination, though Mr John Wood, the Chairman of the Inland Revenue, admitted the examination to be 'a mere form to test hand-writing and knowledge of arithmetic'. During the next ten years the examination for entry as an Excise assistant was extended to include history, English and geography. By the end of the century the Excise tests were considered of a far higher standard than the Customs examinations.

In 1857 the first annual reports of both departments were published, and they have appeared continuously since that date. The idea of a departmental report originated three years earlier in the Post Office. The success of this report persuaded the Treasury to extend it to the revenue departments. The first report of the Customs gave historical notes on the earlier methods of collecting the duties. The Inland Revenue's report contained valuable tables showing the yields of the various Excise duties since their inception. Because these reports contained information not readily available elsewhere, there was a great demand for copies, and they quickly went out of print. The demand was in fact so great that the Inland Revenue reprinted their historical tables in the thirteenth report in 1870.

Despite the system which had been established under the Northcote-Trevelyan Report having proved itself, a further Commission under Dr Lyon Playfair was set up in 1874. The new Commission was requested to investigate the flexibility of staff within the service and the feasibility of employing a lower grade to undertake the less important clerical work. As *Punch* succinctly remarked, 'What the Civil Service needs is less Playfair and more fair play.'

Largely as a result of this new Commission, there was an amalgamation of grades within the Excise. Inspectors were placed into three classes, and senior and junior officers combined into one grade. The Customs were accepted as a 'special category' due to the 'largely technical nature of the work', and they were allowed to form a special grade of 'Customs port-clerks', with promotion rights to collector. Both departments employed a lower grade for the less important work; these were called 'writers' and frequently were in fact aspiring literary gentlemen. By the end of the century more improvements were made in the general conditions of service, annual and sick leave, and the establishment of promotion examinations with the departments. It has been claimed by many that the reforms achieved in the Civil Service during this period were of greater importance than those achieved in the reform of Parliament.

One of the features of the last half of the century was the number of inquiries into the feasibility of amalgamating the two departments. Certainly there was no lack of perseverance by the various proposers of such schemes. The first committee to look into the subject was headed by Thomas Horsfall, M.P. It sat during 1862–3 and published all the official evidence, but no formal report. The draft report 'abstained from recommending the consolidation of the department'. There were no reasons given for this conclusion.

About three years later fresh proposals for amalgamation were put forward, based on the published evidence of the Committee. They suggested that the Post Office, Inland Revenue and the Customs should be formed into one large revenue department, with a Secretary of State for Revenue. The main objections to this scheme were said to be 'the difficulty to obtain a competent person to control and manage such a large organisation' and the 'jealousy and antagonism towards any scheme likely to affect their personal interests, influence or position'.

There were certainly sound reasons for combining the Customs and Excise departments. Both services were closely involved with the main revenue duties, spirits, wines, tobacco and tea. At every port there were separate Customs and Excise staff, and at many of the small ports where the income from Customs duties was not even sufficient to pay the salaries of the Customs officers there was invariably a larger Excise staff. Both services were involved with bonded warehouses, and it appears in retrospect that considerable economies could have been achieved with a merger then of the two services.

For the next twenty-five years several proposals were submitted for the amalgamation, and requests for another committee to re-examine the subject. Finally, in 1888, this pressure was successful, and no less than a Royal Commission—led by Sir Matthew Ridley—was set up. The Commission met from November 1888 to March 1889. It examined the subject in very great detail, receiving submissions from both departments, from mercantile and trade interests and from Gladstone, the grand old man of politics, now in his eightieth year.

The Inland Revenue—whose star was in the ascendancy, due to the recent success of the introduction of beer duty—was greatly in favour of the amalgamation, and suggested that the Customs should be absorbed into their service. They proposed that the Custom House should be sold and the London staff moved to Excise accommodation at Tower Hill, and the Head Office staff to Somerset House. The Customs strongly defended the status quo, maintaining that nothing would be gained from such a merger, and that the building at Tower Hill was insufficient for their needs.

Needless to say, Gladstone was greatly in favour of the amalgamation; he spoke at length of his experience of both departments. He hoped that 'the Inland Revenue would be the dominant servant . . . because the traditions of the Customs did not come up to the excellence of the Excise'. The general view among merchants and traders was summed up by the wine trade: 'Better the evil we know . . .'

The papers submitted by both departments were strongly criticized and attacked by each respective chairman. The acrimony and bitterness engendered during the hearings and subsequent debates remained in both departments for a very long time, and were ultimately to effect the eventual amalgamation in the next century. The final conclusion of the Commission was that the estimated savings were slight (£11,000), and the problems in combining the two staffs, with all the different grades and salary scales, did not justify such an important experiment. The Customs must have breathed a sigh of relief. Little did either service realize that in less than twenty years the matter would be raised once again, only this time it would result in the Customs absorbing the Excise.

During the years between 1850 and 1860, there had been considerable improvements in the conditions of service in the Excise. One of the most welcome of these was the establishment of a Mutual Guarantee Fund in 1852. This fund dispensed with the age-old system of officer's bonds and securities and opened the door to a more democratic entry into the department. Previously all officers had to provide two sureties prepared to give bond for sums ranging up to £3,000; now all that was required was an insurance payment annually to the Fund. Some time later the Customs also introduced their own fund.

Four years later the Excise Board at long last agreed to provide an allowance for the upkeep of a horse, officers receiving £20 and supervisors £30. Such an allowance had been strongly advocated by Thomas Paine, back in the eighteenth century! It seems strange that the Board should now relent, at a time when much of the country could be reached by railways, but even as late as 1897 there were complaints about the insufficiency of the allowance, and it survived into the twentieth century.

One further reform which had been proposed by Paine was finally achieved in 1857. This was the periodical transference of officers. This improvement was largely due to a long and dedicated campaign by a group of officers known as the Edinburgh Committee. They had continually petitioned the Treasury and Parliament, and had gained the support of almost the whole service. Their feelings on the success of the campaign were summed up by their secretary; 'The base and villainous system of "General Removes" is now an atrocity of the past.'

Strangely, during the same period of the campaign for the reform of the removal system other members of the staff were actively engaged on the repeal of another restriction on the officers' freedom. An order had been issued in 1852:

To obviate the great inconvenience and embarrassment, which had arisen from Excise officers marrying before they are appointed to a fixed station. The Board give notice, that all persons entering the Service after this date. will be called on to relinquish (their posts) if they marry before they attain the rank of Ride Officer.

Needless to say, this 'Anti-Marriage Edict', or 'Celibacy Bull', as the order was termed, was greatly opposed by the young assistant officers. They formed a committee to fight it, and called themselves The Inland Revenue Friars. Ultimately they achieved their aims, with its revocation in 1859. The Board allowed them to marry but warned them, 'The requirement of the Public Service cannot be sacrificed to the consideration of individuals, and that as often as a removal is necessary, it must be carried into effect without regard to the existence of a wife and family.'

The one subject that gained the full and immediate support of the whole service was the claim for some improvement in salaries. There had been no increase since 1820, and although prices had shown an overall downward trend since that date, the decade from 1850 was in contrast, showing a marked increase. The salary campaign reached a height in 1857-8, with over fifty petitions to the Treasury, and many presented to Parliament. As the Commissioners commented, 'Considerable discontent prevails among the Excise officers . . . which has occupied our most serious attention.'

Meetings were held all over the country, Members of Parliament were solicited to support the claim and even Excise traders petitioned Parliament in favour of some increase for the officers. All these combined efforts achieved a satisfactory result. A general increase of salaries was approved in March 1858, although the average rise was barely 10 per cent, compared with the general increases in salary outside the service, which were in the region of 30 per cent.

As if to pay for their rise, the next few years saw an increase in the work-load of the Excise officers. In 1864 certain assessed taxes, such as playing cards, patent medicines, and licences for pawnbrokers, were transferred to the department. Three years later the control of dog licences—which had previously been the responsibility of the local parish officials—was passed to it also. The most onerous task to come to the department was in 1866, when the Excise officers were instructed by the Board of Agriculture to collect agricultural statistics of livestock and crops in Great Britain.

From the outset the collection of these statistics was the cause of much discontent amongst the farmers. The returns were due during their busiest time of the year, and since they were not mandatory, very great difficulty was experienced by the officers in obtaining the figures. Frequently farmers refused to give the information, and it was felt by the Excise Board that this defiance was instigated by the large land-owners, who feared that the collection of such comprehensive figures was a prelude to a general land tax. The Excise officers found the work annoying and distasteful, and for many years they petitioned without success for some extra allowance.

Although as we have already seen the Customs had employed women as searchers as early as 1842, they were never placed on the establishment, and acted in a purely temporary capacity. It was the Excise which first employed women in established posts. In 1873 the Excise Head Office reported that 'some use has been made of copying machines'. They had employed five operators, or 'female typewriters', as they were called. Originally the female typewriters had been supplied by the company which had supplied the machines. However, later the Board recruited the 'lady writers' directly, although they hastened to point out that they employed them only on 'simple letters'. The Customs as usual were slower to make use of modern methods, employing 'two type-writers' in 1889.

From the repeal of the beer duty in 1830 the only duty on the drink was that charged indirectly on the materials used in its manufacture. This was mainly on malt, but there was also a small duty on hops. In 1847 sugar was permitted to be used in brewing, and an extra imposition, over and above the normal import duty, was charged on it. By 1860 the duty on hops was abolished in favour of an increased brewer's licence.

For many years there had been considerable pressure to abolish the duty on malt. Most of the objections to the duty had been sustained by various politicians. It was a tax on raw materials, imposing unnecessary Excise interference at every stage of production, and it greatly affected agriculture. These were some of the arguments put forward in favour of its repeal. Its advantages were seen to be that it was the simplest and easiest method of taxing beer, whether produced by the licensed brewers or by the home brewer. Furthermore, it tended to equalize the duty on spirits and beer, being a common ingredient of both. The biggest obstacle to its repeal, in favour of a general beer duty, was the large number of brewers and the vast amount of home brewing. In 1853 there were over 45,000 brewers, and over two million bushels of malt were used in private brewing. In the face of such figures the Excise just did not possess sufficient resources to impose control.

By 1879 the numbers of brewers had decreased by a half, and private brewing had greatly diminished. Now, with the main obstacle largely removed, the way was open for the desired change. In June 1880 the malt duty was repealed and replaced by a beer duty. Malt duty had been collected without interruption in England since 1697, and other than that on spirits, it was the longest surviving Excise duty.

The new beer duty was revolutionary in concept in that it was based on the strength or specific gravity of the beer, which would be tested by saccharometer. The old beer duty had been charged on the bulk quantity of 'strong' or 'small' beer. The new system of Excise control was based on the method used in distilleries, which had proved so successful for many years. The officers were required to visit or 'survey' the breweries very frequently, and to arrange their visits to coincide with all aspects of the brewing process, as well as making evening and weekend visits. The duty was charged on the amount of beer brewed at a standard gravity; however, as a check against fraud and unskilled brewers, a presumptive (or assumed) charge was calculated on the materials used in the brew. Duty was finally charged on the greater quantity.

Gladstone, who introduced the new duty, required it to correspond closely to the old malt duty. It was considered that 36 gallons of beer brewed at a gravity of 1055° was equivalent to two bushels of malt, and so the standard gravity was fixed at 1055° and the amount of duty based on this figure. Because of pressure from the powerful lobby of brewers, Gladstone was forced to compromise and raise the standard gravity to 1057°, which effectively reduced the amount of revenue from the new duty.

The professional brewer, or 'brewer for sale', was required to take out a licence annually, and duty was levied at 6s. 3d. on every bulk barrel of beer produced at the standard gravity. The brewer was, however, allowed to deduct 6 per cent for loss or waste during the brewing process before calculating his duty figure. The home brewer paid a smaller licence duty, and was charged an amount based on the materials used in his brew. There is no doubt that from an administrative point of view the new beer duty was a great advance over the old malt duty, although the brewing industry was far from accepting this.

Some of the large brewers, Mr Bass especially, objected to the idea of Excise officers gaining knowledge of their trade secrets. The official Civil Service newspaper *The Civilian* felt that 'the change is a downward step in the social and official life of the Excise officer'. Certainly many Excise officers were not happy with the change. In some areas—notably the Midlands— every victualler brewed his own beer and the fermenting vessels were housed in dank cellars 'which reeked of foul air and teem with bacteria'. In view of such a comprehensive change in their work, the chance was taken to reorganize the surveying staff. The old titles of 'foot-walk' and 'riding' stations disappeared, to be replaced by first and second class stations. There was a small increase in salary, and despite such a fundamental change, there was no great increase in staff. The new system of control of beer duty has survived the test of time, being virtually that which is in operation today.

In addition to the new beer duty, further new work was placed on the Excise in 1881. Excise officers were made responsible for the granting of probate on estates not exceeding £300. Probate was the oldest of all death duties, dating from 1694, when all estates over £20 were charged 5s. duty. Gladstone changed the existing rates to a straight 3 per cent on all estates, payable by stamps. He also introduced allowances for debts and funeral expenses, before the dutiable value was assessed. It was largely to assist the working classes that this task was given to the Excise: the presence of Excise officers in virtually every market town made it more convenient and cheaper than visiting the few probate registries, or becoming involved in expensive legal fees. During the first year over five thousand cases were dealt with, which doubled in the next year. The work over the years became an appreciable part of a normal Excise station, and most officers found the work very rewarding. The department dealt with probate until 1 April 1968.

Although the advent of free trade had seen a reduction in the old waterside work of the Customs, the following forty years saw a vast increase in the variety of duties they performed on behalf of other government departments. Already by 1854 the Merchant Shipping Act required Customs officers to act as 'Shipping Masters'. This involved them in a great number of duties relating to ships' crews and the interests of seamen generally. This new work brought even more colour to the Custom Houses, as the premises were often thronged with seamen of many nationalities. This frequently led to incidents—so much so that in many ports mercantile marine police were specially employed to ensure the maintenance of good order.

The same Act reiterated the Customs officer's responsibilities as 'Receivers of Wreck'. Since the early days of the seventeenth century the officers, along with sheriffs, J.P.s, mayors and constables, had been empowered to call for assistance for the preservation of ships in distress and for protection of any salvaged cargo. Over the years many officers were involved with wrecks all round the coasts, and the Customs records abound with reports of the problems of securing wrecked goods. Contrary to popular belief, wrecking was not confined solely to Cornwall; the coasts of Wales were notorious for this activity. Hundreds of country people (as they were called in the reports) flocked to any wreck and often spirited away the cargo before any officials could arrive to secure the goods. Frequently officers 'were forced to flee for their lives' faced with the hostility of large bands of 'determined spoilers', and were unable 'to act without the assistance of an arm'd force'.

There was an important change in 1846, when much of the old legislation was amended and officers as receivers of wreck were involved in conducting inquiries into all aspects of wreck work, including disputed claims. Perhaps the most famous wreck the department was involved with was the s.s. *Politician*, which was wrecked off the west coast of Scotland in August 1941, with a large cargo of export Scotch whisky. The subsequent disappearance of a large amount of the wrecked whisky was used by the novelist Sir Compton Mackenzie as a basis for his novel *Whisky Galore*. Work connected with wreck is still undertaken by officers of the department today.

Further legislation towards the end of the century gave the control of copyright on literary and artistic works to the Customs Department. Officers were supplied with a list of copyright works in order to prevent the import of pirated copies. Such copies were seized and passed, with the agreement of the authors, to the crews of lightships and lighthouses. Parallel with this control was the check on the importation of obscene prints, books and paintings; work which is still undertaken by the department on behalf of the Home Office.

In 1883 an Act was passed placing more stringent rules on the marking of imported goods. Examining officers were required to ensure that there were 'no unfair and untruthful marks on goods, which might suggest British origin'. In the first year over 5,000 cases were reported, and for many years this import control caused much extra work and brought many problems. In the same year the collectors were appointed 'Sea Fishery Officers', with responsibilities for British fishing vessels, and also for foreign vessels fishing within British limits.

For the first time in their history Customs officers were employed in inland towns, away from the ports. This occurred when bonding warehouse facilities and privileges were extended to certain inland towns. The first inland warehouses were approved in the large Northern manufacturing towns of Manchester, Halifax, Leeds, Bradford and Sheffield. In the early days these new warehouses were little used, but by the end of the century they were taking much of the trade of the older warehouses at the ports. The control of these warehouses was to change hands in the subsequent years. First they were passed to the Inland Revenue for Excise control, only to be returned to the Customs a few years later, when there was a general amalgamation of the whole warehousing system.

The large reorganization in the Customs in 1860 had not stopped further Treasury inquiries into virtually every branch of the department. The Accounts Branch was investigated, and as a result the historic office of Receiver-General disappeared, and was included in 1870 with the duties of the Accountant General. The new post became the Accountant and Comptroller General. Also for some time there had been disquiet concerning the production of trade statistics. The inevitable committee was formed to examine the procedures, and as a result of their report a special Statistical Office was set up to manage the executive work of the collection of statistics. Matters of general policy, such as the nature, extent and form of the statistics, were retained by the Board of Trade. Also in 1882 the newly formed Statistical Office took over the production of the Bills of Entry from the Customs Fund. These Bills were published daily until the outbreak of the Second World War.

Although these reforms were concerned in the main with the work of the headquarters, the out-ports were also involved in change. The great improvement in both road and rail communications, and the massive development of new and larger docks, had diverted much of the local trade away from the ancient and small ports. Already many of the collectors at these ports had been replaced by a lower grade of official named Superintendent of Customs and Mercantile Marine. A further reorganiz-ation in 1882 reduced ports such as Rye, Deal, Lyme Regis, Chepstow, Carlisle and Lancaster to the status of 'creeks' of neighbouring larger ports, and they were placed under the supervision of a minor official. The decline of these historic ports, with their long and rich history of Customs connections, was a sad loss.

During these times of change and reform the Treasury was being continually inundated with petitions from the lower ranks of the Customs, on their miserable rates of pay and the unsatisfactory working conditions.

The hours were long and the work onerous; the officers attended twenty-four hours a day, in all kinds of weather. The Customs Board were very concerned about the amount of sick leave and the high incidence of early retirement due to ill-health. It was largely for these reasons, rather than in a spirit of paternalism, that the Board appointed a medical officer. The causes of sick leave and early retirement were monitored very closely, and each year a very full report by the medical officer on the general health of the service was published in the Board's annual report.

The Board did very little to remedy the many grievances of the lower grades, and it was left to Mr Goschen, the Chancellor of the Exchequer— bowing to pressure in Parliament—to agree to hold an inquiry into the Customs outdoor service. The outcome of the inquiry was embodied in a Treasury minute dated March 1891, which became known as the Goschen Minute. It recommended the separation of the Landing and Waterguard services, after only thirty years of amalgamation. The duties of the Landing and Waterguard were carefully delineated. From this date until the reorganization in the 1970s, the Waterguard remained a separate branch within the department.

The Goschen Minute was considered by the Board to be the 'unique authority'; however, the staff were not happy with its proposals. It had failed to resolve most of the problems, such as promotion, overtime, pay and the wearing of uniform, which concerned both Landing and Waterguard staffs alike. In the ensuing years further changes were needed. In 1896 the basic grade of entry to the Customs, the outdoor officer, was replaced by a new grade called Assistant of Customs, with a lower salary scale than the equivalent Excise assistant. Boatmen—now known as preventive men—and the lower grades of tobacco-weighers and labourers were formed into one grade called watchers.

In an attempt to ameliorate both the promotion and the salary problems, the Board introduced in 1903 a novel system of allowances for the Waterguard service; this system was based on the granting of stars. Eligibility for the stars depended on length of service, good reports and conduct; the maximum possible number was three, and each star carried an extra salary increment. They could be granted for good conduct, but they could also be removed for disciplinary reasons. The stars were worn on the uniform sleeves. The system was not popular with the officers, and it did not survive for very long.

Other than salary, the most contentious issue was without doubt the wearing of uniform. As far back as 1867, the Board had recognized that 'uniform would be an advantage, both to the Service and the Public, if all officers belonging to the Outdoor Service wore uniform and caps when on duty'. The uniform was extended to officers working in warehouses. Although the Board ordered that the officers should wear uniform, the majority had to purchase the uniform themselves; only the cap badges were supplied officially. Many officers expressed the view that 'the uniforms made them socially inferior', and it was pointed out that Excise officers were not uniformed, even when they worked in warehouses. The landing officer's uniform was retained until after the amalgamation of the Customs and Excise. However, in 1906 the department provided the first free issue of uniform.

Despite the new beer duty, the main Excise revenue was obtained from spirits. The whisky industry had boomed in the decade 1870-80, new distilleries were built at an alarming pace, and many of the famous brands date from this time. By 1893 there were 132 distilleries in Scotland, producing over 32 million proof gallons, at a total duty of £15½ millions.

The battle against the illicit distillers had been won; there were only six seizures of stills in that year. The Excise control in the distilleries was very strict; all vessels were locked with revenue locks, all the pipes were in open view and painted in various colours to denote their content. Every process and operation was controlled and checked by the officer; in fact, he was required to make a complete survey of the premises three times a day. The warehouses attached to the distilleries were kept under similar strict supervision, and were also placed under revenue locks.

With such close supervision each distillery had at least one permanent officer, and some of the larger ones had more officers. During the busy season many Excise assistants were drafted in to help the permanent officers. Because of the remote location of many of the distilleries, the distillers were required to provide the officers 'with a suitable house or lodgings at a rent not exceeding £10 per annum' (1832 Act). As the officers were prohibited from being tenants of the distillers, the department paid the rent. This accommodation became known as a provided house, and in 1881 there were ninety-seven such houses in Scotland.

The rent allowance was increased to £15, to provide 'more superior accommodation', and in 1893 the Board decided to approve plans and specifications for a 'standard Excise house'; hitherto approval of houses had been undertaken locally. The design of the Excise House was impressive, even by today's standards; it was built of stone, had four bedrooms and a maid's room. It was certainly in keeping with the high social standing enjoyed by the distillery officer in the community.

The outbreak of the Boer War in 1899 brought forth a flood of import and export prohibitions, which caused a considerable increase of work. Many of the officers of both services were allowed to volunteer for the armed forces; it was agreed by the Board that their posts would be held open for their return—a far different view than that taken at the time of the First World War.

Some extraordinary events occurred before the Budget of 1900; merchants and traders, in an attempt to pre-empt the expected increase in duty due to the war, applied for release of goods from the bonded warehouses at the pre-Budget prices. This 'forestalling', as it is called, started as a trickle, quickly gained momentum, and within days became an avalanche. It reached a peak during 3–5 March; traders were queueing before the opening hours of the London Custom House. The Long Room, the staircase and the entrance hall was packed with merchants waiting to pay their duty; soon the crowds became so numerous that they were blocking the street, and the police were called in to prevent rioting and maintain order. Similar scenes were enacted at other Custom Houses around the country. In two days over £2 millions of duty was paid, mainly on tobacco goods and tea.

Forestalling was a totally unique experience for the department, although it was never to be repeated on such a scale. Today removals from warehouses during a pre-Budget period may be restricted. The merchants in 1900 were correct in their assumptions; all the old revenue duties, such as those on tobacco, tea, wines, sugar, coffee and dried fruit, were increased. The duty on sugar, which had been abolished in 1874, was reintroduced, accompanied by an equivalent duty on saccharin. Coal, which had also been duty-free since 1830, was now liable to an export duty. At the then large coal ports of Newport, Cardiff and Barry the new duty caused considerable extra work. In fact, all the extra impositions resulted in a total increase of staff by over four hundred.

During 1903 a Royal Commission had been set up to examine the question of alien immigration. Much of the evidence given to the Commission was from members of the Customs Department, who for years had dealt with both alien crews and passengers. During the latter decades of the previous century the officers had handled a very large number of immigrants arriving from Russia and Eastern Europe, the majority en route to the United States. In 1892 the officers were instructed to 'examine them, to ensure that they did not land in a filthy or otherwise unwholesome condition'.

The Commission's report led to the Alien Act of 1905, which established the basis of immigration controls. Many Customs officers were transferred to thirteen large ports and packet stations to act as immigration officers. They were placed under the control of the Home Office. At all other ports the local Customs staff were given depositions to deal with immigration work, in addition to their normal duties.

In spite of the seemingly endless inquiries and the frequent reorganizations suffered by both departments the staff were unanimous in the feeling that both Boards had paid scant regard to their complaints of inadequate salaries and poor promotion prospects. There was a very widespread dissatisfaction in both services, and quite independently both outdoor services actively engaged the support of Members of Parliament for a new Committee of Enquiry to examine their grievances.

Between the years 1906 to 1908 large rallies were organized and numerous petitions were presented to the Treasury. Sympathetic members in the House of Commons put questions about the morale of the revenue officers. All the campaigns received the same reply from the Treasury: 'There is no necessity at the present time, for any further reviews of either

Department.' With hindsight, it is plain that the amalgamation of the Customs and Excise that the Treasury was already planning was seen as an expedient which might cure the ills of both services. However, since the amalgamation worsened the promotion chances of most of the existing staff, it is not surprising how difficult the practical aspects of combining the two services proved to be. It posed more problems than it solved.

CHAPTER EIGHT

A Marriage
has been Arranged

The year 1909 proved to be the most memorable and eventful in the long history of the Customs and Excise; perhaps more important and decisive than the time of the formation of the two departments, back in the seventeenth century. It is doubtful whether anybody serving in either service realized at the time just how far-reaching and fateful the events of the year would prove to be. It was a watershed between the two separate Victorian services—which had evolved out of the many reforms of the late decades of the nineteenth century—and the establishment of a single modern twentieth-century department, which was to remain essentially unchanged until very recent times.

The first event of note, which vastly changed the working life of Excise officers, was the introduction of a non-contributory pension scheme under the Old Age Pensions Act 1908. The scheme was effective from 1 January 1909, and under the Act, Excise officers were designated pension officers. In fact, it had been decided that 'they were the class of men best fitted for this kind of work'.

The duties of the pension officer included the investigation of all claims and reporting the facts of each case to the duly appointed local pension committee, who were responsible for deciding the validity of the claim and the amount of pension payable. The officer would issue the pensioner with a pension order book, and payment was made via a post-office. He had periodically to visit the pensioner at home for the purpose of review. The vast increase of work for the Excise staff could only be undertaken by the transfer of certain establishment licences, such as game, gun, dog, carriage and male servants, to the local authorities for collection. This enabled sufficient Excise officers to be released to cope with the extra burden.

The Act provided for a grant of a pension to every claimant who was seventy years or over, was a British subject and had been resident in the country for the past twenty years. One of the exemption clauses concerned the claimant's annual income: it was not to exceed £31 10s. per year, and it was this condition which caused many of the problems encountered by the investigating officers. Some of the other exemptions were easier to establish; persons on poor relief were not eligible, nor were those 'who had habitually failed to work', or persons convicted and imprisoned within the previous ten years. The maximum pension was five shillings per week—not a princely sum, even in those days.

Preparation work started on the scheme in the first week of October 1908, and some of the administrative problems of establishing the machinery for such a large volume of work soon became very apparent. The deployment of sufficient officers to the various areas was extremely difficult to estimate, largely because of the lack of any reliable figures of the probable number of claimants in any given area. Some areas, like the Scilly Isles, where there were fifty claimants out of a population of two thousand, came under Excise control for the first time. Many of the small islands off Scotland and Ireland created special problems, and vessels from the Fishery Boards helped to convey officers to these remote places. A further complication was the number of monoglot Welsh, Gaelic and Erse claimants; although there were sufficient Welsh-speaking officers in post, in Scotland and Ireland ministers, priests and schoolmasters were used by the officers as interpreters.

One of the practical problems in the investigation of the claims was the establishment of the claimant's correct age. In the majority of claims there was no evidence of age, and many claimants had only a vague recollection of their exact date of birth. This so hampered the verification in the registers of birth that extra staff had to be recruited at Somerset House to cope with all the inquiries. In Scotland Excise assistants were drafted into Register House to do the work, but in Ireland, where the greatest problems were encountered because so few registers had survived, local priests made inquiries in their parishes and their certificates were accepted as bona-fide evidence.

Prior to the commencement of the scheme in January over three-quarters of a million claims were dealt with in three months, and as the Inland Revenue Board admitted, 'There is no doubt that the whole staff worked under the greatest of pressure.' By the first of January over 535,000 pensioners were cleared and in a position to draw their pensions. Nearly 2,600 supervisors, officers and clerks were involved in pension work, and this accounted for almost three-quarters of the total staff of the Excise department, which gives some idea of the size of the operation. When one considers that this mammoth task was undertaken without the means of modern technology, such as computers, great credit must be given to the Excise service for the admirable way they organized their control. There was much criticism in the House of Commons that the qualifying age for the pension was too high; many considered that it should have been sixty-five. There seems no doubt that if the earlier age had been chosen the massive number of extra claims to be processed would have made the scheme administratively impossible. As it was, by March 1909 there were 647,000 pensioners, the majority on the maximum pension, although this figure represented only about $1\frac{1}{2}$ per cent of the total population.

The second event which made the year so memorable also owes its origin to the Finance Bill of 1908. Mr Asquith, the Prime Minister, in giving the financial statement to the House of Commons (a unique situation in itself, which was caused by the very recent appointment of a new Chancellor, Mr Lloyd George) made a short reference to:

> Another and more far-reaching change which I propose to take power to make in the Finance Bill, is to transfer the Excise Department from the Inland Revenue to the Customs. From the point of view of administrative economy and efficiency I think—and my opinion is shared by almost all these distinguished Government officials, who have the closest experience of the inner working of both offices—a substantial gain will result to the public service from the change.

The announcement of the proposed amalgamation was received with amazement by the staff of both departments. It was obviously a very well-kept secret, known only to a few of the highest officials in the Treasury, and obviously to the Boards of the two departments. None of the outdoor officials in either service were consulted. Never before had such a radical change in the Civil Service taken place so suddenly and with so little consultation or previous inquiry. In fact, it was only twenty years since a Royal Commission had looked at amalgamation and had recommended that the proposal should be rejected. Even then the battle between the two departments had been so bitter, and left its marks on both services, that the majority of people had assumed the matter dead and forgotten.

Now one can see that the proposal to amalgamate was wise. However, at the time both services considered that the proposed merger was both undesirable and unnecessary. The Excise officers were the more vehement in their protests; they felt they had more to lose in the change than the Customs. Their main concern was on the question of promotion. In the Excise they had long enjoyed an avenue of promotion to the highest outdoor post, that of collector, whereas in the Customs the post of collector invariably went to staff recruited from the indoor clerks grade. The Excise further felt that they would lose their individuality, and other privileges which they enjoyed, such as the right to move anywhere in the country at their own request. There was also a certain fear of the stricter discipline of the more autocratic Customs Board, compared with the more democratic Excise service, with its right of appeal to the Board.

Quite apart from the misgivings of each set of officers, there was no doubt that such a merger—involving so many different grades and salary structures—would be a most complex operation, and one which would require very careful negotiations. It was obvious from the first discussions that any agreement would produce certain individual hardships and many contentious issues. Prior to the amalgamation the Customs outdoor branch comprised just over two thousand persons, headed by the collectors, of whom there were various classes with a wide range of salaries. Below them the grading structure consisted of inspectors, three classes of surveyors, two classes of examining officers with assistants as the basic grade of entry into the branch. There were also over four hundred clerks covering six different classes, all of whom were recruited by a separate examination. The Excise, although only a department within the Inland Revenue, had a far larger outdoor staff. It followed a simpler pattern than the Customs, with two classes each of collectors, inspectors, supervisors and officers. There were only three classes of clerks, but all the staff were recruited from one common examination, that of Assistant of Excise. This examination was considered by many to be a much more difficult test than that of the Customs, and as such attracted a better class of entrant, a factor which even the Customs Board admitted in 1905.

The Order in Council promulgating the amalgamation was dated 15 February, to take effect from the first day of April 1909; it became known as The Excise Transfer order. The new Board of Customs and Excise was created on the same day. The existing Customs Commissioners were joined by the Secretary of the old Excise Board, and by the Secretary of the Inland Revenue Board. Mr L. Guillemard was appointed the first Chairman of the Customs and Excise. He had previously been Deputy Chairman of the Inland Revenue from 1902 to 1908, and was ideally qualified to head the new combined department.

The move of the headquarters staff was fairly swift; they left Somerset House to join their Customs colleagues at the Custom House, although there were now so many of them that extra accommodation had to be found in Ocean House, a near-by building. There was no equally swift movement of the outdoor staff; it was to be nearly two and half years before a physical amalgamation took place. In the meantime both services acted independently of each other, as if the transfer had not taken place. There was a little interchange of outdoor staff, but only as a temporary expedient, with the officers returning to their respective sides, after the temporary pressure of work had ceased. It was a time of great uncertainty for all personnel, who waited patiently to see what alterations the new Board would propose.

The first positive step towards amalgamation was not taken until February 1910, with the creation of a new post—Chief Inspector of the Customs and Excise. The old equivalent Customs post of Chief Surveyor-General was abolished, its incumbent being appointed Collector, London Port. Sir Arthur Tedder, previously Chief Inspector of the Excise, was appointed to the new post. This appointment, which was the top post in the outdoor service, no doubt cheered the Excise staff, who now felt that the man in control fully understood the problems of their service. He held the post for barely two years before being appointed Commissioner. It was the first time since the days of Thomas Everard that any person entering the service from the lowest grade had been appointed to either Board. Sir Arthur was father of the late Lord Tedder, Marshal of the Royal Air Force.

A committee had been formed in March 1909 under the chairmanship of Mr C. Hobhouse, Financial Secretary to the Treasury, to consider the conditions under which the amalgamation could be carried out. However, because of the sudden General Election in the following January, and of its pressing financial problems, the Committee did not meet to hear evidence until a year later. Its deliberations were long and protracted, and frequently Mr Hobhouse had to defend in the House of Commons the long delay of the committee's report. Unfortunately, the tardiness of the committee only aggravated the uncertainties of the staff as to their future in the new department. Finally, in August 1911, almost two and half years after its inception, the committee reported its findings.

It recommended the establishment of a new post to be called Officer of Customs and Excise, which would perform all the executive duties of the department. This new grade would have a very long salary scale, and entry to this basic grade would be by one common entrance examination for both indoor and outdoor staff. A higher single grade of surveyor was proposed to supervise the officers. Promotion to this would be by a competitive examination based on the officer's knowledge of the laws and work of the department. The overall supervision of all outdoor staff would devolve on a controlling grade of inspectors, and entry to the higher grades would be by selection from the most able surveyors.

The long-awaited report did little to allay the misgivings and dissatisfactions of the two services. Although it was felt that the basis of the report was sound, the Excise were especially unhappy on the questions of promotion prospects and seniority. The Customs, on the other hand, felt that they had an especial grievance in the wearing of uniform. The report had recommended the retention of uniform for Customs officers on landing duties on the quays. The matter was to remain a bone of contention for the next few years, until uniform for both officers and surveyors was abolished in 1914. The question of overtime had been completely ignored by the committee, leaving the problem of payment for extra attendance by both Customs and Excise officers to another day and another committee.

The first formal amalgamation of staff took place in November 1911, when assistants, examining officers, Excise officers and some clerks were formed into the new grade. This was followed in January 1912 with the formation of the new grade of surveyor, out of the existing Customs surveyors, Excise supervisors, some of the junior Customs collectors and principal clerks. During the implementation of the new grades considerable pressure was applied by the various staff federations. Members of Parliament were lobbied on specific grievances, and numerous questions were asked in the House concerning various anomalies in the settlement. The continual pressure brought results; the Chancellor of the Exchequer agreed to meet deputations of the staff to hear their various grievances. In May 1912 he made some concessions: a slight increase in salaries and some extra surveyor posts to improve the promotion prospects. These few minor changes, however, did not settle all the outstanding points. Even in 1914 the Excise officers were still pursuing their case, without much success. Many of the other problems were not cleared up until after the War.

The success of the amalgamation settlement must be viewed in the long term rather than the short term, and on that score it was certainly well conceived. The basic structure devised by the Hobhouse Committee worked well, and lasted within the department for over sixty years. It was dismantled only in the reorganization which took place in the early 1970s. It is sad to recall that the basic rank of Officer of Customs and Excise which emerged from the amalgamation is now what is termed an obsolescent grade.

Besides reorganization of the staff, the system of collection throughout the country was changed as a result of the amalgamation. Prior to 1909 there were fifty-seven Customs collections in England, Wales and Scotland based on the various ports. The Excise had sixty collections, divided into two classes, some centred on ports but the majority on large inland towns. By 1910 the total number of Customs and Excise collections had been reduced to ninety-two and divided into two classes. This was the initial step in a general reorganization of the collections which continued into the two following decades, whereby they were made far larger units of administration. By 1930 the number of collections had been reduced to thirty-nine.

Just as the Budget of 1908 had brought some revolutionary changes, so did the first Budget to be presented by Lloyd George in April 1909. The long debates and eventual rejection of the Finance Bill by the House of Lords caused a grave constitutional crisis, which resulted in the dissolution of Parliament. This left the department in an invidious and apparently untenable position. It was then collecting the increased duties imposed by the Budget under resolutions passed by the House of Commons, without having any legal basis for the extra duty, now that the Finance Act had been rejected by the House of Lords and had not therefore received the Royal Assent.

The Board found themselves in a position which was without precedent, and after considerable discussion it was decided that the best procedure would be to accept the extra duty as a voluntary payment. These sums would be treated as deposits, which would be refundable in the unlikely event of fresh legislation not being passed to make the extra duty lawful. Meetings were arranged with the various trade associations, and their co-operation in the scheme was sought; thus a form of gentlemen's agreement was reached. Indeed, the exercise was such a success that when the Bill was finally passed a year later only about £500,000 remained outstanding, and this sum was collected by June. It was a good start for the new department. Even the Treasury were sufficiently moved to express their appreciation of the services rendered by the Board and their officers.

Besides increases in the duties on spirits, tobacco and tea, the ill-fated

A cartoon on Pitt's consolidation of duties (pp. 74–5)   *HMSO*

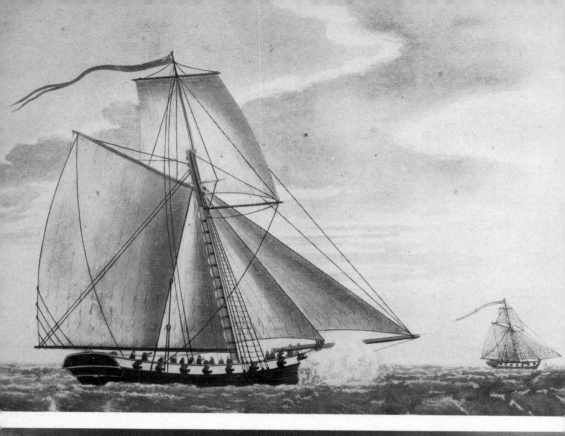

Above left: the nineteenth-century
revenue cutter *Greyhound*   HMSO

Left: the modern Customs cruiser
Challenge   HMSO

Above: illicit distillation in Scotland in
the late nineteenth century   HMSO

Right: copy of a portrait of a nineteenth-
century Distillery officer. *J. Campbell*

AT THE COURT AT BUCKINGHAM PALACE,

The 15th day of February, 1909.

PRESENT:

THE KING'S MOST EXCELLENT MAJESTY IN COUNCIL.

WHEREAS by section four of the Finance Act, 1908, it is enacted that His Majesty may by Order in Council transfer from the Commissioners of Inland Revenue to the Commissioners of Customs the management of any Excise duties which are under the management of the Commissioners of Inland Revenue at the time the Order is made, and any powers and duties of the Commissioners of Inland Revenue which it appears necessary or expedient to transfer in consequence of or in connexion with the transfer of the management of Excise duties, and that all powers and duties so transferred shall become powers and duties of the Commissioners of Customs, and that if an Order is made under the section the Commissioners of Customs shall, as from the date fixed by the Order, be styled the Commissioners of Customs and Excise:

And whereas it is further enacted by the said section that such provisions may be made by the Order in Council as it appears necessary or expedient to make in order to give full effect to any transfer, or in consequence of any change of name effected under the section, and that for the purpose of making the provisions as to the action and procedure of the Commissioners of Customs and Excise under the Acts relating to Customs and Excise respectively uniform, the Order may provide that as to the action or procedure of the Commissioners any provisions of the Acts relating to Excise shall have effect to the exclusion of similar provisions of the Acts relating to Customs, or that any provisions of the Acts relating to Customs shall have effect to the exclusion of similar provisions of the Acts relating to Excise:

And whereas it is further enacted that the Stamp duties on medicines and playing cards shall, for the purposes of the section and for all other purposes, be deemed to be Excise duties:

Now, therefore, His Majesty, in exercise of the powers vested in Him by the

P. C. 19.   I. & M.—26/1/09.

The Order in Council for the amalgamation of the Customs and Excise departments (p. 132)   *HMSO*

Budget produced a brand-new duty, a charge of 3*d.* per gallon on motor spirit. This was defined in the Act as 'that being used for providing reasonably efficient motive power for a motor car'! (Not a particularly exact legal definition.) Not only was motor spirit taxed but the dealers and manufacturers in petrol were required to take out a licence. There were many exceptions to the new duty on petrol: a 50 per cent rebate was allowed for all motor spirit used in taxicabs, trade vehicles, doctor's and vet's cars, and fire-engines. The number of exemptions increased in subsequent years, making the administration of the duty unduly complicated. In the first year it raised only £320,000 but since there were at that time only 40,000 private cars in use, it was a potentially a rich source of future revenue. The duty was, of course, the forerunner of all hydrocarbon oils duties, which have now become one of the largest producers of revenue in the country.

The last—but certainly not least—important event in 1909 (although at the time few people in the service realized the full implications) was the first successful crossing of the English Channel by aeroplane. As the Collector Dover reported on 25 July:

> I have to report that M. Blériot with his monoplane, successfully crossed the Channel from Calais this morning, and landed in a meadow on the East side of Dover Castle, about two miles from our watch house shortly after 5 a.m., having occupied 33 minutes in crossing . . . I visited the spot where he landed at 6.30 a.m. and got into conversation with an individual largely interested in the Wright aeroplane, who gave it his opinion that although airships [*sic*] will never come into commercial use, there are great possibilities in store for them, and I think that a time may come when this Department will have to treat their arrival seriously, and take steps to ensure that no opportunity be given for Revenue interest to suffer through indiscriminate landings of airships in this country.

Although the Collector had given strict instructions to his staff that any attempt to impose Customs regulations on anyone engaged in 'aerial navigation would only tend to bring the Department into ridicule without doing any practical good', Mr Camburn, the preventive man on hand, had interviewed M. Blériot and issued him with a quarantine certificate, thereby treating the aeroplane as a yacht and the pilot as master and owner. Mr Camburn by using his ingenuity had thus set a precedent for treating all aircraft as vessels. The Board decided that the time had not yet arrived for any action; little did they realize that within the next ten years they would be forced to consider the problems of control for this new form of travel.

The years leading up to the First World War were traumatic times for the staff of the new department. They were continually faced with new work; each year and each succeeding Budget brought increasing burdens on an already hard-pressed and overburdened staff. The compulsory retirement of officers over the age of sixty-one had caused much bitterness, and the cessation of promotion due to the merger of the two staffs had aggravated the discontent. This unrest was set against a background of anxiety and uncertainty arising out of the unresolved problems caused by the amalgamation. The morale of the officers was at a nadir; and it was only the advent of war, with its consequential demands on patriotism and loyalty, which restored their spirit of unity, so that they could face the new and extra responsibilities being forced on the service.

In April 1910 a new, revised procedure for Excise licences for spirit and beer dealers and retailers was introduced. The intention was to produce a uniform system throughout the country, and since the rates had not increased for over forty years, an increased source of revenue. The new system appeared unduly complicated and cumbersome; varying rates of duty were imposed according to the annual value of the licensed premises, with allowances made according to the population of the area. To complicate matters even further, reduced rates were brought in for hotels and restaurants, these licences being based on the proportion of the licensed rooms to the total area of the building! As can be imagined, this led to some most involved calculations and many contentious cases. Generally the new procedure caused an appreciable amount of extra work for the Excise, which was certainly not commensurate with the increased revenue raised by the new rates. Also, for the first time private clubs were charged with licence duty, which was based on their annual purchases of liquors. In areas where these clubs abounded, such as South Wales and the North of England, this work was most onerous, especially since it was in these same areas that old-age pension and probate work were the heaviest.

Further new work was placed on the Excise in 1912, when the National Insurance Act became law. Officers were required to investigate and report on the various claims and rates of contribution. The general discontent of the service was so great that many officers resigned and obtained posts with the new Insurance Commission. The number of officers who applied for transfer was so great that the Board placed an embargo on the moves, and refused to allow the majority of applicants to transfer. In the event only a handful of junior clerks were released. There was now no doubt that the Board was aware of the feelings of the mass of Excise personnel.

The influx of new work into the Excise was in addition to that on the old-age pensions, which had been further complicated in the previous year, while there were now nearly a million pensioners in the country. Moreover, the normal Excise work continued—that is to say, relating to breweries, distilleries, warehouses, tobacco, licences, probate, agricultural statistics and some income-tax work on behalf of the Inland Revenue. It is not surprising to find that within the Excise service much concern was expressed on the question of overwork. The staff journal was full of letters from officers, who complained of the 'serious amount of double duty being performed', and many instances were quoted of 'great distress and illness caused through overwork'.

Perhaps it is more surprising to find that this concern received the attention of Members of Parliament. In the years between 1911 and 1913 there were many questions put to the Chancellor of the Exchequer on the incidence of 'considerable overwork in the Excise Service'. One of the most persistent Members was Philip Snowden, one of the first Labour M.P.s, who had been an Excise assistant in the last century, but had been forced to resign due to ill-health. The official line was stoutly maintained in the House that there was no overwork in the Excise, although after continual pressure by Snowden Lloyd George finally admitted that in the previous two years there had been forty-four deaths of Excise officials while still in post. He added, however, 'only three of these might be attributed to pressure of work'!

The controversy reached a climax in 1913, when the sad case of the suicide of a young officer in Scotland caused a considerable outcry. This officer had recently transferred from the Customs to an Excise station, which had not had a permanent officer for over eight months. It was strongly rumoured that he had left a suicide note blaming arrears and pressure of work for his action. The sad incident was brought up in Parliament by Snowden, who, not satisfied with the answers to a series of questions he had asked, badgered the Government continually for a statement of the situation in the Excise. Finally Lloyd George made the following statement: 'There is no doubt that there has been a good deal of overwork in the Excise, especially in connection with old age pensions, but that it is now generally passing away. A searching Department inquiry into the suicide of an officer has been conducted and there was no evidence found to substantiate the claim that overwork was the cause of this unfortunate death.' The campaign had achieved a slight increase in staff, which eased the pressure of work, but not for long.

During all these years of change one branch of the service had been particularly excluded from the general upheaval within the rest of the department. As their work was solely Customs, the Waterguard had not been greatly involved in the amalgamation, although due to the agreement they had lost some of their higher posts to the new controlling grade. What did concern them, and had been a bone of contention for a number of years, was the question of overtime. A departmental committee was duly set up in 1912 to examine not only overtime but the staffing generally within the branch, and their report recommended an increased complement of supervisory posts, with increased powers over the staff. The changes made the Waterguard almost autonomous in its control of work and staff, a situation which was to prevail until the 1970s. It was an opportune time to reorganize the Waterguard service, because with the advent of the war they were given far greater work and responsibilities.

It was during 1913 that the department became rather reluctantly involved with the women's suffrage movement. In December of that year the Collector at Plymouth received a request from the police to assist them in arresting Mrs Pankhurst on her arrival from New York on the s.s. *Majestic*. The Collector arranged for Waterguard officers in plain clothes to meet the vessel in Plymouth Roads and clear Mrs Pankhurst before the arrival of the vessel in Plymouth. Much to the dismay of her large band of followers and the press, Mrs Pankhurst was landed at Devonport dockyard, and taken direct to Exeter Gaol. Because of 'the sundry wild threats made by her followers of injury to government buildings if she was arrested', guards were placed at the Custom House. No damage was sustained, but several arrests were made.

A similar occurrence happened later in the same month. Mrs Pankhurst was released from prison after a hunger strike, but she broke her parole to attend a meeting in Paris. Once again on her arrival at Victoria Station the police requested assistance to re-arrest her. She was cleared by the Waterguard en route from Dover, and was spirited away once again out of sight of her ardent supporters.

One of the last surviving links with the seventeenth century disappeared in 1914. Since the very early days of both services bonds had been required from all staff to ensure good conduct, and as security for the duties they collected. Until 1852 these bonds were required to be secured by two guarantors, but in that year the Mutual Guarantee Fund was established, which secured the bond in the form of an insurance policy. It had been over forty years since any bond had been placed in suit, and as they were now an anachronism and no part of a modern service their departure was universally welcomed.

At 11.17 p.m. on 4 August 1914 the Board received the following telegram:

> The Under Secretary of State for Foreign Affairs presents his compliments to the Secretary of the Customs and is directed by the Secretary of State to inform you that Germany has declared war against this country.

By 2 a.m. the following morning a specially printed note was received with the message: 'A state of war exists between Great Britain and Germany.' For more than three years before the outbreak of war the Board had been represented on the committee which had been set up to determine what action would be necessary at the ports in such circumstances. Sealed copies were deposited with collectors, which were only to be opened on receipt of a certain codeword. By the end of July, when war seemed imminent, the codeword was sent out, and the collectors were aware of the action required, and were able to plan accordingly.

Within an hour of the Board receiving the first telegram, all collectors had received the further codeword for action. The first priority was the seizure of every German merchant vessel in the ports of the United Kingdom. The ships were not only to be seized but also prevented from sailing by 'the removal of some vital part of the machinery'. To this end engineer surveyors of the Board of Trade were called in to give assistance. The Chairman of the Board was able to report: 'By seven o'clock every German vessel in the United Kingdom was safely tied up.'

All these vessels were detained for the duration of the war, and their cargo was treated as enemy cargo. It was a different matter for vessels seized at sea, they were condemned as prizes of war, a memory of the days of Nelson. The only vessel that was in fact seized at sea by the Customs was a large German merchant ship called the *Belgia*. This vessel was anchored in the Bristol Channel awaiting a berth in Newport Docks. The Collector at Newport felt that this ship would escape if he did not take some steps to arrest it. He requisitioned the dock company's tug, and along with several officers boarded the *Belgia* about seven miles from the port. The vessel was brought into Newport docks, the wireless was dismantled and guards placed on board. The Collector's prompt if somewhat unusual action caused some embarrassment at first, although he was later praised for his efforts. He subsequently applied to the Prize Court of the Admiralty for a share of the prize money, the vessel having been valued at £750,000. However, he was informed that a reward was not applicable in the case. It is interesting to note that he had been on duty continuously for thirty-seven hours, which resulted in a breakdown of his health, and his being away on sick leave for over two months.

Within the next two months the department was placed on a war footing. A series of stringent controls were imposed on imports, exports, coastwise traffic, stores and coal and oil fuel for bunkers. The new controls placed considerable extra work on all grades of staff in the Customs. Prior to their introduction exports, other than dutiable goods and arms and ammunition, had required only a very cursory check. The new controls required all goods to be pre-entered before shipment, and a full examination was needed at the ship-side to prevent any illegal shipments to firms or persons on the black list, which was a record of neutral firms considered enemies of the State.

The import control was altered from a fairly informal system—most goods were free of import duty—to a rigorous and elaborate system of certificates of non-enemy origin and interest. The control of all stores and bunkers was entirely new work. Each shipment required prior Customs permission, and in this matter the department worked in very close consultation with the Admiralty and the Board of Trade. This supervision proved to be a powerful weapon in controlling the movements of neutral ships and compelling them to adapt their trade to serve the interests of the Allies.

During the next few months even further duties were imposed on the Customs. The Foreign Office required that all ship's papers and cargo manifests should be scrutinized, in order to extract information on the movements of cargo world-wide; this work proved to be the most onerous of the department's war duties. There was also a much closer control imposed on the arrival and departure of alien passengers and crews, for obvious security reasons. Over forty officers were seconded to approved ports, the only places where aliens were allowed to land. The Waterguard officers were used by the Admiralty to give confidential verbal messages to the masters of outgoing vessels as to the routes they should follow. The masters of incoming vessels were de-briefed for information, which was then passed to the Intelligence Branch.

Although nearly all of this new war work had fallen on the Customs, the Excise did not escape. By September 1914 the control of separation allowances was entrusted to them. These allowances were granted by the War Office and the Admiralty to the dependants of unmarried soldiers and seamen. The work was very akin to that on old age pensions, and required the patient and careful examination of all claims. In six months the number of such claims had amounted to one and a half million, and the work was further increased when an appeals procedure was set up. Later war compensation claims by the dependants of killed civilians were dealt with by the Excise, as well as the additional allowance of 2s. 6d. per week granted to pensioners 'suffering special hardships in consequence of the war'.

Again this work was in addition to the normal revenue work, which as the war progressed also drastically increased. There were considerable staff shortages, despite the re-employment of retired officers and a large influx of temporary clerical staff, mainly women. The dedication of the officers was such that it extracted from the Board the following appreciation:

TO ALL MEMBERS OF THE CUSTOMS AND EXCISE SERVICES

Now that the War has lasted some months, the Board wish to place on record their appreciation of the spirit shown by the Service at a time of National need.

A mass of important work of a novel character arising out of the War has been thrown upon the Department, and the staff concerned from the highest to the lowest, whether at Headquarters, or on the coast or inland, have responded loyally to the call made upon them, and have shown their ability to master new duties and to adapt themselves to strange conditions. They have also, in common with other members of the Service, who have not been directly occupied in the performance of the special War work, proved themselves ready to forgo accustomed privileges, to surrender leave and leisure, and, in some cases, where it has been impossible to give permission to volunteer for military service, to sacrifice their own patriotic inclinations.

Taking the work as a whole and having regard to its volume, and the complexity and responsiblity of much of it, the success with which it has been carried through in every part of the United Kingdom reflects great credit upon all concerned, and constitutes a record of which the Service has a right to be proud.

Board Room	L. N. GUILLEMARD
Custom House, E.C.	F. S. PARRY
11th December, 1914	A. J. TEDDER
	N. E. BEHRENS

To publish such a eulogy was without precedent; such a handsome expression of approbation from the Board went some way in bridging the gap that the various problems of amalgamation had caused. The friendly atmosphere between the Board and their staff did not prevail for very long. Soon the two sides were locked in a battle over voluntary enlistment, and for the next year or so this subject engendered much passion and acrimonious debate.

In the early days of the war the only members of the department allowed to enlist were those who were members of the various reserve forces, and only then if there was no serious detriment to the service. In fact by April 1916 less than eight hundred officers had been allowed to enlist.

The Board considered that the service occupied an altogether exceptional and unique position. The collection of revenue, as well as the other special duties, was essential to the war effort, and the Board found the department to be one 'essentially organised for war', or as the Prime Minister stated, 'they are serving their country in the most effective way possible to them'.

Despite these views, the Board early in 1915 agreed to the issue of buttonhole badges inscribed 'On War Service 1914' only after considerable pressure from the various staff associations. However, as the recruiting meetings throughout the country stirred great enthusiasm for enlistment, the younger officers had been placed under an intolerable strain; this was a time when eligible young men were being accosted in the streets and branded as cowards by the presentation of white feathers. The letters in the staff journals clearly show the passion this subject aroused, and it was only as a result of intense pressure from the officers that the Board finally agreed in December 1915 to introduce a new recruiting scheme. All eligible officers were allowed to enlist, and they were then issued with a certificate stating that they had expressed a desire to join the Army and were allowed to wear an armlet bearing the word 'Enlisted'. The concession did not amount to a great deal, because within three months conscription was introduced.

At the outbreak of the war the revenue from the Customs and Excise had began to fall; to account for the estimated deficit of almost £4,000,000, the duties on tea and beer were increased in the first war Budget. However, due largely to the increase of wages caused by war work and a vast increase in the consumption of both tobacco and spirits by the troops, there was a surplus of revenue rather than the expected deficit. As the war progressed even more finance was required to sustain the war effort, and as in previous war economies, the duties drastically increased. In 1915 there were large increases in the duties on tea, cocoa, coffee, tobacco, sugar and petrol, but the biggest increase was that on spirits, where the duty was doubled. This was more of a social than a fiscal measure.

Excessive drinking in the munitions industry was concerning the Government, and causing serious impairment of the war effort. Lloyd George said, 'We are fighting Germany, Austria and Drink.' As well as the large increase in duty, restrictions were placed on the delivery of raw spirits from warehouses; only spirits which had been warehoused for three or more years were allowed to be delivered. The amount of brewing was curtailed, and brewers were compelled to brew weaker beers, thus producing the same liquid quantity but of far less strength. The licensing hours were shortened—in fact the afternoon gap in the hours is a lasting memorial to the war. Lloyd George was convinced that the only answer was the complete State control of the liquor industry, but he had to be content with partial control in areas where there were large munitions factories. Carlisle was perhaps the most famous of these, State control surviving until 1971.

Throughout the months following the first Budget in 1915 there was a growing demand for some form of taxation on imported goods. In May a coalition government was formed with McKenna as Chancellor of the Exchequer. This new Government was under great pressure from City financiers in particular to impose some form of import duties. (It is to be remembered that the majority of the Cabinet, including McKenna, were dedicated proponents of free trade.) In the second Budget of the year, which was presented in September, McKenna proposed the imposition of a Customs duty of $33\frac{1}{3}$ per cent on motor cars, clocks and watches and musical instruments, and also a special duty on cinematograph film. The parliamentary history of these new import duties was very stormy. They were attacked with great vigour by the free traders in the House of Commons, who felt they were merely a prelude to the introduction of a general tariff. It is difficult to comprehend, in these days of tariffs, the passionate arguments in favour of free trade—an essential part of Liberal policy, ever since the time of Gladstone. In fact, since 1860 the country had been virtually free trading. Before gaining parliamentary approval for them the Prime Minister promised that these taxes were 'limited in amount, temporary in their duration and experimental in their character'.

The duties were finally approved for one year only, but up until the end of the war their annual renewal did not cause any controversy. It was not until the 1920s that the McKenna Duties, as they became known, became the centre of a bitter political battle. The new work fell to the already burdened Customs officers; as the Chancellor succinctly commented, 'Every new tax imposes a new burden upon the Customs and Excise; they are an admirable staff.'

This comment was equally applicable in the following instance, when again the Budget introduced new work for the department. This time it was a new and revolutionary duty—entertainments duty. This was a charge on all payments for admission to any form of entertainment, which was defined as including all sports, exhibitions and amusements. The idea of taxing entertainments was not particularly novel; as far back as the late eighteenth century such a form of taxation was being considered, as it was on several occasions in the following century; however, each time it was rejected because of the difficulties of collection of the duty.

The rates of tax introduced in 1916 varied from $\frac{1}{2}d.$ on payments under 2d. to 1s. on payments over 7s. 6d. It can be seen that the rates of duty were not proportionate; the lower the admission charge the greater the percentage paid in tax. This aspect of the tax was roundly attacked in the House of Commons; some members considered it as being 'grossly unfair and unequal'. The proposed tax structure was defended by the Chancellor on the grounds that the object 'was not to prevent people from going to the theatre or cinema, but to make them pay some contribution to the war effort when they went. It is a temporary duty solely for raising revenue.'

The Chancellor felt that the main source of revenue from this new tax would be the picture palaces. During the Bill's passage through the House of Commons certain concessions were granted to entertainments devoted to charitable and philanthropic purposes, as well as relief for those of a wholly educational nature. These exemptions were to cause many thorny liability problems for the department throughout the duration of the duty, which for a temporary duty (so called) was quite long; it survived until 1960.

In the same Budget, Mr McKenna, the Chancellor, introduced another new duty, this time on matches. The Chancellor in proposing the duty said he was 'undaunted by the example of Mr Lowe'; he was referring to the abortive attempt in 1871 by the then Chancellor, Mr Lowe, to place an Excise duty on matches. Because of the considerable opposition both inside and outside Parliament, the proposed duty was withdrawn, but not without the Chancellor suffering for some years under the nickname 'Lucifer' Lowe. The 1916 duty was imposed on both imported and home-produced matches; British manufacturers were required to take out a licence, and their operations came under the control of Excise officers. To ensure equality of treatment, a corresponding duty was placed on mechanical lighters.

The Chancellor further demonstrated his scant regard for controversial duties when he reintroduced the duty on cider and perry. The resurrection of this old Excise duty certainly did not cause the outcry that it had in the eighteenth century; and it was destined to be of only short duration, being repealed in 1923. This prolific Budget raised the Customs and Excise revenue to an unprecedented level; and from 1916 until the end of the war no new extra duties were introduced, much to the relief of the overworked staff.

At the onset of war the major railway companies had come under direct Government control. In 1916 it was decided that the checking of the railway-passenger duty accounts was an unnecessary burden on the department. Therefore, with effect from 1 January 1917, the payment of railway-passenger duty was suspended in the case of railways controlled by the State. This left only twelve small railway companies still paying duty; in 1919 this figure amounted to only £7,393, compared with £270,000 collected in 1916. The period of Government control came to an end in August 1921; and under the Finance Act of that year the famous 1d. per mile disappeared, after having being in existence since 1844. The first year after de-control saw the duty increase to £½ million, the highest figure since the 1880s.

One of the lasting effects of the war on the department was the increased employment of women. In 1914 there were only twenty-one women on the establishment, all 'female typewriters'. By the end of the war there were over 1,400 employed, mainly as temporary clerks. The temporary clerks had first been employed in 1915 to assist officers on the separation allowance work, but by 1917 they were largely used on old-age pension work—so much so that a new grade was formed called women pension officers. They were normally employed in large towns, where they could be grouped for easier supervision, and in 1918 there were sufficient numbers working in London to justify the appointment of a woman welfare supervisor. At present the number of women in the department has risen to over 8,000, almost 30 per cent of the total staff. In November 1964 Mrs D. C. L. Johnstone CBE was appointed to the Board, becoming the first woman commissioner in a revenue department.

A unique memorial service was held in Westminster Abbey on July 11 1918 to commemorate members of the Civil Service who had died in the war, and was attended by the King. It was the very first service of its kind to be held, and strangely enough was conducted four months to the very day from the Armistice. Of the total of 1,927 Customs and Excise men who had served in the war, 123 had been killed. After the war a memorial plaque was set up in the Long Room of the London Custom House, and since then a remembrance service has been conducted on the closest working day to Remembrance Sunday.

The problems of the two amalgamated services which were present at the outset of the war had not disappeared in the succeeding four years; the vastly increased work-load had only exacerbated them. The staff expected that there would be a large increase in the complement to deal with the vast amount of new work taken on, and they were also looking for the establishment of reasonable working hours, with fair payment for all work undertaken in excess of the normal. To the Customs this meant overtime, a problem which had remained unresolved for the last ten years. On the other hand, the Excise officers expected some scheme to compensate for the long hours they were working without any extra payment.

One of the pressing problems was salaries. Prices had doubled during the war years, and despite the various awards in the form of war bonuses, the officers felt that they had not been adequately recompensed compared with their pre-war standards, and more especially outside industry. Although in 1919 there were some salary increases given to certain grades, each award was accompanied by the condition 'without prejudice to the ultimate revision of salaries after the war'.

The general mood of euphoria at the end of the war was clouded in the department by the number of problems remaining to be solved. These included the return of the Servicemen, the establishment of women clerks, salaries and extra payments, reintroduction of promotion, and the general adjustment of the workload, as the service returned to its peacetime role. It therefore seemed inevitable that in facing these realities the department would once again be involved in large-scale changes, which would only lead to another reorganization.

CHAPTER NINE

Have You
Anything to Declare?

The newly combined Preventive forces—consisting of the Coast Guard, the Mounted Guard, the Revenue Cruisers and the Coast Blockade—had achieved some moderate but encouraging success. During 1822 over a million gallons of spirits, some $22\frac{1}{2}$ million lb of tea and $11\frac{1}{2}$ million lb of tobacco were seized. This steady increase in seizures, and the much greater risk of capture, forced the smugglers to resort to far more ingenious methods to land their goods successfully.

These changes in smuggling techniques have been called by several writers on smuggling the scientific period. Certainly the emphasis changed from the all-out confrontation of large gangs, landing their cargoes in defiance of the revenue forces, to a variety of methods which ranged from sinking cargo to careful concealments on the vessels themselves. One of the most popular devices was to weight spirit tubs with sinking stones, dump them overboard and leave them attached to a recovery line with a buoy marking the spot. The smugglers were then able to retrieve their cargo at a more opportune moment. Most of the smuggling vessels had a special rail fitted on the hull of the vessel and known as a tub-rail. This carried the tubs ready for the sinking operation, which was called 'sowing the crop'. Many revenue vessels and boats patrolled close to the shore using grappling irons, which were pulled along the sea-bed in the hope of discovering the sunken goods. This operation—called creeping—was very unpopular with the revenue crew: it was tedious and time-consuming, and rarely produced any seizures.

The smugglers now were forced to use hiding-places close to the shore to store the goods until they could move them. In 1822 some Custom House officers searching a house in Margate found a secret entrance in the basement which led to a narrow passage 'just large enough to admit one man crawling upon his knees'. The passage—which was over 300 yards long—came out on the beach, and its entrance was boarded over and covered with chalk and earth. It was estimated that the tunnel must have taken eighteen months to construct, at a cost of £200. Natural caves close to the shore were obvious hiding-places, and frequently the spirit tubs were buried in shingle. Around the chalk wastes of Kent and Sussex a popular concealment was to stack the tubs at the bottom of a cliff and cover them with chalk to resemble a cliff fall.

All these contrivances had the disadvantage that the cargo had to be left, and there was the continual risk that it would be discovered. The smugglers soon came to the conclusion that it would be much simpler to hide it on board the vessels themselves, where their goods would be under their constant surveillance. The wooden sailing-vessels were particularly suited for a variety of concealments—false bulkheads and hulls, hollowed-out masts, special compartments in holds, false ceilings in cabins. In one ship, for instance, a double hull measuring about 18 inches in width was fitted to the outside of the vessel in which to conceal the smuggled goods. The contraband was often hidden under the legal cargo in ballast, and in many instances in the cargo itself. One example was kegs of butter, in which was found a large quantity of coral. Tobacco was frequently found in coils of rope, sacks of flour, bales of cotton and even inside barrels of pitch. The Custom Board were well aware of the various contrivances—in 1822 they issued an instruction to all officers:

> to use their best endeavours to detect the various schemes and devices adopted by smugglers to defraud the Revenue, particularly in the construction of concealments in coasters, colliers and other traders, by means of false bottoms, false bulkheads and other means.

During the next thirty years as each new concealment was discovered the Customs Board passed on the full details to the officers to ensure that they were aware of any new method.

Perhaps the most difficult type of smuggling to prevent was that undertaken by the fair traders. Vessels, especially colliers, would clear out coastwise from a port laden with coals, and on their voyage would rendezvous with foreign vessels and load contraband goods—stow them under the coal, and proceed onwards into an English port. The smuggled goods could then be discharged long after the Customs officers had lost interest in the vessel. In 1829 the Coast Guard were instructed

> to be upon their guard against a common practice amongst vessels returning from a voyage with coals, to any foreign port, of putting Contraband goods on their return into light vessels for London on the coast, but chiefly to Cobles and Fishing Boats at sea.

Despite the greatly strengthened revenue forces, there were still attempts to land smuggled goods in the old-fashioned way. The coast blockade service especially was involved in frequent battles with 'bands of armed smugglers numbering two hundred or more'. Between 1821 and 1824 five officers had been killed and over thirty seriously injured. Their main opponents were members of a most successful and dangerous band known as the Aldington

Gang. George Ransley, their leader, had set up his headquarters at Aldington Fright, a deserted area between Folkestone and New Romney. The gang was relatively small in number—probably not more than twenty-five or so—but well trained and disciplined by Ransley's brother-in-law Samuel Bailey, a deserter from the Navy.

The final downfall of the gang resulted from a run of spirits on the beach near Dover, which was intercepted by the coast blockade men. In the ensuing battle a Richard Morgan of the blockade service was murdered. This 'dreadful outrage', as one of the newspapers called it, stirred the government into action. During the following weeks the gang continued their smuggling activities, but two men were captured and another member of the gang came forward to give information as to the names of their associates. With these as witnesses, and choosing a wet and windy night, a large force of men surrounded every house in Aldington, and Ransley and the whole of his gang were captured without a fight.

In January 1827 the sixteen prisoners were tried at Maidstone, all appearing in the traditional smuggler's smock. The Crown had prepared a very strong case, with the Solicitor-General prosecuting, and all pleaded guilty. Two were acquitted, and the rest given the death penalty, which was remitted to transportation. The judge's comments on passing sentence showed the difference in outlook and opinion since the days of the previous century when smuggling was condoned as an 'honest and romantic form of criminal activity'.

His Lordship said that they had pleaded guilty to an offence of a most heinous nature, which struck terror into every well-disposed mind. They had assembled in numerous bodies to aid the running of uncustomed goods, and in so aiding had fired upon persons who were only doing their duty. . . . Prisoners had admitted that they assembled in gangs of as many as eighty—a gang numerous enough to overcome the peaceable part of the community. These things could not be suffered to go on with impunity. He trusted that the present proceedings would have a proper effect, and convince the offenders that the arm of the law was long enough, and sufficiently powerful, to reach and punish even the most distant and most desperate. It must be made known throughout the country that if an offence of this nature were again committed no mercy would be shown to the offenders. . . . If persons in the highest stations of life were not to purchase smuggled goods there could soon be an end to smuggling, but many persons laboured under the delusion that defrauding the revenue was no crime. It was a serious offence against the laws of God; and smuggling led to the commission of the greatest crime, that of murder.

These impassioned comments were a far cry from the all too recent days when no jury in the smuggling counties would convict any smuggler. The conviction of the Aldington Gang virtually marked the end of the large smuggling gangs. The last battle the coast blockade fought was in 1828, when a large body of smugglers landed several hundred tubs of spirits at a desolate part of the coast near Bexhill. The blockade men endeavoured to intercept them, but the force of the smugglers was too great, and reinforcements were sought. In a short time a force of over forty men, all strongly armed, was gathered, and finally met up with the smugglers at Sidley-green, a small village some miles inland.

The smugglers 'drew themselves up in a body in a regular line and a desperate fight took place'. They fought with great determination and courage—so much so that the blockade men were forced to withdraw, with their quartermaster killed and several of the men injured. The smugglers 'were all armed with bats and some with firearms and Collins, the quartermaster had his brains literally beaten out'. The following morning one of the smugglers was found dead 'his bat still grasped in his hand, the weapon being almost hacked to pieces by the cutlasses and bayonets of the blockade men'. Some days later one of the smugglers came forward with information as to the names of all the gang, and slowly each member was rounded up and convicted.

The last important smuggling run occurred a year later, when a large band of smugglers conveyed a train of carts and horses loaded with spirits and tobacco through the streets of Lydd. It was reported that the townspeople cheered the smugglers. Little did they realize that they were witnessing the passing of an era. The battle had been largely won; at all events sufficiently for the Coast Blockade Force to be lifted, and the Coast Guard to take over their duties.

The number of revenue vessels operating had greatly increased: in 1823 there were thirty-three in service as part of the Coast Guard, and by 1839 the total had risen to fifty, stationed around the coasts. The majority of the vessels were commanded by naval lieutenants and were divided into three classes; the first class exceeded 140 tons, the second class was from 100 to 140 tons, and the third below 100 tons. The pride of the fleet was the *Vulcan*, the first steam vessel to be employed in the service. This vessel had been built in Cowes, and was launched in 1834. Considering the experimental nature of steam vessels at this time, such a departure showed a very adventurous outlook on the part of the Customs Board. *Vulcan* was stationed in South Wales, Dartmouth and Ireland before being paid off in 1849. The Commissioners were delighted with their steam vessel and used it on a variety of tasks; on one occasion it was used on the west coast of Ireland 'to convey considerable sums of money to pay the wages of the numerous laborers employed on the Relief works'.

In the 1820s, the famous novelist and naval officer Captain Marryat had been employed on revenue duties; his vessel *Rosario* was given the coast from Portsmouth to Start Point to patrol. His views on smuggling were expressed in a memorandum sent to the Admiralty. He found the whole preventive service insufficient and badly organised' and felt that if revenue cruisers 'were not at anchor so much' there would be less incidence of smuggling. His ultimate solution to the problem was a complete blockade of the smuggling ports, such as Cherbourg, Flushing and Roscoff. In his opinion, 'the Cruisers would have a far better chance of falling in with the smugglers, than when dispersed over a wide area of coast'. Captain Marryat used his experience of the smugglers as material in some of his novels.

Although *Punch* described the Coast Guard stations as 'Castles of idleness, where able bodied men spent their time looking through long glasses for imaginary smugglers', this was far from the reality. The conditions of the service were particularly arduous, the hours were long and discipline was strict, in tune with naval tradition. The men were continually reminded that 'the sole object of their appointment is the Protection of the Revenue', and they frequently worked a sixteen-hour shift. To avoid any collusion with the smugglers, they were informed of the area of coast to patrol only at the very last moment. The discipline was harsh, with misdemeanours and offences punished by fines and dismissals. One such order was issued by the Comptroller-General: 'that a list will in future be kept of every person serving at a station, within which a run took place and that no such officer or man will be considered eligible for promotion or entitled to any mark of indulgence or favour'.

In 1831 Sir James Graham, the First Lord of the Admiralty, suggested that the efficiency of the Coast Guard would be improved by 'rendering the Service in all its branches essentially naval', and further that the Coast Guard Service be composed of naval men 'available for great National objects, independent of the benefits it will confer by the protection of the Revenue'. The Treasury agreed in June 1831, and thus the Coast Guard now became the reserve for the Royal Navy, greatly enhancing the chances of promotion for all ranks. New recruits were henceforth required to sign an agreement to serve on naval vessels abroad if requested, and formal training was given at Royal Navy Establishments.

At the same time the organization of the riding officers—now known as the Mounted Guard—was drastically altered. Many of the older officers had retired, some at the age of eighty! In future all the new entrants were required to be over twenty years of age and under thirty years, with previous experience in a cavalry regiment. A system of day pay was introduced, hopefully as an encouragement for the men to patrol the coast regularly. Ranks from sergeant to private were brought in, all under the direct control of the Chief Officer of the Coast Guard. By 1849 the Mounted Guard was costing over £15,000, and was considered an expensive luxury, with doubtful advantages. It was therefore decided to reduce the numbers to a mere handful of men stationed at places like Deal, Folkestone, Hastings, Isle of Wight, Swanage and Fowey—the old notorious smuggling areas.

Although the Customs Commissioners still controlled the combined Preventive forces, they were now in essence a military force, the Coast Guard and the revenue vessels being commanded and manned by naval personnel, and the Mounted Guard recruited from the Army. There was no doubt that this combined force was achieving some success—the quantity of goods seized during the years 1839–43 greatly increased. However, despite the undoubted improved efficiency of the revenue control, probably the greatest single factor in the reduction of smuggling was the introduction of free trade, with its vast reductions in import duties. The advice of economists over the years who had argued that the only answer to smuggling was to reduce duties appeared at long last to have been heeded (though Sir Robert Peel, in all the debates on tariff reform, never once instanced smuggling as one of his reasons for his free trade policy).

Some of the reductions had made the smuggling of many goods no longer a profitable occupation. The illegal trade in tea, wines and silks had virtually ceased. The only goods which remained worth smuggling were spirits and tobacco. Spirits, largely because of their bulk and smaller profitability, were smuggled far less; for the rest of the nineteenth century the main commodity of the smuggler was tobacco. A report issued in 1844 which examined the conditions in the tobacco trade alleged 'a considerable amount of tobacco is daily brought into the United Kingdom and can be obtained anywhere for 2s. 6d. per pound [the duty alone was 3s. 2d.]'. Evidence was presented that special establishments had been set up in Flushing and Nieuport for the express purpose of packaging tobacco for the smuggling trade. Much of the smuggled goods was brought ashore by ships' crews. A captain of a Boulogne steam-ship maintained that all his men smuggled tobacco; they were deliberately paid low wages because 'they have the power to make a venture'.

The worst areas appeared to be the Humber, Tyne/Tees and the Bristol Channel. In 1843 over 145,000 pounds of tobacco was seized, much of this by the revenue cruisers at sea. The largest haul was taken by the *Lapwing* cruiser off a Dutch vessel found hovering near the Lincolnshire coast. Over 3,700 pounds were found by local Customs officers in Tynemouth; the goods were concealed in an inn, and were believed to have been landed from one of the colliers. However, the majority of seizures consisted of small amounts found concealed on board, either in the cargo or in the accommodation, and as such a formidable task to prevent.

Captain Hornsby, the Commander-General of the Coast Guard, gave his opinion on the question of reducing the tobacco duty as follows:

> unless you take the duty off altogether, you would not prevent smuggling. I know the habits and practices of the fishermen along the coasts of Kent and Sussex contiguous to France; they would carry on smuggling however small the duty, because they have greater facilities for it than the fair trader; they get their living by working in boats, they have no port dues to pay; they have no lights to pay and have none of the expenses attending upon merchant vessels, therefore they would undersell the fair trader, even if the duty was low.

In 1849 the Coast Guard consisted of ninety-six districts, each under a Commander of the Royal Navy, and there were seventy cruisers operating around the coasts. The total establishment was over 6,000, at an annual cost of £510,000. It was decided that the numbers of cruisers could be reduced without greatly affecting the efficiency of the force, 'as runs by swift sailing cutters are seldom now attempted, smuggling where it prevails is generally effected by means of contraband goods secreted under cargoes or in carefully contrived places of concealment'. Twenty-one cruisers were paid off, with a resultant saving of £29,000. A replacement for the *Vulcan* steam vessel was urgently required, as 'one screw vessel can do the work of two cutters, and defeats the smuggler's reliance upon the state of the wind and the weather'. The replacement steam vessel was called *Argus*, and was brought into service in 1852.

With the outbreak of the Crimean War in 1854 three thousand Coast Guard men were drafted into the Navy, their places being filled by pensioners, and many of the revenue cruisers were placed under the Admiralty. They operated very successfully, capturing eleven Russian vessels, of which eight were condemned as prizes. *Argus* captured the first Russian prize off Beachy Head, a barque called *Troja*, laden with salt and flying Russian-Finnish colours. It is interesting to note that during the war all seizures of tobacco were sent to the Crimea for the Army.

By the end of the war it had become obvious that the protection of the revenue was only one of many reasons for the existence of the Coast Guard, and in 1856 it was decided to transfer the control of the service to the Admiralty. The Customs Board made very strong representations to the Treasury on the inconvenience that they considered would result from such a change. The Treasury informed them that the responsibility for the change rested entirely with Her Majesty's Government, and the Customs Board would stand 'entirely exonerated, if any inconveniences apprehended arose to the detriment of the public service'.

On 1 October 1856, therefore, the control of the Coast Guard was transferred to the Admiralty under the Coast Guard Service Act. The preamble of the Act laid down their duties as 'The defence of the coasts of the Realm, the more ready manning of the Navy in the case of war, and emergency and the protection of the Revenue.' The Customs Department was now left with one revenue vessel, the *Vigilant*, and a number of small rowing-boats at the various ports, with a comparatively small force of land and tide waiters. From the date of the transfer of the Coast Guard, Customs officers were no longer armed, although the Coast Guard themselves remained an armed force, largely because of their defence responsibilities.

The first report of the Customs, published in 1857, took a very optimistic view of smuggling:

> With the reductions of duties and the removal of all needless and vexatious restrictions, smuggling has greatly diminished and the public sentiments with regard to it have undergone a very considerable change. The smuggler is no longer an object of public sympathy or a hero of romance, and people are beginning to awake to the perception of the fact that his offence is less a fraud on the Revenue, than a robbery of the fair trader. Smuggling proper is now

almost entirely confined to tobacco, spirits and watches; though lace, silk and
other trifling articles are still occasionally seized on the person, or in the
baggage of some unprincipled or inconsiderate passengers; but all these cases
are on the decrease and in the last ten years have diminished to about one-
third. The thoughtless habit, however, of so packing dutiable articles within
the folds of ladies dresses as to answer this purpose, or at least to give the
appearance of fraudulent concealment, still prevails among passengers
arriving from abroad, and gives rise to many disagreeable disputes. This
practice is the more indefensible because the very parties who thus
dishonourably endeavour to frustrate the purpose of a partial, rapid and polite
search are the loudest and most vehement in their complaint, if that search be
minute or tedious.

The same report recorded the discovery of large-scale smuggling in Swiss
watches. A seizure of watches from a seaman off a cross-Channel boat led to
the leader of a large smuggling ring, a London dealer called Lucien
Marchand. He had been operating the illegal trade for about four years,
using both seamen and passengers as couriers. He was finally found guilty
and fined £3,510. In an attempt to combat smuggling in the maritime
counties the police in these areas were issued with the authority to seize
smuggled goods. The Essex police were the first force to receive such
commissions, and in 1856 they seized 3,000 pounds of tobacco at Dedham. In
1860 the Hampshire Constabulary had a notable success, in finding 1,981
pounds of tobacco. These were the outstanding seizures; other county police
forces secured very little, although the Commissioners felt that 'the
preventive effect had been good'. Similar authority was given to the
Admiralty police in H.M. Dockyards. From very early days the Royal Navy
had the privilege of duty-free stores; there is a record in the Customs and
Excise Museum of the stores granted duty-free to be placed on H.M.S.
Victory, only a month or so before the battle of Trafalgar. Naval seamen had
always received duty-free tobacco, but for a number of years this privilege
had been abused by the majority of seamen smuggling small quantities
ashore. The action of the Admiralty helped to control the trade; their police
were given very strict instructions to seize all quantities of tobacco, however
small, although the smuggling by naval personnel was a continual problem
for many years.

    The Isle of Wight appeared to be one of the last bastions of the old-time
smuggling. It was suggested in 1860 of the area around the southern tip of the
island that 'the whole population are smugglers . . . here are fishermen, who
do not fish'. This opinion was borne out by the number of seizures made in
the area. Poor old William Arnold must have turned in his grave! During
1867 tubs of spirit were being landed on the shores as in the good old days;
seizures of spirits were made at South Yarmouth, Totland, Small Hope, and
in December 1868 there was an abortive attempt to land 72 small casks,
containing 205 gallons of brandy, on a beach near South Yarmouth. Because
of the dark night all the smugglers managed to escape, but at least they did

not resort to violence, and all the casks were secured. On another occasion over 150 tubs of brandy were found in 'a cliff near Cowes, for which, a notorious smuggler named Stamp was convicted and punished'. The last recorded seizure of spirits on the island was in 1874, when 17 kegs of brandy were discovered near Freshwater.

With the further reductions in import duties after 1861, many dutiable goods were found being smuggled in goods that were now duty-free. Tobacco was found hidden in a wide variety of goods from casks of potatoes, bales of hops, and even in the middle of baked German bread. Cigars were now becoming a favourite commodity of the smuggler. At Liverpool over 1,000 pounds of cigars were found hidden in a consignment of toys, and in 1870, 21 pounds of cigars were found in the crinolines of two female passengers from Ostend. This new type of smuggling forced the Customs Board to introduce a more vigorous examination of duty-free goods, especially from countries where the sale of tobacco was unrestricted. The London police became more active in preventing goods being removed out of the docks: 250 pounds of tobacco were found in a cab at East Greenwich, followed by similar seizures from cabs at Millwall and Bermondsey. Perhaps the most cheeky attempt at smuggling was in November 1874, when four men were arrested in the act of putting 180 pounds of tobacco—brought ashore from a vessel from Antwerp—into a cab in Lower Thames Street, 'within sight of the London Custom House'!

During the 1870s the incidence of tobacco-smuggling appeared to be on the increase, judging by the number of seizures made, some of which were quite large. The Customs Board reported in 1875 that 'the temptation to smuggle offered by the high duties imposed on tobacco must always induce attempts to defraud this Revenue'. Most ports were fairly successful in finding smuggled tobacco and cigars, although 'the general use of steam has greatly increased the difficulties of the rummaging officers, spaces in connection with the machinery, which can only be searched when they have become cool, are becoming favourite places of concealment'. (The numbers of engine-room men who were convicted for smuggling offences greatly reinforced this opinion.)

The largest hauls were still made on the deserted coasts. At Deal over 200 pounds were found hidden in the sand, and at Littlehampton, Sussex, a small vessel was searched and nearly 11,000 pounds of tobacco was discovered. The largest haul was in 1871, when the *Sunrise* cutter was boarded in the river Itchen and 8,000 pounds of tobacco was found on board. This led the officers to over 6,000 pounds hidden in a house at South Stoneham. The owner of the cutter, William Mitchell, a well-known smuggler, was convicted and fined £2,000. It became the practice to pack manufactured tobacco in waterproof bags, which were placed in a case and thrown overboard on arrival at places agreed upon between the crews and their confederates on shore, who picked them up. Frequently consignments of tobacco were found 'washed ashore on the beach'. In Newcastle a plank was found in the river, floating but stationary; on investigation a rope was found running down to a sunken box containing over 100 pounds of tobacco.

The Excise service were involved in some rather large seizures of tobacco, which were hidden in large reels of paper. In 1877 a paper manufacturer in Bradford had offered a tobacco merchant tobacco at a price lower than the duty. The merchant informed his local Excise officer, who along with police searched the paper mill. Over 500 pounds of tobacco were found, also information as to tobacco at other premises in Leeds, where a further 1,600 pounds were discovered. The Yorkshire area seemed to be a particularly notorious area for smuggling, and Hull was the centre of a large tobacco operation. The regular tobacco merchants complained bitterly to the collector that their business was 'being injured by the scale of smuggled tobacco'. During April and May 1880 a combined operation was mounted by the Customs, the Excise and the police, which resulted in over 13,000 pounds of tobacco and cigars being found in various premises in Hull and the surrounding villages.

The peak year for tobacco smuggling was 1882, and from then until the end of the century the figures slowly declined. In 1887 the Customs Board commented that the smuggling of tobacco was still a problem, with the crews of large steam vessels trading from Europe and America as the main offenders, but added that it was 'believed that this illicit trade has been considerably checked by the vigilance of our officers'. The same optimistic view was taken of smuggling by passengers: 'It is diminishing in frequency and importance.' It was admitted, however, that some of the attempts were clever—fourteen pounds of tobacco concealed in a belt worn by a passenger, as well as a variety of false bottoms and sides to trunks. Due to the number of small or petty seizures, the Board of Customs introduced a system in 1884 whereby the offender was offered the option of depositing a sum of money with the collector, 'to abide by the Board's decision', or to be proceeded against before a magistrate. The amount of the deposit was fixed at treble or double the duty plus value of the goods, according to the circumstances of the case. The officers were to exercise 'their best judgement in favour of the passenger'.

A new notice to the public was introduced in English and French: 'If you have any tobacco, cigars, gold or silver plate, Eau de Cologne, or Spirit of any sort, it is obligatory that you should declare the fact previously to the examination of your baggage. The importation of merchandize with baggage is prohibited.' Before the examination of baggage, the passengers were asked to read this notice, and if they did not read it, then 'the officer should proceed as if they had'!

The procedure of passengers' deposit in cases of smuggling that had been used with passengers was so successful that in 1888 it was estimated that the work of the officers had been reduced by under 50 per cent. The procedure was not extended to smuggling by members of ships' crews, in an attempt to demonstrate that the owners and officers of a vessel had some responsibility to ensure that the crew obeyed the revenue laws. A system of fines was imposed: if a ship's officer was caught smuggling, or if no owner could be obtained for smuggled goods found on the vessel, there was a fine imposed on the ship, to be paid by the owners of the vessel. It is debatable how successful this measure has been; it is certainly true that in the early days many shipping companies dismissed any crew member who was caught smuggling, and a note was recorded in his seaman's book, which made it difficult for him to obtain another ship.

When the commander of the sole remaining revenue cruiser *Vigilant* died the opportunity was taken for a thorough inspection of the vessel. It was found that the cost of complete overhaul was not warranted by the expected life of the vessel, and it was therefore decided to replace it with a small screw steamer. The new *Vigilant*, the sixth vessel to bear the name, became operational in 1866. The advantages of the steam vessel were said to be that it can 'always move about indifferent of wind or tide, and can follow behind large foreign steamers up the river to London and prevent their unshipping or throwing overboard contraband goods'. During its first ten years of operation it had proved very useful, the crew rummaging on average eighteen hundred vessels each year.

So practical and successful was the *Vigilant* that the Board of Customs considered replacing the existing small sailing vessels at the various out-ports with small steam launches. The first ones were built for just over £1,000, and were stationed at Southampton in April 1872, and at Gravesend in December of the same year. The Board felt it desirable to judge the practical effect of these launches before extending them to other ports. In 1873 steam vessels were built for Falmouth, the river Tyne and later Liverpool. By 1901 there were twenty such steam vessels in operation, and the department was now considering replacing some of the rowing-boats with motor-propelled vessels. In 1899 it had experimented with a ¾ h.p. motor driven by paraffin on a boat used at Portsmouth. It was the first large authority to operate motor-boats. The experiments with the motor-boats proved successful, and in 1905 specially built motor-boats were adopted for their use. The fleet of vessels had so increased that in 1907 the Board established a separate branch of the Waterguard Service, called the Launch Service, specially to man and service the boats.

The proposals of the Goschen Minute of 1891, which separated the Landing and Waterguard staffs, established the modern Waterguard Service, whose main purpose was the prevention of smuggling. The Chancellor of the Exchequer had particularly in mind the value of rummaging, which he said

> may be considered the first line of defence of the Customs Revenue, while the size and the complicated construction of modern vessels tend to render such searching more difficult. It is necessary, therefore, to provide carefully for its due supervision and the evidence of experienced officers, who had spent their lives in Waterguard work, was given to the effect that rummaging cannot be

properly supervised except by officers who have had practical experience of
this duty themselves.

By the beginning of the twentieth century the amount of tobacco smuggling
had reduced considerably; in the Board's opinion this was due to the
vigilance of its officers. The average number of seizures each year was 4,000,
totalling some 8,000 pounds of tobacco, and these figures hardly changed
until the outbreak of the First World War, when the figures nearly doubled.
In the period before the war the department was faced with the problem of
'coopers'. These were virtually floating spirit and tobacco ships, which
hovered around the herring fishing fleets to supply them with duty-free
tobacco and drink. All were of Dutch nationality, and there were about eight
of them operating around the coasts. Their presence, as well as the problems
of preventing the landing of their goods, 'was a constant source of anxiety to
the Department'. They normally operated outside the three-mile limit, and
were thus free from British control. However, in 1906 two of them were
found operating within the river Humber, and were arrested by H.M.S.
Argus, their cargoes of tobacco and spirits being seized. This was a rare
occurrence, for normally the only method of combating the trade was to
increase the Waterguard staff at the fishing ports during the herring season.
The Orkney and Shetland Islands and the north-east coast of Scotland were
especially vulnerable to this trade. In 1913 the last cooper was arrested
operating off the Shetlands. With the advent of war, this form of trade
disappeared, and it did not re-emerge.

In addition to the marked increase of tobacco smuggling after the war,
there was a rise in the incidence of saccharin smuggling. When the duty on
sugar had been reintroduced in 1901 an equivalent duty had been placed on
saccharin. It was a perfect commodity to smuggle: the duty was very high
compared with its bulk. During the 1820s there was obviously a considerable
amount of commercial smuggling, and many seizures of saccharin were
made. The cleverest attempt was made in 1921, when a consignment of
teddy bears were imported into London, and found to be tightly packed with
bags of saccharin. An ominous sign of the not too distant future was the
seizure in 1922 of a large quantity of cocaine from a vessel in Grimsby. The
seaman had bought the drug in Hamburg, being assured that it would show
a nice profitable transaction.

Many changes had been made in the Coastguard Service since its
departure from the Customs Department; the number of stations and men
had been drastically reduced. In 1906 the Customs Board felt moved to ask
the Admiralty as to their future plans for the service. The Admiralty
intimated that they considered the latter's extensive patrolling as a
precaution against smuggling to be no longer necessary. The inevitable
reorganization of the Coastguard service was delayed until after the war; in
1922 a committee was set up to examine the whole question. One of its
recommendations was that the Board of Customs and Excise should establish
its own force of coast-watching staff.

The new force—which was known as the Coast Preventive Force—would act as a supplement to the existing Waterguard officers and perform all the preventive duties hitherto carried out by the Coastguards. It came into being on 1 April 1923, and the new-style Coastguard was placed under the control of the Board of Trade. Once more, after nearly seventy years, the department was in full control of all the revenue protection services.

During the inter-war years the department was constantly under attack from the popular press concerning the inadequacies of the resources devoted to the prevention of smuggling. There were allegations of 'Midnight yachtsmen making fortunes running goods', 'The Isle of Wight—a paradise of contraband' and 'A smuggling boom in the Channel.' All the articles suggested that smuggling was now easier than it had ever been. In 1931 the *Daily Mail* attempted to demonstrate this point by running some goods into the country. They chose a beach near Shoreham on an August Bank Holiday; two reporters landed a consignment of spirits and loaded them into a car, all without any revenue interference. The story duly appeared the following day under the headline 'Thrilling Smuggling Exploit.'

Certainly the preventive measures existing at the time were sparse and scattered by previous standards. There was only one revenue cruiser, the *Vigilant*, which was to all intents and purposes a flag-showing vessel, used mainly by the Commissioners. The Special Enquiry Staff, the forerunners of the Investigation Division, comprised only ten officers, mainly involved in *ad valorem* duty frauds and illicit distillations. The system of patrol by the Coast Preventive Men was grossly inadequate: only two hundred of the approved complement of four hundred had been appointed. These men were each expected to cover some twenty miles of coast, both night and day, and were under the direction of a Chief Preventive Officer, who was normally based up to thirty miles away, with no means of transport to visit his men. The local Preventive Officer, who had the best knowledge of the area and the potential dangerous spots, had no voice in either the timing or direction of the patrols. The Waterguard officers at the ports were fully involved in the rummaging of vessels, and had become fairly successful in reducing the amount of smuggling by the ships' crews. However, they had no means of transport to visit the smaller ports and creeks to examine the small coasters and yachts, which had increased in number since the War. One report suggested that the revenue was losing £10 millions each year by smuggling.

It is difficult to judge the accuracy of this estimate. Certainly few smugglers were caught, but whether this was an indication of the lack of smuggling or the lack of success by the department is a very debatable point. The Board were obviously concerned about the revenue protection services, because in 1928 they appointed a special committee to examine and review the position. Its report generally discounted the lurid newspaper articles as 'wildly exaggerated fabrications', but it did recommend certain improvements, such as an increase in the Special Enquiry Staff, the establishment at each port of specially trained rummage crews to be used as flying squads, closer attention to be paid to yachts and periodical visits to private aerodromes with greater co-operation with police in regard to the reporting of unauthorized landings. The report was fully accepted by the Commissioners, and all the recommendations were brought into operation.

The few large smuggling exploits that were detected during these years received full coverage in the Press, if in somewhat colourful terms. In 1936 Captain Hayter—a Red Cross pilot, or as the Press called him a 'hero of the Abyssinian wars'—was one of the few persons sentenced for smuggling by aeroplane. He landed at a small aerodrome at Wickham Bushes, near Dover, with a consignment of cigars. He and his partner were caught while trying to sell the cigars to tobacconists in Margate. In the same year two chartered yachts were seized at Burnham-on-Crouch after the police received an anonymous letter about large-scale smuggling in the area. The four smugglers were caught hawking brandy around the public houses in the vicinity. (The prosecuting counsel said, 'The story of this escapade is like those I used to enjoy as a boy'!)

One of the most organized smuggling attempts was uncovered in 1935, when the chartered vessel *Hawarden Castle* was searched at King's Lynn. Over 1,000 pounds of tobacco was found under the cargo; during the search of the captain's cabin documents were found made out in an intricate code, which gave full details of consignments and names of customers. The smuggled goods were loaded into a rowing-boat at night, taken to a storehouse up-river and then delivered to customers in Manchester and Leeds. The operation had been working successfully for over three years. One newspaper exhorted the authorities, 'If this lucrative, highly organized and expensively equipped illegal business is to be suppressed, the maximum sentence of six months for smugglers must be abolished. Send the smugglers to gaol for a long stretch to provide an effective deterrent.'

Perhaps the most unusual smuggling case in the thirties was the smuggling of greyhounds from Eire. The greyhounds—each valued at £60-£70—were bought in Cork, taken across Eire, smuggled over the land boundary and taken on board a coastal collier in Belfast. The dogs were brought to Penarth Docks near Cardiff, and were carried off the vessel late at night and delivered to the greyhound tracks in Cardiff and Merthyr Tydfil. The local Customs officer received some information about this trade, and on the vessel's next arrival in the port it was thoroughly searched. Three greyhounds were found in the forepeak. The master admitted that he had smuggled in nearly sixty dogs in the previous eighteen months. With the duty of 40 per cent, he had defrauded the revenue of nearly £1,500.

The conditions at the end of the Second World War were ideal for a resurgence of smuggling. High tariffs, punitive rates of purchase tax, rationing and a general scarcity of goods were all incentives for the profitable illegal trade. The Waterguard service was weakened through the lack of suitable recruits, and—perhaps most important of all—there was a pool of demobilized Servicemen eager to involve themselves and their gratuities in any exciting and profitable trade. It is therefore not surprising to find that smuggling escalated in the immediate post-war years. The Waterguards found themselves stretched to the limit in an attempt to combat and control the smuggling boom, especially as they were deeply involved in training the new staff, who had been recruited mainly from the returning ex-Servicemen.

Apart from the regular smuggled goods, such as cigarettes, cigars, tobacco and spirits, anything that was in short supply or rationed was profitable to the smuggler, including tinned foodstuffs, butter, cosmetics, razor blades, records, fountain pens, lighters and saccharin—the list was almost endless. The item which appeared to be favourite, and whose smuggling became a post-war phenomenon, was nylon stockings. The fibre had not been introduced until 1939, and nylons were virtually unobtainable in this country. They cost around 7s. to 8s. in America, and could be sold in this country for £1 to 25s. a pair. Virtually every vessel that came from America carried large amounts of smuggled nylons. It was reported that a firm in New York supplied large quantities to British crews on credit terms. Many seizures were also discovered in the parcel post, hidden in all manner of goods. One famous seizure was in tins described as 'Matzas for the Passover'. Although the supply position in this country had eased somewhat by the 1950s, large quantities of nylons were still being smuggled and seized, and the trade did not disappear until the end of clothes rationing.

The so-called luxury goods, which carried a high rate of duty and purchase tax, were obvious favourites with the smugglers. Goods such as cameras, jewellery and last but not least watches were the most frequently smuggled goods. Before the war over eight million watches had been imported annually into the country; during the war virtually none had been imported, and in the immediate post-war years import and currency restrictions curtailed the number of imports to two million. Thus with the duty at $33\frac{1}{3}$ per cent and a high purchase tax (in the case of gold watches 100 per cent), they were obviously a very profitable commodity. The Continental centres for watches were Antwerp and Brussels, where there was an industry to supply special cheap watches for the smuggling trade. A great variety of devices were used for smuggling, including hollowed-out books, false heels, false-bottomed suitcases and specially made body belts. The most serious problem for the department was the commercial smuggling trade. One of the normal methods of concealment was to use cars with the watches hidden in the upholstery or in hollow parts of the chassis, and often cars were discovered with specially constructed compartments. In 1950 at Dover over 7,740 watches, valued at over £20,000, were found in such a compartment. In the same year over sixty thousand watches were seized.

Perhaps the most famous smuggling case of the post-war years was the ultimate capture of the smuggling craft *Dawn Approach*. The escapades of this ex-naval motor torpedo-boat were used by the late Nicholas Monsarrat in a novel called *The Ship that Died of Shame*. The *Dawn Approach* was used on twenty-three successful runs on various parts of the coast, and the frequency of its journeys interested the then newly formed Investigation Branch. The craft was watched by an Investigation officer at Cherbourg, where it loaded watches and made for Beaumaris in North Wales. The discharge of the watches at Beaumaris into a car was observed, and the car followed to London in the hope of discovering the organization of the gang. However, the officers were forced to intercept the car on the outskirts of London, and the thirteen thousand watches were seized. The vessel was also seized, and the hiding-place for the watches—a hollow bulkhead—was discovered.

Faced with a marked increase in smuggling, the department considered that the coast defences should be strengthened. They decided that the best method was to revive the cutter service. Already in 1946 the *Vigilant* had been replaced, when a former naval minesweeper was purchased at a bargain price and converted to revenue purposes. Two years later two further vessels were purchased from the Admiralty, both harbour defence launches, which were ideal for revenue work. They were named the *Valiant* and *Vincent*. The three vessels gave admirable service throughout the fifties; although their number of seizures were not large, they provided an excellent preventive control around the coasts, which was their main function.

Because of the numbers of ex-naval men in the Waterguard service—well-qualified and experienced in handling small vessels—volunteers were called for from the Waterguard to command and crew these vessels. The manning of the Customs vessels from within the service set a precedent, and from that time all members of the cutter service have been recruited from serving personnel. Nowadays the selected officers receive training at the RAF Marine Training School.

The Customs cutter service was increased in 1962, when a fourth vessel was acquired and named the *Venturous*. This vessel was specially built for the department, and was the first cutter for over a hundred years to be constructed to the department's design. A new *Vigilant*, the tenth in the line, was introduced in 1965, followed by a replacement for the *Valiant* in 1968. The cutter service has grown rapidly in the last five years. New patrol vessels built by Fairey Marine have been introduced to reinforce the existing preventive measures being taken against smuggling, and to further assist in the exclusion of rabies, a vital necessity which has received much coverage of late. These vessels—*Gazelle, Swift, Active, Alert, Challenge, Champion* and *Safeguard*—are all named after Customs vessels which operated in the heyday of smuggling. The only departure from this practice was the naming of a new fast patrol vessel, built by Brooke Marine Ltd, which was launched in February 1979 and called *Searcher*, thus reviving the name of an ancient Customs post which dated back to the very early days of the department.

Highly organized commercial smuggling of jewellery, expensive watches, cigars and spirits is still a serious revenue problem. The greatly enlarged Investigation Division has a special commercial smuggling team to meet this challenge. The rapid development of direct road container services from

Europe has greatly increased the smuggling risk, for in some instances false bulkheads have been found in these containers, designed to conceal a large quantity of goods. A further complication has arisen from the country's accession to the EEC; the fraud potential in all aspects of the Common Agricultural Policy is large, because of the vast differences in the complicated structure of levy rates. There have been recent cases of foodstuffs—notably butter—being smuggled both in and out of the country to avoid levy payments. A recent report suggested that there was a large-scale smuggling of pigs across the Irish border to cash in on the different rates of farm subsidies in operation in member countries. Also a recent imposition by Eire of a sales tax of 2 per cent on farm animals has been responsible for an increase in cattle-smuggling across the Border.

The various import licensing controls also create scope for frauds. In 1973, after a long and painstaking investigation by the Licensing team of the Investigation Division, a large-scale fraud in men's suits was uncovered. The suits were manufactured in Romania and routed through Vienna, where false invoices and documents were made out, declaring them to be of Austrian origin, and thus falsely claiming EFTA rates of duty. The evasion of duty in this instance was over £150,000. The sanctions against Rhodesia led to several investigations into attempts to break the embargo on both the import and export of goods. The import of gold coins, notably Krugerrands, has caused the department concern.

Since 1947 the Customs and Excise has been responsible for the control of the export of currency. In recent years the decline in the sterling rate of exchange has given a great incentive to the smuggling of money out of the country for the purpose of the purchase of foreign properties or deposit in foreign bank accounts. In 1977 over £1½ million was confiscated, largely as a result of the selective checks on passengers. However, the department, working in close liaison with the Treasury, has investigated large-scale and complicated frauds. In January 1975 a number of persons were convicted of illegally transferring large sums of money from the United Kingdom to Italy. This investigation, which disclosed a very involved system of fraud connected with antiques, jewellery and works of art, became known as the Italian Connection. Ultimately fines in excess of £200,000 were imposed on the guilty persons.

These diverse and challenging aspects of modern smuggling are a far cry from the simple and straightforward smuggling of tobacco and spirits of yesteryear. The more sophisticated methods of smuggling and the intricate evasions of import restrictions by the use of false documents, combined with betting duty, the duties on hydrocarbon oils and VAT frauds, have imposed considerable demands on the Investigation Division. It is not surprising to find that in recent years the division has expanded greatly in an attempt to control the situation.

The greatest expansion has been in its investigation and control of drugs. The division has established small but highly specialized teams for the three main drugs—heroin, cocaine and cannabis. These teams work very closely with the Scotland Yard drugs squads, Interpol and other international agencies. Many of them visit and work on investigations in foreign countries, for the control of drug-smuggling depends on close international co-operation. In 1978 separate mobile task forces were set up in a number of centres around the country, to operate in close co-operation with the main specialized teams and the police. At the end of the year the department set up a force of drug-detection dogs, after experimenting with police dogs and RAF Police dogs. The dog-handlers were recruited from within the department and include the first female drug dog-handlers in the world. The dogs and their handlers were trained at the RAF Police School, and are based at Dover, Liverpool and Bristol.

Hardly a week passes nowadays without some newspaper report of a seizure of drugs by the department. At the end of 1978 over £22¼ millions in street values of drugs were seized, which was about double the quantity seized in the previous year. Such a large increase in seized drugs inevitably poses the question as to whether the department's control is becoming more efficient and effective, or whether there is a vast increase in smuggling. The answer appeared to be a combination of the two. Certainly the new improved detection methods have resulted in a greater number of seizures, yet it does seem obvious that London has become the international transit centre for drugs, especially for heroin destined for use in the United States. Previously Holland, and especially Amsterdam, had been used as the European centre of operations, but due to increased vigilance of the Dutch authorities the operations were moved to London.

Heroin accounted for over a half of the 1978 drug-seizures; the centres of distribution are in the Far East, with Bangkok, Singapore and Hong Kong as the most likely sources. The majority of heroin is smuggled into this country by couriers, students, young women and 'straight' businessmen being used. Some of the methods of concealment were specially constructed briefcases, body belts, cigarette cartons and tins of talcum powder. Two 'pregnant' women were stopped at London Airport and were found to be carrying heroin valued at £2 millions. In November 1978 an important American gang was broken up by the arrest of three American women couriers, who was paid 5,000 dollars to make the trip from Bangkok to London. A month earlier 32 kilos of Chinese heroin, worth over £6 millions, were found in the tyres of cars from Malaya.

Eight million pounds' worth of cannabis were seized in 1978, and two incidents received very wide publicity. In September the seizure of cannabis valued at nearly £¼ million was the culmination of a major investigation into a drug-smuggling ring which operated in the West Indies and Luxembourg. The drugs were seized from a Piper Aztec aircraft at a small private airfield near Scunthorpe, in Lincolnshire. The aircraft was prevented from taking-off again by one of the Customs officers leaping on to the wing.

Another long investigation culminated in a seizure of 196 kilos of cannabis worth about £300,000, in circumstances very reminscent of the old-time smuggling. The prosecuting counsel summed up the case as 'a highly sophisticated and skilful drug-smuggling operation, involving detailed planning, substantial finance and ingenuity. It also involved the use of ship-to-shore radio, a chartered yacht, inflatable boats, and skill only matched by the Customs and Excise.' The gang had previously used a minibus to bring drugs from Morocco, but some recent successes by the Spanish Customs had decided them to change to a chartered yacht. The vessel was called the *Cornish Lady*, and was used to bring drugs to England. However, the various members of the gang were kept under close surveillance by the Investigation officers, and when the *Cornish Lady* appeared off Exmouth it was closely shadowed by the revenue cutter *Alert*, and its progress up the river Exe radioed to the waiting officers. The officers watched while seven sacks of cannabis were off-loaded into a dinghy and placed on board another vessel. When the transfer was completed the officers boarded the vessel to seize the drugs, while officers from the *Alert* intercepted the *Cornish Lady*. The four men involved each pleaded guilty and were sentenced to seven years imprisonment.

This exploit—so redolent of the smuggling runs of two hundred years ago—clearly shows that despite the vast changes in international trade and tariffs the smugglers themselves do not greatly change. From the owlers of the early days through the gangs of the eighteenth and nineteenth centuries to the drug-smugglers of today, the common factor is the enormous profit to be made from smuggling. Today this is to be found chiefly in the illegal importation of drugs, and with this incentive there are enough desperate and cunning people to risk all. It is unlikely that smuggling will ever be eradicated; each new age brings its own distinct problems for the department. The best one can hope is that the measures devoted to the prevention of smuggling are sufficiently adequate and successful to make the trade of smuggling a much more risky and far less favourable enterprise.

CHAPTER TEN

The Age of Tariffs

The Civil Service, along with the rest of the population of the country, was hoping that Lloyd George's brave promise of 'a new and better country for the returning heroes' would bring some extensive improvements in the conditions prevailing in the service. They had worked long hours with little recompense, and coped with an increasingly large burden of work with little demur. Although virtually all the special wartime departments disappeared, the number of civil servants in 1919 was double that at the start of the war. The immediate post-war years saw considerable changes in both the conditions and the organization of the Civil Service generally, which set the pattern for the next fifty years. The most far-reaching of these was the establishment of three basic classes: administration, executive and clerical.

Perhaps the most important achievement to come out of these times was the foundation of the Whitley Council. For the first time in Civil Service history, official negotiating machinery was set up whereby conditions of service, salary and other grievances could be discussed between management and staff. The Council was named after Mr J. H. Whitley M.P., who was chairman of a committee which had proposed the establishment of such councils to deal with the unrest in various large industries. The Treasury were loath to accept that such bodies could play a useful part in the Civil Service, or whether in fact they had any place at all in the Service. However, they finally relented and agreed to their introduction, and the first National Whitley Council met in July 1919.

Most members of the Customs and Excise felt that their own special grievances could be resolved only by a complete reorganization of the department. The various staff associations in the service had quickly appreciated the advantages of the new Whitley Committees to achieve these aims, and lost little time in promoting 'Whitleyism' within the department, whose first Departmental Whitley Council met on 23 December 1919. At this first meeting constitutions were approved for grade, sectional and local committees, so that within six months of acceptance of the principle of Whitleyism in the Civil Service the department had a comprehensive system of negotiation from local right up to Board level.

The various section and grade committees were deeply involved in the comprehensive reorganization of 1920. This was a milestone in staff relations; for the first time the staff had an appreciable influence in the final outcome of the organization. The scheme was approved in March 1921. The main features as far as the outdoor service was concerned were the transfer of old-age pension work, at least in the large cities, to a new permanent grade of woman pension officer and the removal of much of the clerical work undertaken by the surveyors and the officers to a new grade, to be called departmental clerical officers. There was a general appraisal of work undertaken at each grade, from the chief inspector right down to the officer, and many of the duties were devolved and reallocated. There were changes in the Waterguard: the grade of preventive man was abolished, to be replaced with a new basic grade of assistant preventive officer. The headquarters staff were aligned to the general classes in the rest of the Civil Service—administrative, executive and clerical.

In common with the rest of the Civil Service, entry into the service was opened to men who were over the normal recruitment age, but who had served in the war. These entrants qualified in what were known as reconstruction examinations. Similar types of examination were also introduced after the Second World War. Many of the conditions of service were improved, the hours of work were reduced from forty-eight to forty-four, new leave scales were approved and special rates of disturbance allowances were agreed. The success of the reorganization was such that virtually all the contentious issues which had been present since 1909 were finally settled. It can be said that the amalgamation of the Customs and Excise had taken almost twelve years, but the new-look department remained virtually unchanged for the next fifty years.

One of the seemingly insoluble problems facing the reorganization committee in the Excise was arriving at some figure for determining the normal workload of an Excise station. Excise officers were not on time attendance basis, with overtime payments for extra work, as was the case in the Customs. As new duties were imposed on the Excise, or new firms moved into the area, the only solution to overworked or 'heavy' stations was to transfer blocks of work from one station to another, or by a general rearrangement of stations boundaries. This system was very inflexible, time-wasting and generally grossly inefficient.

In 1921, as part of the reorganization scheme, a new system for the measurement of Excise work was introduced. This new method was based on 'units'. A year was calculated as containing 1980 working hours (this figure allowed for deductions in respect of Sundays, public holidays and Saturday half-days). There were two types of units devised. The first, called Schedule I, were set-time allowances, which had been agreed with the staff, for a wide variety of regular Excise work. For example, a brewery visit or survey was allotted ⅓ of an hour to 1½ hours, depending on the size of the brewery; or 18 hours per year might be allowed for every hundred old-age pensioners in the area.

The second type of units were called Schedule II, and were used for non-recurring work. Here the time allowance claimed had to be agreed locally with the surveyor and collector. Even travelling within the area was calculated on a time basis—three miles per hour for walking, and double for public transport. In theory the unit system enabled the workload of an Excise station to be calculated to a very fine degree, and any new work introduced into the area could be accurately measured. Any units over the normal 1980 hours were eligible for payment of an Excess Unit Allowance quarterly, the Excise officer's equivalent to overtime.

The system worked fairly well in theory and with experience worked well in practice. In a very short time most officers became adept in the calculation of their units, and expertise in this field became as highly related as any of their more normal duties. The unit system gave for the very first time a reasonable assessment of the annual work of an Excise station, and was a feature of Excise life for the next fifty years, only disappearing (to the regret of many) in the reorganization of the 1970s.

One of the most urgent and pressing problems to be solved after the war was the settlement of a permanent salary scale. During the war salaries and wages had been adjusted by a system of war bonuses, which were temporary additions to the various salary scales. In 1920 a general wage agreement was reached for the whole of the Civil Service; in future all salaries would be paid in two parts. The first, that of the basic scale, would be settled in respect of the assessment of the salary at 1914, and in the terms of 1914 money values. These scales could only be increased on evidence of new and extra responsibilities. The second part of the salary was to be a cost of living bonus, which would be adjusted according to the change in the purchasing power of money since 1914.

The cost of living bonus was based on a Ministry of Labour system which had been arrived at by investigations made as long ago as 1904. The scheme had taken the 'average expenditure of a normal working-class family' as its basis, and included a very high figure for food (60 per cent) and a very low figure for rent (16 per cent). Throughout its operation the system was roundly criticized by all the staff associations on the grounds that it was not only grossly out of date but that its make-up had little bearing on the 'expenditure of middle-class Civil Servants'.

During the ten years from 1921 to 1931 when it was in operation, there was an average reduction in salaries by about 35 per cent. During the economic crisis of 1931 salaries were reduced by 10 per cent. However, in that year a Royal Commission recommended a return to a consolidated salary scale, and in 1933, a new salary scale was agreed within the department, and the cost of living bonus was abolished.

Louis Blériot and his monoplane, 1909 (p. 135)   *HMSO*

A view of Croydon Airport, *c.* 1930 (p. 167)   *HMSO*

The clearway system at London Airport (p. 178)   *HMSO*

Above right: a unique view of VAT Headquarters, Southend (p. 133)   *Evening Echo*

Below right: another VAT problem?   *Punch Publications Ltd*

"*I have here, God help me, a warrant to search these premises.*"

Left and above: cannabis seized from an
Aztec aircraft, September 1979 *HMSO*

Below: Part of the largest seizure of
heroin ever made in this country
(1980) *HMSO*

In July 1921, in the general reorganization, the Board themselves offered their own economies; they recommended to the Treasury that of the four Commissioners only the Chairman and the Deputy should remain. The other two posts should go to the Director of Establishments and the Secretary of the Board. These two ex-officio Commissioners would retain their original salary but received no extra recompense for their seat on the Board. This step achieved a saving of £3,000 per year. For almost forty years, except for a short time when two Deputies were appointed, the department was controlled by only Chairman and Deputy Chairman.

The development of flying during the later stages of the war opened up great possibilities for the commercial exploitation of this new mode of transport. The first scheduled commercial flight from this country took place in 1919 and already the department was involved in an International Conference on Air Navigation, which attempted to devise international regulations for the control of aircraft. As a result of this Conference an Act was passed in 1920, setting out the conditions for foreign aircraft flights. The regulations bear a very close resemblance to the international rules for vessels. The aircraft (or aeroplanes, as they were called) were only allowed to land or take off from Customs-approved aerodromes. The details of journey, cargo, crew and passengers were required to be reported to the Customs within twenty-four hours of landing. Only four such aerodromes were approved—New Holland in Lincolnshire, Hadleigh in Suffolk, Lymne in Kent and Hounslow Heath. The latter was the London aerodrome, and was sited slightly east of the present London Airport.

During the 1920s, as commercial flights became more commonplace and more frequent, Hounslow Heath had been replaced by Croydon as the international aerodrome for London. In May 1928 a new control tower and large terminal buildings were opened, and Croydon became the first specially built Customs aerodrome. By the thirties it had become a very busy aerodrome, with most of the main airlines having regular scheduled flights. The main user was the famous Imperial Airways. By 1936 there were over 7,000 flights per year. The Customs officers who controlled both Croydon and Heston, the second London aerodrome, were based in London Port, and were sent to the aerodromes on monthly spells of duty. Besides Heston, where Neville Chamberlain's plane landed after Munich, other aerodromes were approved around the country, although Cardington in Bedfordshire was approved for airships only.

By the end of the Second World War there were only twelve authorized airfields but over five hundred usable airfields, not including the military ones. Commercial pressure was applied not only to increase the number of approved airfields, but also to provide an airport for London, one that was capable of being developed and extended as needed. The site chosen had originally been a grass airfield, belonging to Richard Fairey the aircraft-manufacturer, and the first recorded flight there had taken place during 1929. In the war the airfield had been used by RAF Transport Command.

The new London Airport was opened for scheduled flights in May 1946, and in the early days both the Customs and the passengers were accommodated in tents until huts could be erected. The first terminal buildings were not erected until 1955.

As with Croydon previously, the new London Airport was placed under the control of the Collector, London Port, but by January 1951 the traffic had so increased that the airport was made a collection in its own right. Until the change in the control of passengers' baggage the airport had a voracious appetite for Waterguard staff. Most officers were either employed for spells of detached duty in the busy summer months, or on gaining promotion to preventive officer invariably found themselves at the airport. The collection now employs the greatest number of Customs staff, and the airport is the busiest international airport in the world.

Most cities have their own Customs-approved airports, which in addition to the other 'international' airports such as Gatwick, Prestwick and Manchester and the phenomenal growth of holiday charter flights at airports like Luton and Stansted, has vastly increased this aspect of Customs work. In 1978–9 there were 345,000 aircraft arrivals, well over double the number of vessels reported. It is a very far cry from the single flight in 1909—quite a growth in less than seventy years!

A most important landmark occurred in 1919 in the history of tariffs in this country. For the first time a lower rate of duty was introduced for goods imported from the Empire. For a number of years various politicians had advocated some relief for goods originating from the Empire—indeed, for many years several countries of the Empire had operated a scheme whereby British goods were admitted at reduced rates of duty. The Act provided for a general reduction on all goods by one-sixth of the full duty, and on the McKenna duties by one-third. The intention of the Imperial Preference, as the reductions became termed, was to encourage trade from the Empire. Most of the goods then liable for duty were the old revenue goods such as tea, sugar, tobacco, spirits and raisins, most of which already had a large share of the British markets. As a result of the introduction of the new preference rates there was a large loss of revenue, which was not compensated for by any appreciable increase in the amount of imports from the Empire. It was only when higher rates of duty were introduced under a protective tariff that the Empire goods benefited, and took a large share of the British market.

With the introduction of special rates of duty for Empire goods the principle of a protective tariff had been established, and was thus extended to other goods. The intention of the new rates of duty can be clearly seen in the name of the Act—The Safeguarding of Industries Act. Certain large industries, such as chemicals and optical and scientific glassware, were considered so essential to the economy that they required some form of protection from imported goods. This protection was afforded by high rates of import duty; in the case of the Safeguarding of Industries Act the duty imposed was 33⅓ per cent. The industries that were so protected became known as key industries, and as this policy was developed over the succeeding years the special tariffs imposed were known as Key Industry Duty, or K.I.D. for short. K.I.D was a feature of the British tariff for the next fifty years, until our entry into the European Economic Community.

The Act had made provision for any specific industry to apply to the Board of Trade for import protection if it believed that it was suffering from unfair foreign competition in the British market. A special Import Committee was established to consider the merits of each case and report as to whether the imposition of a special duty was considered necessary. If a duty was deemed expedient it would be introduced into a Finance Act, and would normally be imposed for a set period of years. During the twenties such diverse goods as lace, cutlery, gloves, buttons and kitchenware were protected in this way. A similar type of duty exists today, under the general name of anti-dumping, which protects goods produced in this country from unfair competition from the import of cheap or highly subsidized foreign imports.

The Acts not only set precedents for the general introduction of a protective element in the British tariff, but they gave the department valuable experience in all the resultant problems of *ad valorem* duties. The establishment of the proper basis of value proved to be the most difficult, as did the evidence of Empire origin for Preference goods. This experience proved invaluable for the future, when a more general protective tariff was introduced.

The Irish Free State was established as a Dominion on 6 December 1921. However, under an arrangement with the provisional government the Customs and Excise duties remained unchanged, and continued to be assessed, levied and collected as previously. This interim arrangement came to an end in December 1922, when the Free State Government assumed direct control of the Customs and Excise in the country. The actual duties remained uniform until March 1923, during which time the department co-operated with the Revenue Commissioners in Dublin on matters of organization and administration. Staff were loaned from Headquarters to assist in the establishment of the revenue service in the Free State. Officers already working in Ireland were given the option of transferring to the Free State service.

As from 1 April 1923, trade with the Free State became foreign trade, and the department was faced with the establishment of a Customs land frontier. The main features of the land boundary control once again resembled the old and well-proven system of Customs control. There was a series of approved roads, the only authorized routes for both passengers and goods, which channelled all movements to a number of Customs stations, for the clearance of goods and passengers. Movements across the border by the unapproved roads were illegal, and to prevent smuggling a large number of boundary posts were set up.

The physical problems of control were considerable; the border was over 250 miles in length and much of it, certainly in the west, was wild and difficult country. The control problems were further aggravated by the prolonged dispute as to the actual line of the border, a dispute which continued for almost ten years. The number of approved routes were relatively few in number in proportion to the vast number of small country roads which crossed the boundary. The boundary posts were manned by a new grade of staff called land boundary men, but the actual patrol of the border to prevent smuggling was the responsibility of the mobile forces of the Royal Ulster Constabulary. It was not until January 1952 that the Waterguard took over the patrol of the boundary from the Ulster police.

In 1932, when the Fianna Fáil party came to power in the Free State, with Éamon De Valéra as Minister for External Affairs, steps were taken to make the Free State completely separate from Great Britain. The relations between the two countries worsened, and finally led to an outright trade and tariff war. In 1932 a duty of 20 per cent was placed on all dairy products and meat imported from the Free State, and this duty was later increased to 40 per cent. A year later a specific duty was introduced on live cattle imported from the Free State. The rate of duty was varied according to the age of the animal, which caused no end of problems for the examining officers in determining this. Within a short time of the duty being imposed the officers working on the boundary became known as cowboys, and very lurid tales appeared in the staff journals about life on the 'Wild West border'.

Some of the guidance given to the officers for determining the age of the animals now seems amusing: 'Apart from the general appearance of the animal (size, shape and girth), the state of the teeth furnishes useful evidence for estimating the animal's age.' There follows a long list of the number of molars and incisors each animal should have, depending upon their age. The smuggling of cattle to evade this duty was rife, and almost impossible to combat. It is clear from local papers and official reports just what problems this duty caused, and there is no doubt that the department greeted the ending of the Act in 1938 as a blessed relief.

Entertainments duty, the 'temporary expedient in times of war', had developed into the most contentious and troublesome duty that the department had dealt with for many a long year. Despite Parliament after Parliament vigorously attacking the duty and calling for its repeal, and several Chancellors openly expressing their dislike of the duty, it remained like 'an ancient monument', as one Member put it, and was fast becoming a permanent feature of the revenue. Throughout its history sundry attempts were made to ease the burden on various types of entertainment, and at one stage there were thirteen classes of exemptions.

The continual arguments and debates centred around the interpretation of the terms 'wholly educational, charitable and philanthropic'—each qualifying an entertainment for exemption from duty. During the course of the existence of the duty almost every type of entertainment was considered eligible for an exemption, and protracted discussions were held on the merits of each case. They ranged from auctions, agricultural shows, the Boat Race, Burns Night dinners, choir festivals, cricket matches, historical pageants, flower shows, the National Eisteddfod, the Lord Mayor's Show, and Royal processions to village concerts and Shakespearean productions. Compared with the liability problems, the actual Excise control was relatively simple. The majority of duty was collected by weekly returns; for the smaller or less regular shows there was a system of Excise Revenue stamps. The duty reached a height in 1945–8, when over £50 millions were collected annually. This increase was largely due to the expansion of sport after the war and the high attendances at the cinemas. The duty slowly decreased as further exemptions were applied, and by 1957 it was levied only on cinemas and television. Largely as a result of the closure of many smaller cinemas, increasing pressure was applied for its repeal. In April 1960 the Chancellor announced 'The continuation of the duty is no longer justified.' By its nature entertainments duty has left a fascinating selection of archive material relating to the social life of the period.

The brief, ill-fated and very unsuccessful betting duty introduced by Winston Churchill in 1926 deserves a place in the history of the department. Sir James Crombie, Chairman of the Board from 1955 to 1963, suggested that its name was inscribed on its collective heart! Certainly Excise officers who were involved with the duty never forgot what an ill-conceived, ill-managed and, in terms of revenue, wasteful exercise it was.

The idea of a betting duty dated back to the 1870s, but it was then shelved because of the problems of collection; in those days all off-course betting was illegal. In 1925, when the duty was once again considered, the department advised that the only effective control would require all off-course cash betting to be legalized in licensed betting shops. This suggestion was approved by the Home Office, but was bitterly opposed by the combined forces of the Church, the Jockey Club and the large credit bookmakers. Public opposition to betting shops was so strong that this suggestion was not pursued, but undeterred, Churchill settled for a duty on legal betting only.

The new duty imposed a levy of $3\frac{1}{3}$ per cent on all bets made on off-course credit betting, and a lower rate of 2 per cent on betting at the racecourses. Bookmakers were required to pay a licence fee of £10, and an additional £10 apiece for all other premises. The duty was collected by weekly returns or by the issue of revenue tickets issued directly on making a bet. A special betting duty branch was set up in the Custom House in London, and was controlled by Mr Adams, a retired Chief Constable. He had a staff of about sixteen ex-policemen, whose duties were to visit the racecourses to control the duty. The visits made to the credit bookmakers were undertaken by the Excise officers. The administration of the duty was never easy; problems arose over bad debts, the liability of various accumulated bets and the basic difficulty of checking bets which were made by telephone.

Despite it being a time of depression in the country, betting flourished, although most of it was illegal and thus escaped the duty. Most of the betting took place at street corners and in the factories and in the public houses, and to prevent it was an impossible task. The whole operation of the duty suffered from some rather odd legal decisions which made the whole system unworkable. In one case the betting by 'totalizators'—then a relative innovation—was not considered 'betting with bookmakers', and was therefore ruled exempt from the duty. There appeared to be no alternative but to repeal the duty, and this was duly done in 1929.

In the same year two old Excise duties also were repealed. The duty on tea, which had been continually taxed since its introduction into the country nearly three centuries ago, and then stood at 4*d.* per pound, was abolished. The other duty to disappear was railway passenger duty, which had only been reintroduced in 1922 with the emergence of the four main railway companies from government control. As *The Times* recorded, 'The abolition of this duty is thoroughly sound, for generations this tax has been an absurd anachronism—a survival of the days of the old stage-coaches.'

Winston Churchill was instrumental in introducing yet another new duty, but this one was destined to survive. The old duty on petrol which had been introduced in 1909 had been repealed in 1921. It had been abolished largely because there was no exact legal definition of motor spirit, which had caused considerable problems, and furthermore the number of exemptions and rebates had made the administration of the duty particularly difficult and complicated. The rapid expansion of motor transport had made it a new and rich source of revenue, if only some precise and accurate system of control could be devised. Churchill set up a special committee to establish a precise and legal specification of light oil used for dutiable purposes. In his inimitable style he co-opted on to the committee representatives of the oil companies, the foremost experts in motor engineering and members of the department. This 'specification' committee was unique; it was the first time that non-departmental persons had been involved with the planning of any new duty.

The committee reported in March 1928, and in April Winston Churchill introduced the duty on light hydrocarbon oils. The committee's definition of light oils appeared in the Act, and so exact and precise was it that it has largely remained unaltered over the years. The second lesson learned from the earlier duty was to avoid the extensive and complex system of exemptions. Churchill made the following comment on the new duty: 'So far as this duty is concerned we are like people in a diving bell; we cannot afford to open a single chink, otherwise the water will rush in and we shall all be drowned.' The new duty was broadly based, being charged on all light oils, irrespective of their use. It was charged after the refining process, and thus required all oil refineries and installations to be bonded. Heavy oils on delivery to industry were granted a full rebate of the duty.

During the thirties, in order to protect the coal industry, heavy oils were charged with a nominal 1*d.* per gallon duty. The most significant change was the development of the diesel engine. The diesel vehicles proved to be more economical to run than the petrol-engined kinds, and furthermore used oil at the lower rate of duty. Their popularity posed a danger to the oil revenue. In 1935, therefore, heavy oils used for road vehicles became liable at the basic rate, then 8*d.* per gallon; this fuel became known as DERV (Diesel Engine Road Vehicles).

After the Second World War the duty on road fuels doubled, and by 1960 it was a very important part of the Customs and Excise revenue. A new system of control of DERV was introduced in 1962. Heavy oils not intended for use as road fuel were designated by means of chemical markers and a colouring substance. A system of mobile testing units (RFTUs) was introduced to sample vehicles and test them at random for the presence of the marked oils. This deterrent method of control proved to be a great success. With the growth of the petrochemical industry and its extensive use of oils, new methods of exemptions and duty-free uses have been introduced. The duties from hydrocarbon oils amount to one-fifth of the total revenue of the department, second only to value-added tax.

The Import Duties Act of 1932 is considered by many to mark the date when overnight the country changed from free trade to protection. It is more accurate to think of the Act as a natural consequence of the policies followed in the 1920s, with the reintroduction of the McKenna duties in 1925, and the extensions of the key industries duties. The 1932 Act owes more to the financial problems of the country at that time than to a positive shift in economic policy. The flow of imports, and the flow of currency out to pay for them, had to be restricted, and the answer was thought to lie with the imposition of a General Customs duty on all goods.

The Act placed a 10 per cent duty on all goods, other than a small number in the 'free list' and goods already chargeable with duty. An 'Import Duties Advisory Committee' was set up to advise the Treasury on extra duties to be imposed, over and above the general 10 per cent. At an Imperial Conference held in Ottawa in August agreements were signed with the major Empire countries, granting them exemption from the new duties and generally reaffirming the broad principles of Imperial Preference.

The Import Duties Act made a vast change in the department, for an extra 1,300 staff were required. Some of these came from other government departments, but the majority were recruited by direct open examination. From 1932 onward, as further import duties were imposed, the size of the department steadily grew. By 1937 there were over 15,000 employed, compared with 11,000 at the end of the First World War. The new import duties brought fresh administrative problems; the assessment of value caused the greatest concern, for the old assessments could not survive the increasing complexity of world trade. For this reason a valuation branch was established to administer the involved valuation problems.

The demands on the Customs officers involved in the introduction of the new duties had been so great that in 1934 an Industrial Court had suggested that the Commissioners might consider the payment of some form of gratuity to these officers. The Board decided that instead of issuing a blanket allowance, they required individual officers to submit and justify a claim for the gratuity. In actual fact, very few claims were received and even fewer approved, and the average allowance granted only came to 3 per cent of their annual salary.

During the pre-war years the general tariff was used as a trade bargaining weapon. In the five years leading up to the war eighteen trade agreements were signed with different countries, each involving different rates of duty and complicated quota agreements. The control of these quota certificates became incorporated in the general management of the Customs duties. After the war the quota system was replaced by import and export licences, which although issued by the Board of Trade, were administered by the department.

By the early 1950s the many and varied Acts relating to import duties that had been passed since 1915, with their different and complex provisions, were in sad need of consolidation. Already in 1952 the more general Acts and provisions relating to the other work of the department had been consolidated into the Customs and Excise Act 1952. (This Act, incidentally, was one of the first to receive the Royal Assent by the new Queen.) The new consolidated Import Duties Act was introduced in 1958, and authorized the change of the British tariff to the principles of a new international tariff, called the Brussels Nomenclature and based on a uniform classification of goods. The handy pocket-sized British tariff thus disappeared as the new large tariff came into use in January 1959.

One of the most disturbing events of the 1930s was the discovery of a large brewery fraud in Edinburgh. The greatest matter of concern for the department was that the fraud had gone undetected for almost eight years. Grave misgivings were expressed over the efficacy of the system of Excise brewery control, which had been in operation since 1880. As a result of the full departmental inquiry changes were made in the surveying procedure, and increased checks were made on breweries. In future all the official books relating to breweries were required to be closely scrutinized every month by the collectors, to ensure that the close physical controls were being maintained. The profound effect the fraud had on the Excise generally, from the chief inspector right down to the newest recruit, lasted for a long time. Like the ill-fated betting duty, the Edinburgh Brewery Fraud became a legend in the department.

With the outbreak of the Second World War the department was entrusted with similar duties to those it had carried out in the previous war, although two new areas of work were introduced. The first was concerned with the administration of compensation for war damage. Excise officers controlled all the claims and investigated those submitted for immediate relief on the grounds of undue hardship. When the scheme for rationing clothes and footwear was introduced in June 1941 the officers were involved in the supply of supplementary coupons to those people who had suffered loss of clothing as a result of bombing. During the seven years that this scheme was in operation they dealt with over 2½ million claims, and issued some 144 million coupons.

The history of currency control dates from the early days of the war. In March 1940 the department undertook the control of currency transfers outside the sterling area. The work involved investigations into financial transactions for the purchase of imports from America, Sweden and Switzerland; on average over 2,000 applications were received weekly, and over 30,000 firms were recorded on a special index. After the war the currency control was formalized under the Exchange Control Act of 1947, and the duties became a part of the examination of passengers.

There was a positive change in policy from the days of the First World War as regards enlistment. The work of the department was not considered war work, and as such all staff between the ages of twenty-one and sixty-five were required to register. In total over 2,900 Customs and Excise staff served in the Forces, out of a total complement of 15,000 as at 1939. During the progress of the war the numbers of staff employed fell dramatically, and by 1944 there were less than 10,000 employed. The shortfall was made up by the re-employment of retired officers, an extension of the retirement age, and once again by a large influx of temporary women clerks. The hours of work were extended and annual leave was curtailed, although if officers volunteered for harvesting work at the special agricultural camps they were allowed an extra week of leave.

Various Custom Houses around the ports suffered from bombing, those in Liverpool and Plymouth both being severely damaged. However, the London Custom House was the first to suffer; during the night of Sunday 29 December 1940 the east wing was badly damaged by bombing. The Board Room was completely destroyed, as were many of the Commissioners' rooms. The staff on duty guarding the building were praised for their efforts to control the fire, and to save precious records from the near-by Ocean House. They 'displayed the vigour and courage that was expected of them, in circumstances of great personal danger and distress'. One member of the staff was killed and two injured in the raid.

The Board were forced to find alternative accommodation for themselves and for most of the headquarters staff. In Feburary 1941 they moved into City Gate House, Finsbury Square, and this building remained the headquarters of the department for the next eleven years. It was in 1952 that they transferred their headquarters to a new building in Mark Lane, quite close to the Custom House. The new building was named King's Beam House, after the long associations with the weighing of goods at the King's Beam. The east wing of the Custom House was skilfully restored to blend with the existing building, and was opened by the Queen in June 1966.

The most important new work to arise from the war period was the introduction of purchase tax. The Budget of April 1940 was the first attempt to introduce the new tax. It was proposed to levy a single rate of tax at $33\frac{1}{3}$ per cent on almost the whole range of sales from wholesaler to retailer levels. The proposal was severely criticized, being attacked especially on the grounds that it taxed necessities at the same rate as luxuries. The Bill was withdrawn, and a new purchase-tax scheme was proposed in the second Budget in the autumn. The major change in the Bill was the introduction of a basic rate of $33\frac{1}{3}$ per cent, but with a reduced rate at half the figure. The schedule of goods liable to the new tax clearly showed that the Government had honestly tried to meet many of the criticisms of the earlier Bill. Luxuries were charged at the basic rate, necessities at the lower rate and essential items for families were exempted from the tax.

The new tax came into operation on 21 October 1940, and like most wartime taxes was considered only a temporary expedient. It was levied on the wholesale value of the goods, and it required all manufacturers and wholesalers in taxable goods with a turnover of £2,000 per year to register with the department. In November 1941 this rather high figure was reduced to a more realistic £500. The registered trader was required to charge purchase tax on any sale of taxable goods to any unregistered trader— normally a retailer—and make a return of all purchase tax so charged at the end of each quarter. By March 1942 there were over 45,000 registered traders, and in the first full year of collection the tax exceeded £98½ millions, over 20 per cent above the estimated yield. It was certainly proving a very profitable new tax.

There is an interesting story about the name of purchase tax. The scheme that was drafted by the department was called sales tax, but the Chancellor, Sir John Simon, for some reason did not like the name, and purchase tax was suggested as an alternative. The Chancellor accepted this as an improvement, making the comment that he did not want to stop people selling; what he wanted to do was to stop people buying.

Within a short time of its commencement a higher rate of $66\frac{2}{3}$ per cent was introduced, and by 1943 this rate was increased to 100 per cent. An added complication was brought in during 1942, with an exemption from the tax of 'Utility' clothing, footwear and furniture. These 'utility' goods were made under strict regulations imposed by the Board of Trade, and as such were subject to a very stringent price-control. The 'utility' mark of two three-quarter black circles enclosing the number 41 became famous throughout the war.

To undertake such a massive influx of new work at a time when the resources of the department were already fully stretched by other war work, and by a general shortage of experienced staff, was a formidable task. Much of the less important work was shelved, and visits were reduced to the breweries and similar traders. In March 1941 the Chancellor sent the following message to the department:

> From the reports received, it is evident that the difficult task of introducing this
> novel tax has been well performed. The goodwill of the traders upon which the

tax depends, has been obtained in large measures and the daily administration is proceeding smoothly despite the obstacles of wartime conditions.

The Board added for good measure, 'All members concerned have done a good job and the Board take pleasure in recording it.'

One way in which the control of the tax was made somewhat easier was in the establishment of purchase-tax centres, area offices, which contained staff solely concerned in the control of the tax. The first such centre was established in London, followed by similar ones in Nottingham, Glasgow, Leeds, Bradford and Birmingham. These centres became a feature of the control of the tax, and remained right up to 1973. Other than at these centres, purchase tax became an increasing part of the work of a general Excise station, and as such widened the field of revenue activity into many more industries and trades.

After the war the tax was used by successive governments as the main instrument in the reduction of consumer spending. By 1947 there were four different rates of tax, the highest being 125 per cent! Ten years later there were seven rates, although from this date the number of rates fell. At the demise of the tax in 1973 there were over 70,000 registered traders, and it accounted for almost a quarter of the total revenue collected by the department.

With the ending of the war the size of the department rose dramatically, partly as a result of returning Servicemen, but mainly because of the numerous 'reconstruction' examinations. New pay scales were introduced consolidating the war bonuses, which again had been a feature of the wartime salaries. Slowly the department was moving to peacetime normality. Early in 1946 the formidable task of training the new influx of staff was started, when the department's training centre was reopened. The permanent instructors were all volunteers, and visiting officers came to give lectures on specialist subjects. Separate courses were established for the Outdoor, the Waterguard and Clerical services, and were a blend of theoretical and practical training.

With effect from 1 April 1947, the administration of the old-age pensions was transferred to the Assistance Board, after almost fifty years of Excise control. Thus departed the doughty women pension officers, many of whom, if all the tales are true, could strike terror into the hearts of their colleagues, let alone what they did to the poor pensioners!

In the immediate post-war years the Waterguard was greatly developed. It was the first service to have its salary restructured and its conditions improved. The increase of passengers, at both ports and airports, new currency work and a sharp rise in smuggling brought an increase in the complement of officers. The new appointees from the reconstruction competitions brought a fresh image to the uniformed service. For the next twenty years its star would be in the ascendancy, gaining more and more improvements to its service and, as many felt, to the detriment of the other outdoor service. Since more and more people came into contact with the Waterguard at the ports and airports, to them the Waterguard was the Customs and Excise.

Language allowances were introduced for Waterguard officers serving at certain ports, and a new grade of uniformed staff was introduced—that of women search officers, who came quite some time after the early women searchers of the 1820s. A boost was given to the service in 1949 with the introduction of a new uniform which closely resembled that of a naval officer. The main feature of the uniform was the new cap badges, in the form of the now familiar portcullis.

The formalized portcullis crowned with chains flying was now officially adopted as the department's emblem. The word literally means sliding gate, and symbolizes those who controlled trade at the gateway to the approved ports. It has long connections with the department; many of the old seals bear this heraldic device, as do many of the bindings of the old books of the Customs Board. The device appears now on all publications, notepaper and the new flag, and the name has been used for many of the department's buildings around the country, as well as the department's monthly journal.

Within ten years of the end of the war the number of passengers entering the country had rapidly increased. In 1950 day-trips to the Continent were reintroduced, and their popularity brought extra work for the Waterguard. The majority of passengers arrived and left during the months of June and September, causing a seasonal migration of Waterguard officers to deal with the passengers. By the early 1960s the number of passengers were increasing at an alarming rate, and by 1963 there were $5\frac{1}{2}$ million arriving during the summer months. The department set up a working party to look at the problem of passenger control. As a result of its findings the duty-free allowances were approved, and for the very first time the amounts of the concession were publicized. The layout of baggage halls was changed to a more informal style of smaller benches and desks. Cash registers were introduced to speed up the payment of duty.

These new improvements brought only temporary relief to the problem, and as the annual number of passengers continued to grow alarmingly it was becoming obvious that some radical change of policy was needed in the control of passengers. It was decided that some system of selective examination was required. The various passenger controls in other countries were examined, and the system in operation in Sweden was considered the most appropriate for use in this country. It incorporated a red and green channel, with a self-selection by passengers, and became known as the clearway system. The new system required a change in the law before it could be put into operation, and this was achieved in 1968. The first clearway system was tried in Harwich, and in early 1969 it came to London Airport. It proved to be so successful that it was slowly extended to other ports and airports, and was adapted for the control of accompanied vehicles. At the present time $31\frac{1}{2}$ million passengers arrive from abroad, and of these over 12 million enter between the months of July and September.

In 1951 a committee was appointed to review the organization of the department, and its report was produced two years later. It expressed general satisfaction with the soundness of both the structure and the organization, and had no fundamental criticisms to offer. However, the main grade of the outdoor service, the officers of Customs and Excise, were certainly not happy with their situation. They became involved with the Board in a protracted and at times acrimonious dispute over their various grievances. The grade had a very long salary scale, a promotion system which did not operate until a minimum of fifteen years' service, and they were involved in a considerable amount of clerical work.

The officers considered that they had suffered a decline in their standard of living compared with their pre-war salary. (It is interesting to note here that between 1932 and 1939 their salary had increased by some $20\frac{1}{2}$ per cent, while during the same years the cost of living and prices had fallen by almost 30 per cent.) In fact, those years prior to the war could be said to be the golden years of the grade; the standard of living achieved had never before been bettered, and has never again been repeated. In an attempt to resolve all these problems an independent committee, chaired by Sir Harold Parker, was appointed. Although it gave consideration to splitting the grade into senior and junior officers, and the classification of stations into first and second class, its report finally recommended the retention of the existing structure. It did, however, suggest a greater concentration of stations to enable the delegation of much of the clerical work. Even the pay settlement after the report did little to assuage the officers' complaints, which remained largely unresolved until the massive reorganization of recent years.

Strangely (considering the internecine struggle going on within the department) the officers had even collected a fighting fund and were prepared to do battle with the Board over their grievances. A Select Committee of the House of Commons could report in 1957:

> The Sub-Committee were impressed by the relationship between the traders and the representatives of the department associated with them, and they heard many commendations. They were also impressed by the esprit de corps within the Department, which must be of great value and of which it may be justly proud. Your Committee are satisfied that the high tradition which springs from many years honourable service is being fully maintained.

Such comment shows scant appreciation or understanding of the unrest in the officer grade, which after all was the most numerous of all grades in the department.

The decade from 1960 saw considerable changes in the work of the Customs and Excise. The first computer was introduced to assist in the production of statistics, and was based in Southend. This caused the dispersal of headquarters staff to Southend, a policy which has continued over the years and more notably of late, with the establishment of the VAT Headquarters there. 1960 had seen the death of entertainment duty and eight years later the Excise officers were relieved of one of their older tasks, when the probate work was passed to the district probate registries, after nearly eighty years in the Excise.

The biggest change for the Excise was the introduction in 1966 of a general betting duty. Since 1947 there had been a form of betting duty in existence. It had been first imposed on football pools, and was later extended to totalizator betting. These duties had been relatively easy to collect, as they were concentrated into large firms, which made them readily controllable by the Excise officer. With the establishment of off-course betting shops in 1959 the pressure for a full betting duty increased sharply. When the new duty was introduced it was based on a uniform rate of $2\frac{1}{2}$ per cent on all bets. From the experience gained in the 1926 duty, the department introduced a system of prepaid betting sheets in various denominations, which each bookmaker had to purchase before commencing business. They recorded their daily takings and the duty liability on these sheets, and were thus paying the duty in advance.

The control of the new duty was centred at Manchester, and the Excise officers regularly visited the racecourses and betting shops in their area. They at once found problems with something as intangible as a bet. Betting slips could easily be suppressed, and credit betting by telephone was wide open to abuse. For a number of years a wide range of control tactics had to be employed, the most popular method being test betting, whereby officers visited betting shops to place bets, which were subsequently checked through the accounts to ensure that the bookmaker was including all the bets. The success of this control depended on the betting officer not being recognized as such by the bookmaker, and in some shops, where there was a certain type of clientele, it meant that the officers visiting such shops to place the bets had to dress the part. Many bookmakers were quite unaware of the officers' activities, and as such the necessary charade proved to be successful. For the first time ever there was a comprehensive duty on all betting and gaming. In the same Act gaming and gaming machines, one-armed bandits, were made liable to a licence duty. At the present, over £2,898 millions are staked on the various forms of betting, and in this total, the duty amounts to £338,557 per year.

The changes in the Customs were fairly revolutionary. The first trials of an 'open warehouse' system took place in 1965. This system gave a relaxed series of regulations in place of the hitherto strict control of physical checks on the stock and comprehensive audit of the accounts. Containers were now becoming a feature of shipping work, and this led to the first approval of inland clearing depots, warehouses well away from the ports, where goods could be directly delivered from the ports, for examination and clearance locally. The rapid development of container traffic has meant considerable changes in the various ports. Many of the old docks have lost much of their old traffic to the new container berths, which are situated closer to the mouths of the rivers. Tilbury has taken over much of the trade of London Port, as has Portbury in the case of Bristol trade. Other ports, like Felixstowe, have grown rapidly as a result of container trade.

The Customs were involved in two unusual schemes intended to help the balance of payments problems. The first was introduced in October 1964, and involved a temporary charge on imports (T.C.I.) of 15 per cent. This levy was collected on certain goods, and was in addition to the Customs duty. Its imposition incurred the wrath of our EFTA partners, as it was considered contrary to the trade agreement. It was, however, of a relatively short duration, being withdrawn in November 1966.

The other scheme was introduced two years later, and was described as very novel by the Chancellor, Mr Roy Jenkins. It imposed an import deposit of 50 per cent on all imports, which would be repaid within 180 days of payment. Many doubts were expressed as to the department's ability to repay the import deposits on time. However, the machinery set up to arrange for the automatic repayments worked very well, and, with very few exceptions, there were few complaints. In January 1967 the Chancellor was able to report, 'The scheme is working smoothly, and I would like to thank all the Customs officials, who are dealing with the extra work with great speed and efficiency.' The exercise ended in December 1970.

The most significant feature of the post-war years was the growth of international co-operation on many diverse matters. The war had greatly increased both trade and tariff restrictions, and with the freeing of international trade as countries recovered from the aftermath of the war the question of tariff became vitally important. The first tangible progress was made in 1947, with the signing of the General Agreement on Tariffs and Trade (GATT); over twenty-three countries were involved, and well over a hundred separate agreements were concluded.

The formal signing of the Treaty of Rome in 1957, which established the European Economic Community, forced this country to look elsewhere for a wider European trade area. The result was the formation in November 1959 of the European Free Trade Association (EFTA). The ultimate aims of the Association were the abolition of all tariffs between member countries and the reduction of tariffs on imports from other European countries. The aim of free trade was ultimately achieved in December 1966. A new trade agreement was signed with Eire, greatly reducing the existing tariffs—a far cry from the days of the 'cattle war'.

With the accession of the United Kingdom to the European Community a vast new dimension was added to the work of the department. Problems regarding to Community Transit, the Common Agricultural Policy, the reshaping of the British tariff in line with the Community tariff, new requirements on valuation, duty-free allowances, harmonization of Excise duties, and the old revenue duties, had to be solved and brought into line with the EEC policy. There is now a Commissioner responsible for all international aspects of Customs operations, as well as a number of head-quarters divisions solely dealing with the work.

In January 1972 a new system of non-reciprocal tariff preferences for goods imported into the United Kingdom from the developing countries came into operation. The scheme allowed duty-free entry for nearly all manufactured goods and raw materials, the principal exemptions being textile goods and all revenue duty imports. The scheme—which is called a Generalised System of Preferences, or G.S.P.—affects over a hundred independent countries and more than fifty dependent territories.

Perhaps the most exciting and successful project introduced in recent times was the development of a data processing scheme for London Airport. This scheme, known as LACES (London Airport Cargo Electronic Data Processing Scheme), became operational on 23 August 1971, only four weeks behind schedule. It had first been planned in 1969, and was the most complex commercial real-time computer system in the country, providing as it did an inventory of goods imported into London Airport. The system monitors the information fed into it via some 200 visual display units located in airline, forwarding agents and Customs offices in the airport, calculates the duty and other charges and selects the entries for examination of documents or goods or for release without examination. It is a combined system, involving the airlines, the agents and the Customs. It was the first time that real-time techniques have been applied to Customs clearances, and the system was unique, being at least two or three years ahead of similar systems being developed in other countries.

The most dramatic event of the post-war years for the Civil Service generally, and the department in particular, was the appointment on 8 February 1966 of a committee to 'examine the structure, recruitment and management, including training of the Home Civil Service'. The committee was chaired by Lord Fulton, and it found certain basic faults in the existing service. It discovered that the service was still essentially based on the philosophy of the gifted amateur, especially as regards the administrative grade. The committee felt that there were too many different grades and classes, each with separate recruitment, and that there were far too few specialist posts. Grave misgivings were expressed about the quality of management, and serious criticisms were made of the personnel management and career planning.

The report was published in June 1968, and most of its recommendations were designed to cure these basic faults. One of the major proposals was the formation of a Civil Service department to take over the management functions of the Treasury, and also to absorb the Civil Service Commissioners, the recruiting department. It recommended the abolition of the three basic grades, administrative, executive and clerical, and maintained that there should be one unified grade structure from top to bottom. It proposed that there should be increased training in both administration and management, with the establishment of a Civil Service College. Furthermore, organization and methods units should be established in all major departments to ensure the better and more efficient use of resources.

The report had serious repercussions within every government department, and not least the Customs and Excise. The department was already working on plans for its own reorganization, and these ideas were now channelled into the guidelines recommended by the Fulton Committee. The avowed intent of the reorganization was to establish

> a more appropriate organisation to handle current and future work, i.e., one flexible enough to meet seasonal and other changes; free from unnecessary barriers which may hinder movement of staff or lead to duplication of effort, and still sufficiently well constructed to provide a sound foundation for any extension of the duties laid to the Department. In addition, the aim is an organisation capable of making the best use of available talent and providing an improved career structure.

Stirring words indeed, which promised a brave new world!

Prior to the reorganization, the department comprised three separate and very distinct services. Headquarters consisted of a Secretaries Office, with a staff of 3,200 disposed in a hierarchy of administrative, executive and clerical grades. Then the second, and largest, service was the outdoor, controlled by the Chief Inspector's Office, which acted as technical advisers to Headquarters. The service had nearly 11,000 staff, from Officer of Customs and Excise right up to Collector, and ultimately to the Chief Inspector. Last, but not least, were the Waterguard service with 3,600 mainly uniformed staff, from Assistant Preventive Officer to the Inspector General of the Waterguard.

The first moves in the reorganization exercise were the compression of three Headquarters grades into one unified grade, stretching from Clerical Officer to Assistant Secretary. A new training and staff development division was set up with training units being formed in each collection. These units played an integral part in the task of retraining the combined staff in their new duties. The merging of the Chief Inspector's Office with the Inspector General's Office were the first steps in the reorganization of the Outdoor and Waterguard services.

Prolonged discussions were conducted on the framework of the further steps to be taken, with involved and complicated schemes for the assimilation of the various grades into a common grade structure. The promotion prospects of all staff were carefully considered, as were the reserved rights for the staff in post. A document setting out the broad principles of the reorganization was signed on 2 July 1971: the full reorganization could commence immediately, and it was destined to last for several years. The Chairman of the Board considered it 'a milestone in the history of the Customs and Excise'. (However, a cartoon in a staff magazine portrayed the signing of the agreement as similar to the signing of the First World War Armistice agreement, with the staff-side representatives depicted as the defeated party.)

The main objectives of the exercise were a large unified grading structure that would allow free movement between the Headquarters and the

Outfield, the integration of the two separate outdoor services, more personnel management and improving the scope for the employment of women in all areas of work. The Waterguard and outdoor services disappeared as separate branches and became known generally as the outfield. Many of the old and traditional titles vanished, especially in the Waterguard, and were replaced by a general grade of officer, from assistant to senior. The name of Officer of Customs and Excise was retained as an obsolescent grade (Officer CX), but by the 1980s it should have faded out.

By 1974 the reorganization of Headquarters was completed with the **amalgamation of the Secretaries Office with that of the Chief Inspector. By** then much of the outfield had been altered with the establishment of multiple Customs and Excise stations undertaking the full range of duties, with the work classified according to the various grades. This reorganization was the largest and most comprehensive ever undertaken by the department. In the various exercises carried out on during 1971–2 to fill the new stations over 5,800 personnel moved. This in itself was a major task, and proved to be valuable experience for a similar large-scale movement on the advent of VAT.

The celebrations that took place in September 1971 to commemorate the three-hundredth anniversary of the granting of Letters Patent to the Customs Commissioners may be viewed in retrospect as equally celebrating the passing of an era, with the end of the old department and the beginning of a new one. Many present members of the department feel that the service they entered thirty or so years ago has changed beyond all recognition, and not necessarily for the good. I have no doubts that the same misgivings were expressed by their past colleagues at similar changes throughout the long history of the department. It is perhaps fitting that this chapter should end as it began, with reorganization. This demonstrates the ability of the service to adapt to changing circumstances without losing its essential character, which has been forged over the last three hundred years. '*Plus ça change, plus c'est la même chose.*'

CHAPTER ELEVEN

VAT – A Simple Tax

Value-added tax or VAT, as it is more commonly known, has become an all too familiar part of the life of the country. Since its emergence as one of the main forms of indirect taxation, much has been spoken and even more has been written on the subject; hardly a week passes without some comment or correspondence being published in the press on various aspects of the tax, and questions on it figure prominently in the daily business of the House of Commons. No modern tax has produced so much controversy; indeed, one is tempted to cite the introduction of the Excise in the seventeenth century as a suitable comparison.

The omnipresence of VAT is such that it affects every member of the community to a varying degree. For the majority of people it is an unnecessary addition to the prices paid for a wide range of goods and services. For the minority, totalling about one and a quarter million, the tax means their active participation in the charging, collecting and accounting for VAT on business activities—and some consider this involvement a rather onerous burden.

Since the introduction of the tax the effect on the Customs and Excise department has been traumatic; involving its staff in virtually all aspects of the business life of the country, from the 'shop on the corner' to the large national and multinational companies, as well as the majority of the professions. This vast extension of the department's activities has quite naturally brought it into the forefront of public interest, and in the process it has suffered considerable criticism. Some of these strictures have no doubt been justified; however, I feel that scant appreciation has been given to the very considerable achievement in establishing the machinery, administration, and control of such a comprehensive tax within a relatively short time.

I do not intend to write a technical exposition on VAT, or to offer an apologia for the tax. To evaluate the efficacy of VAT after such a short duration would be unwise and unfair: six years is but a short time in the development of any tax. As we have seen, the most successful ones have taken many more years to develop and refine. Nevertheless, VAT now plays such a major role in the Customs and Excise that no narrative of the department would be complete without some account of the tax, however recent that history may be. Furthermore, some assessment should be made of its overall effects on the public, a subject on which many misconceptions have been expressed.

Since the days of the introduction of the dreaded foreign Excise in 1643 virtually all the new duties and taxes introduced in the United Kingdom had the merit (albeit a dubious one!) of being home-produced, devised for the particular circumstances prevailing in the country at the time. Entertainments duty, purchase tax, betting duty and selective exployment tax are some recent examples. Value-added tax is without doubt foreign in origin, owing its inception to Europe, and in some small part to the United States of America. It can now be considered the fastest growing tax in the world. In 1965 it was in operation in only France and some of the states in America, yet now it is the main form of indirect taxation in the European Economic Community, as well as operating in the Scandinavian countries and Austria. Its introduction is moreover being considered by other countries.

Prior to 1970 few people in this country would have been aware of the existence of VAT, although in the early sixties a committee was formed to inquire into the practical effects of the introduction of a form of turnover tax to replace the existing purchase tax. At this time certain economists felt that the country's poor economic performance compared with other European countries could in some sense be attributed to the existing taxation system.

The committee (which was chaired by Mr Gordon Richardson) reported its findings in March 1964. It said that purchase tax provided the more logical, efficient and economical method of taxing consumer expenditure in this country. Furthermore, the committee felt that a value-added tax would not assist exports or economic growth, and would involve a far greater administrative burden for both business and the tax authorities than did the system operating at that time.

In view of a report which had categorically dismissed VAT, it seems rather strange that three years later the National Economic Development Office—or NEDO for short—should instigate its own inquiry into the tax and the likely implications for business should it be introduced into the country. The need for a fresh inquiry was no doubt occasioned by developments in the EEC. In April 1967 the Council of the Community had adopted VAT as its official indirect tax, and had issued a directive on the harmonization of turnover taxes. Henceforth some form of value-added tax became a prerequisite of entry into the EEC.

This fresh inquiry examined the types of value-added tax then in existence in Denmark, France, Germany and the Netherlands, and perhaps more importantly canvassed the views of a wide range of British industry on the subject. The committee's report was published in August 1969, and on the whole was much more in favour of the tax than the earlier report. Certain advantages could be seen for such a tax given the right conditions, although the report expressed misgivings about the very real administrative problems for both government and industry in introducing the tax. The conclusion was drawn that providing the devised system was as simple as possible, two to three years were allowed for the preparatory work, and sufficient publicity was given to the administrative changes and arrangements, such a major alteration in the taxation structure could be achieved with only temporary and initial difficulties.

The reports of both committees received due publicity, but caused little general interest outside the esoteric world of finance and taxation. It was not until May 1970 that VAT came into more general prominence, when it was introduced to the unsuspecting public in the Conservative Party's manifesto for the June general election. The manifesto (entitled *A Better Tomorrow*) stated, 'We will abolish the selective employment tax, as part of a wide reform of indirect taxation, possibly involving the replacement of purchase tax by a value-added tax.' With the election of a Conservative government there was now a distinct possibility that some type of value-added tax would become the instrument for its avowed reform of indirect taxation.

The uncertainty of whether such a tax would indeed be introduced was sustained for almost nine months, but finally in March 1971 the Chancellor, Mr Anthony Barber, announced in his Budget speech that purchase tax and SET would be abolished, to be replaced by a broad-based value-added tax, which would come into operation in April 1973. A Green Paper on the new tax was published, which laid down the basic principles of the system and was intended as a basis for discussion and consultation with the various trade and professional associations and other interested bodies. The most important statement in the Paper as far as the department was concerned was that the tax would be administered by the Customs and Excise. In many quarters it had been assumed that if such a tax was to be introduced its control would be assigned to the Inland Revenue. However, the new tax was to be based on transactions and invoices, a field in which the Customs and Excise had far greater experience.

The die was now cast, and the department was faced with the very formidable task of preparing for such a fundamental change in taxation in only two years. The time factor was critical: every other country that had introduced a similar tax had taken far longer to achieve such a radical change. It was therefore the consensus of opinion that all the preparatory work could not be undertaken in such a short time, and thus the introduction of the tax would be delayed.

With the publication of the Green Paper over eight hundred trade and professional bodies, as well as many individual firms, made representations to the department on various aspects of the tax. Over three hundred meetings were arranged, besides numerous conferences and seminars, which were addressed by members of the department. A series of discussion papers were circularized for comment. Such a measure of consultation and discussion was unique—never before had a government department instituted or encouraged such public debate prior to the introduction of a new tax. As one of the Commissioners closely involved in the consultations has commented, 'the amount of education, advice and assistance that we received from the representative bodies was immense'.

The broad outline of the system of departmental control had been worked out in the early planning stages. It was to be based on a central computer, which would keep the registration and tax records of all the traders. The issue of all the forms and returns would be controlled by the computer, which would also be able to provide statistical, management and other information to facilitate the tax. The actual control of the VAT traders would fall to the lot of staff in local offices throughout the country.

As early as 1970 estimates of the number of staff needed to administer the tax has settled on 8,000; they had been arrived at without any firm knowledge of the final form of the tax. As the planning progressed this figure became accepted as the staff ceiling for VAT. Allowing for the 2,000 or so staff already involved in some way with the control of purchase tax, the net requirement would be 6,000. An increase in size of the department by almost one-third in such a short time was a daunting prospect: the problems of recruitment and training would be formidable, but the most urgent and pressing need was that of accommodation. About half of the VAT complement was to be based at the local offices, employed in visiting the registered traders. It was decided, rather than to try to enlarge and extend the existing Customs and Excise offices, to establish separate special VAT offices in the cities and major towns; each office covering a wide area based on post codes.

The Ministry of Public Building and Works and the accommodation staff both at headquarters and in the collections were involved in the search for suitable offices. Early in 1970 a partially completed building in Southend, large enough to house the computer and the necessary staff, was found. The building was due for completion before 1973, and was in an area which already housed a large number of headquarters staff who had been dispersed from London. This building became the headquarters of the VAT control, and was formally opened in October 1972. The search for offices in some seventy areas throughout the country now became a major undertaking, and while there were problems in a few areas, suitable offices became ready for occupation in 1972. Considering the size of the operation, and the strict time factor, its success deserves praise indeed.

The White Paper which would form the basis of the VAT Bill had been promised by the Government for late 1971. However, on the 9th of November the Chancellor announced that there would not be a separate Bill for VAT, but that the requisite legislation would be included in the Finance

Bill in 1972. This change was viewed by many as the first step to a delay in the introduction of the tax. *The Times* thought that the postponement indicated that the drafting of the Bill was proving more difficult than expected. However, the Chancellor saw the delay purely as an extension of time to allow for further discussions with trade and industry on the implications of the tax. Nevertheless, the postponement raised many complaints from industry and accountants, who maintained the delay in publishing such vital details as rate—or indeed rates—and scope and coverage of the tax, made considerable problems for companies; especially those who would need to re-programme their computers.

The long-awaited White Paper was eventually introduced on 21 March 1972, the draft clauses and schedules of the proposed Bill being produced as an appendix. It was stressed that one of the main objectives in planning the new tax was to keep it as simple as possible. This aspect was further emphasized in the subsequent debate on the Paper, when the Chancellor stated, 'If we are to have the simplest VAT in Europe, which I am determined we shall have, it is essential that the Customs and Excise, in its discussions with trade and industry shall not be hamstrung in any way.'

The essence of this simple tax was that all goods and services supplied in the United Kingdom in the course of a business were liable to a standard rate of tax; exceptions to the tax would take the form of either exemptions or zero-rating. Zero-rated goods or services would be liable to VAT, but the rate of tax would be nil. The Act would require any person whose taxable turnover in taxable goods and services exceeded £5,000 to be registered with the department, to account for tax on all transactions and to make a return once a quarter. If a registered person should supply another registered person, he would be required to issue him with a tax invoice, although in the case of retailers (where no invoices are issued) special schemes would be introduced to enable them to calculate the VAT from their gross takings. The rate of tax was announced as 10 per cent, although the Chancellor retained the option to vary the rate in the range $7\frac{1}{2}$ to $12\frac{1}{2}$ per cent. The actual rate to be imposed would not be disclosed until the 1973 Budget.

In the simplest terms, registered traders would calculate the amount charged by them to their customers and deduct from this figure the amount of VAT charged to them by their suppliers of goods and services. The net amount so calculated would be paid to the department at the end of each quarter. If a registered person was trading wholly or mainly in zero-rated goods or services (on which the tax was nil) they would receive a repayment of VAT from the department on the goods or services used in their business. By this method no hidden tax would fall on such goods as food, fuel, water, transport, books and newspapers and exports.

One large item of consumer spending was selected for special treatment. A special tax of 10 per cent would be introduced in April 1973 on motor cars, and based on the wholesale value of the vehicle. This car tax was intended to compensate for the revenue which would be lost on the abolition of the 25 per cent rate of purchase tax. When in operation it would virtually be the only living reminder of the old purchase-tax system.

Another novel feature of the new tax was the special appeals procedure; independent VAT tribunals were to be established in London and six provincial centres to hear appeals on a number of matters in relation to the tax. A full-time president and chairman would be appointed, as well as part-time lay members. The intention of the tribunals was to enable all registered traders to present their cases for arbitration and it was planned that the hearings would be of an informal nature to encourage the small traders to use the appeals procedure without recourse to legal representation and without undue difficulty. The first case to be heard was in January 1973 and concerned the Llandudno Cabinlift Co. Ltd and the liability of the fares of the cabin-lift to VAT. The company lost the case; the tribunal decided that the fares were liable to the standard rate of VAT.

'Britain's value-added tax is a monument to sane reform' was the opinion expressed by *The Economist* after the publication of the White Paper. Some of the other comments were not quite so laudatory, but the consensus of opinion was favourable—largely on account of the apparent simplicity of the system—and universal relief was expressed over the avoidance of a multi-rate tax. For the majority of the public VAT was still an unknown factor, and their reaction to the new tax would not be apparent until the department's publicity campaign commenced later in the year.

Considering the important and comprehensive changes that VAT would bring, much of the Budget debate was taken up with discussion on the reforms of corporation tax and personal taxation. It was not until the Bill reached the committee stage that the various VAT provisions were debated in any great detail. The most contentious issues were those relating to the proposed processes of enforcement—that is to say, the methods by which the department would ensure that the registered traders obeyed the rules. In particular the powers of entry and search and the proscribed offences and penalties were rigorously attacked. The Bar Council and the Law Society considered the various powers to be 'unconstitutional', 'draconian' and 'an intolerable invasion of privacy'. *The Economist* likened the legislation to a return to the thumbscrew, and considered the powers invoked wholly disproportionate to the puny rate of VAT at 10 per cent.

The various clauses in the Bill were debated for almost two days, and although minor amendments were made, the enforcement and control provisions remained largely unchanged. One clause greatly concerned and worried the business world: that providing for the interchange of information between the two revenue departments. It was argued that such a provision brought 1984 and Big Brother a step closer to reality. The offending item was in fact accepted by Parliament with very little debate, on the assurance that such exchange of information would be exercised at an appropriate level. Nevertheless, this particular aspect caused small traders considerable concern, judging by the number of questions raised on it in the subsequent months.

There were long hours of debate, and many little jokes were made on the liability of various items. (The discussion on fish and chips—taxed if eaten on the premises, and zero-rated if taken away—occupied an inordinate length of time.) Eventually, however, the Bill emerged relatively unscathed from the various attacks. The only major concession was on children's clothing and footwear. These goods, which had been exempt from purchase tax, would now be taxed for the first time, so a special committee was set up to look at the problems and report its findings before the 1973 Budget.

The Bill received the Royal Assent in July and by this time many of the detailed tax machinery provisions were being dealt with by subordinate legislation. Discussions were continuing with the various trade bodies on special arrangements for retailers and transactions on certain second-hand goods. It was not until the end of August that the department produced their four special schemes for retailers to enable them to deal with both taxable and zero-rated goods sold at the shop counter. Although the schemes 'sounded dreadful'—according to *The Economist*—they were in fact not unduly complicated, and allowed the retailer the option of selecting the most suitable method for his business.

The build-up of the department's staff commenced in 1972, although the majority of the required new staff were recruited by direct examination. Many were transferred from other government departments, and for some time became known as 'OGDs'. During the summer of 1972 there was a major movement of staff to fill the complements of the new VAT offices which had been established around the country. This massive transfer of officers, including the subsequent filling of residual vacancies, made it one of the largest dispersals of staff ever experienced by a government department. Although the exercise enabled the majority of staff to transfer to more desirable areas, it also meant that in addition to coping with the new tax they had all the attendant problems of the sale and purchase of property and the consequent upheaval to their families.

With the majority of the staff in situ in the new VAT offices, the department launched a major publicity campaign aimed at the trading community, to ensure that those who were required to collect and account for the new tax were fully aware of their obligations. Detailed information was supplied to national and trade newspapers. A special eight-page booklet for small shops and businesses was produced, over four million copies being made available at post offices as well as being fully advertised in the press and on television. BBC Television, in conjunction with the department, made a colour film entitled *VAT Special*, which gave a detailed account of the VAT system, an explanation of who was to register and a broad outline of the accounting procedure. The film was first shown on BBC1 on 24 September with the Deputy Chairman of the Board answering questions on the tax.

Copies of it were made available for hire, and by March 1973 they had received over 1,500 showings.

During August 1972 over a million and a half information packages were distributed to all known businesses. These 'VAT packs' (as they became known) contained a general guide to VAT, a notice explaining the scope of the tax and a form for registration. They also contained the first issue of the *VAT Bulletin*, a leaflet designed to be published at regular intervals to inform the business world of new developments in the tax. The launching of an official bulletin dealing with taxation matters was an innovation, and the first issue contained a message from the Chancellor of the Exchequer explaining why the Government was introducing a value-added tax and why he considered it 'a much better and fairer system of levying indirect taxation'.

However, the department, recognizing the public's inherent lack of enthusiasm for any official literature, decided that the best and most reliable method to inform the traders of the tax and its operation would be by individual visits from officers. It was planned that every registered person would receive an 'educational' visit (as they became known), but with an estimated 1,500,000 registered persons such a formidable programme could not be achieved before VAT commenced, or indeed before the first returns were due. The visits commenced in early September, and in many ways proved to be equally educational for the visiting officers. They gave them a valuable insight into the workings of many businesses, as well as demonstrating a wide variety of accounting methods (and in the case of many small businesses showed the sad lack of any formalized records or accounts). Furthermore, in many instances the officers found the 'VAT packs' unopened and were greeted with the comments that they did not have time to read all that official rubbish!

In order to convey the information about VAT to a wider field in the relatively short time before April, the department actively encouraged public meetings about the tax. Speakers were provided for meetings, seminars and conferences organized by various trade and professional bodies throughout the country. These meetings were always very well attended, and clearly demonstrated the trading community's interest and concern over the implications of the new tax. Most colleges and institutes organized evening courses on VAT, using local Customs and Excise staff as the lecturers. Again, these courses were well subscribed. In many areas, particularly the more rural, mobile teams of officers held VAT surgeries in village and parish halls. In addition each local VAT office (or LVOs as they were known) had a special inquiry section open to the public to answer problems on VAT. In the early days these sections were the busiest in the office. The time and effort spent by members of the department in explaining the requirements of the tax was completely unprecedented; never previously had any change in taxation occasioned such a vast educational programme. The proviso of the earlier NEDO report that sufficient publicity should be given to the administrative arrangements had been amply fulfilled.

The visits, meetings and courses gave the department an insight into the areas of the tax which were concerning most traders, and also highlighted problems which hitherto had not been appreciated. It was mainly the small businesses and retailers who feared the introduction of the tax the most. They were concerned with the extent of accounts they would need to keep, how they would differentiate between taxable and zero-rated goods, the problems with credit customers, Green Shield stamps and generally the completion of the VAT return form. Small firms in the building trade were worried about the liability of various types of repair and alteration work, but all in all the most pressing problem for retailers appeared to be that of dealing with goods which had paid purchase tax and from 1 April would become liable to VAT.

It had been decided in order to avoid double taxation that goods which were easily identifiable should be purchased on a sale and return basis—i.e., no tax charged until the goods were sold. Other types of taxable goods would be granted a 'tax pause' of an undefined length, when purchase tax would be removed to allow retailers to dispose of their stocks. Both schemes were considered unsatisfactory by the majority of traders, and continual pressure by the various interested parties—especially the CBI and the TUC—to find a more satisfactory scheme eventually achieved its aim.

On 7 November 1972 a special rebate scheme was announced in the House of Commons: 'Thanks to the tenacity and ingenuity of the Customs and Excise, I have now been able to decide that there will be a full rebate or repayment in respect of all tax-paid stocks.' The essence of the scheme was that goods which had borne purchase tax, as well as certain excisable goods which were in stock at midnight on 31 March 1973, would be eligible for a refund of tax. The scheme required the trader to be registered, and that a full stock account should be taken. The refund of the tax would be automatic, the amount claimed would be deducted from the first VAT return. In total over 325,000 such claims were presented, for £280 millions tax. The operation of the scheme caused considerable extra work for the local staff, who were involved in verifying a percentage of the larger claims, as well as posing many problems for the computer staff in Southend.

The registration schedule commenced on 1 October, and it was preceded by an extensive press and television campaign. The programme was designed to be spread over four months, allowing two months after the end of January as a safety margin. However, by the end of November the number of completed forms received was well below the expected number, and by the beginning of December only 300,000 forms had been received. Of these about 8 per cent were incorrect, and had to be returned for amendment. The more common errors found on the forms were listed in an article in the *VAT Bulletin* as a guide to future applicants. This article became the subject of much criticism by the press. It was suggested that this was an official admittance of a bungle, and one newspaper commenting on the shortfall of registration forms suggested that the department was learning that you just cannot direct the British public. A senior consultant in the computer industry prophesied that the registration programme was going to be a disaster.

Early in December the Opposition in the House of Commons tabled a motion to delay the introduction of VAT for a year in order to give more time to reconsider the whole matter. Obviously the slowness of the registration programme had added fuel to the fire, as did some newspaper reports that the strain imposed on the Customs and Excise by the introduction of the tax at such a speed could lead to a 'mutiny'. The Chancellor, commenting on this rumour, assured the House that the Chairman of the Board had informed him that there was no truth in it. The Chancellor added that the Customs and Excise staff responsible for VAT had operated magnificently in the challenge which had been set them. The press reports had come somewhat as a surprise to the VAT staff; they were too involved with educational visits, meetings and registration programme to consider any form of industrial action. Indeed, the majority of staff realized in retrospect that this educational period was the most enjoyable and rewarding time they had spent in VAT. Any discontent in the department could be attributed mainly to the Government's intransigent policy on Civil Service pay—and in some part to certain reorganization problems—rather than to the hasty introduction of the new tax.

The debate in the House was interesting, as some of the views expressed highlighted many of the misconceptions and misgivings surrounding the tax; it also featured as the main protagonists Mr Barber and Mr Healey, till recently the only Chancellors to be responsible for VAT. During the debate it was suggested that over fifty thousand persons would be required by trade and industry, as well as mountains of paper, in order to control the tax; food bills would drastically increase, small businesses would close and it would be the death of many theatres and cinemas. Even the Football Association was quoted as saying that it was a killer tax because the increase in gate money would force many of the smaller clubs out of business. Mr Healey—who was destined to introduce a multi-rate VAT somewhat later—considered it 'a feast for fiddlers', and that 'its introduction in April would cause a disaster for at least the first six months on the scale of the Dunkirk disaster'. It seemed that VAT would be responsible for all manner of ills for the country, except perhaps the British weather!

The Chancellor stoutly defended the tax and maintained that the yield from VAT would be some £700 millions less than the taxes it was replacing, and that many items would in fact be reduced in price. He pointed out that food would be zero-rated, and with the abolition of SET many food prices should be reduced. The other points were dismissed as scaremongering. The motion was defeated, and the introduction of VAT was set fair for the first of April—All Fools Day, an appropriate day according to many.

By the middle of February 1973 about a million traders had been registered for VAT. This figure was particularly due to an intensive campaign of visits by staff to traders' premises all over the country. It was now fairly obvious that the original estimate of 1,500,000 was incorrect, and that there would now be fewer traders on the register. The shortfall could be accounted for by the fact that a significant number of potential repayment traders who were below the compulsory limit had not opted to register, and that many associated companies had registered as a group.

The Budget had been brought forward to the beginning of March to allow sufficient time for the last-minute arrangements. It confirmed the standard rate as 10 per cent. The committee's report on children's clothing and footwear recommended zero-rating, which was accepted, but the surprise of the Budget was that sweets, chocolate, ice cream and crisps etc. (which had previously carried purchase tax) would not be liable to VAT, thus adding to the list of exceptions. The press had a field day calling the Budget 'Kid's stuff' and 'Children's Party Budget'. With it over the department could direct its attention to another vitally important problem.

For many months there had been considerable speculation and discussion on the effect VAT would have on prices. It had been anticipated that consumer prices would increase overall by about 1 per cent, but with the Budget concessions this figure was adjusted to an estimate of only 0·8 per cent. However, as the Government was deeply involved in a counter-inflation policy it was greatly concerned that the public should be fully informed as to the likely increases and decreases in the prices of various goods and services.

The Economist had undertaken a survey in early December on these lines, and some of the goods it recommended for purchase in order to have 'a VAT-happy Christmas' were cookers, pets, pianos, new telephones and yachts (all due to increase after VAT), whereas cameras, radios, televisions, furs and watches should be bought as Easter presents (Easter was late in 1973). It was decided that the department would be responsible for all the publicity on the VAT price changes, and although the local VAT staff were the obvious choice for both monitoring price changes and investigating the complaints from the public, it was felt that they had sufficient work without taking on this fresh responsibility. The work therefore devolved on the inspectors of weights and measures.

The publicity campaign commenced on Tuesday 13 March, and was deliberately concentrated into the final weeks before the changeover to gain maximum effect. There was extensive coverage in the national and selected provincial newspapers as well as use of peak television viewing time. A special leaflet was published, designed as a guide for shoppers, and listing over 170 goods and services, ranging from cars and caravans down to a packet of razor blades, and showing how prices should change. By the last week of March 5,500,000 copies were made available for free distribution through post-offices. The whole advertising campaign cost £728,000, and it remained to be seen just how effective it had been.

The last pre-VAT week had shown 'gadarene panic buying' according to

The Times; certainly many large stores reported spending sprees on expensive items, with sales over 50 per cent up on the previous year. One large London store sold 184 pianos in the week, as well as large numbers of cookers, carpets and lawn-mowers. The first day of April fell on a Sunday, so the public's first experience of VAT had to wait until Monday, except in the case of cafés and restaurants. The reaction to VAT seemed to vary according to the newspaper one read: the *Daily Mirror* had 'muddle Monday' and the *Daily Express* 'VAT blunders itself in', while *The Times* claimed 'VAT arrived as softly as the rain.' The general opinion was that, like decimalization, it was a non-event. Supermarkets and large stores were showing reductions on a wide variety of goods, and the Retail Consortium— which represented 90 per cent of the High Street traders—reported few difficulties. The biggest area of confusion arose in cafés and canteens; during the whole of the monitoring period on prices, half of the 21,000 complaints received concerned food. The public seemed well aware of the price changes—in fact, many of the smaller retailers seemed to be less conversant with the tax than their customers.

By the middle of April the main complaints appeared to be with restaurants, corner sweet-shops, hairdressers and car parks. However, Sir Geoffrey Howe, the Minister for Trade and Consumer Affairs, reported that the changeover to VAT was going reasonably well, and the great majority of price adjustments were being fairly made. This view was reiterated by the Chancellor in the House of Commons on 19 April. Certainly the tax had not been postponed as many of its critics had prophesied: there were now 1,100,000 traders registered, while there had been no strike of shopkeepers as there had been in Belgium on the introduction of their VAT. The department could feel justifiably pleased that the tax had been introduced within the short time available, and moreover that it had been achieved with the minimum of friction.

By the time the first returns started to filter in some fresh problems arose: the number of errors on the forms was far higher than expected, with almost one return in five requiring some form of amending action. The resultant clerical work was far greater than anticipated, and the situation was aggravated by problems associated with the purchase tax rebate scheme and the sheer misfortune of certain technical difficulties with the computer. To meet the crisis staff from local VAT offices were temporarily transferred to Southend to assist with the inquiries, while many queries being sent to the local offices for correction by visits to the traders concerned. The problem fortunately was of short duration, and although it was considered within the department to be a disappointment, there was never any risk of a serious breakdown in collection.

One year after the introduction of VAT a representative of the retail trades association commented, 'The introduction of the tax in April last year seems now to have been a fairly unspectacular event . . . now one can sit back and wonder what all the fuss was about.' Whether many of the smaller retailers shared this view is doubtful; during the year rumours were rife of the number of small businesses which had sold out because of VAT, and there were some extraordinary claims of the time spent completing the VAT records and forms. Nevertheless, by and large the vast majority of the trading community had accepted the tax—though not without complaint—and were now finding its workings not so formidable as they had first feared.

The educational programme came to an end in April 1974 with over 700,000 visits completed. As there were now nearly 1,200,000 registered traders, the shortfall of visits was about 40 per cent. It was regretted that not every trader had been visited, since it was generally agreed within the department that traders who had received such a visit were more likely to operate the tax properly, keep better records and complete the returns correctly. The Chairman of the Board, giving evidence to the Public Accounts Committee in January 1975, expressed the view that had more visits been made, the department would have had fewer problems.

The department was now faced with the long-term problem of the control of the tax. During the next three years it was planned that each trader would have at least one inspection or control visit and some more than one, depending on the size and complexity of the business. The intention of the control visit was to ensure that the traders fully understood the works of the tax, to verify the returns they had submitted by examination of their books and accounts and to ensure that the records were consistent with the nature and extent of the business.

In first year over 250,000 such control visits were made, and as this was usually the trader's first personal contact with a VAT officer a fairly thorough inspection was considered necessary. The vast majority of the visits passed without incidents or complaints—in fact, many traders commented on the helpfulness of the visiting officer—but about one visit in four produced some inaccuracies in the returns. Sometimes the errors were in favour of the trader, but more frequently they were in favour of the department. In the first year of control the amount of VAT underdeclared which was found on these visits amounted to £20 millions. One of the difficulties was to relate the number of deliberate errors and dishonest returns to the genuine mistakes due to misunderstandings.

Shortly before the end of the first control year considerable publicity was given to allegations that certain VAT officers had exceeded their powers and had acted in a very unreasonable manner. All the complaints were thoroughly investigated, and no justification for the accusations was found. The press publicity given to one case (where the officers were likened to 'VAT bullies' and 'A Gestapo squad') was particularly vicious. All the officers working on VAT felt that they had been very unfairly criticized, and the slur did great harm to the good working relationship that the officers had built up with the trading community. All the ensuing publicity led to a number of Parliamentary questions and much correspondence. Finally in May 1975 the Chancellor of the Exchequer, commenting on the complaints, said, 'But in truth, despite all the publicity there have been very few complaints and even fewer have disclosed any impropriety. After all over 8,000 visits each week were being made without incident.' The furore died down, but it unfortunately left a mark, both within the department and with the trading community.

The tax had not really been allowed to settle down before the first changes were made. Foodstuffs (which had been zero-rated in the first VAT Budget) were now included in the 10 per cent rate, as was petrol. Perhaps more ominous was the announcement that the department should consider and consult the various trade bodies about the procedural changes needed if additional rates of VAT were introduced. The early hopes of a simple tax seemed to be rapidly receding. In July 1974 the standard rate of tax was reduced to 8 per cent. This in itself caused problems: many traders found the fraction of 2/27ths which was applied to tax-inclusive prices much less intelligible than 1/11th, and quite a number of traders had not found that particularly easy to understand. As one economic correspondent commented, 'The change in VAT is a bonus for the makers of pocket calculators.' However, worse was to come in November, when the rate of VAT on petrol was increased to 25 per cent. The department and many traders were now faced with a multi-rate tax. In May 1975 many more traders were faced with the problems of a multi-rate tax when the higher rate was extended to a range of so-called 'luxury' goods, such as radios and television sets, cameras, furs, boats, jewellery and caravans. It was just like the old days of purchase tax with discriminatory rates on luxury goods. The simple tax of 1973 had disappeared like melting snow.

The three rates of tax of necessity complicated the calculation of VAT and added weight to the traders' claims that they were unpaid tax-collectors. From the early days small businesses especially had complained of the amount of time and money spent on the compilation of accounts and the completion of VAT returns. Now many of the small firms proposed deducting an amount from their returns to compensate them for all their VAT work. The department stressed that there was no provision in the law for them to allow any payment for the cost of meeting their VAT requirements. It was additionally pointed out that the VAT accounting arrangements gave the trader an average of two and a half months to obtain payments from their customers before accounting for the tax to the Customs and Excise. This system operated with particular favour to retailers, who are trading on a cash basis, thus giving them an enhanced cash flow in their business.

The department had always envisaged that the numbers of staff required to operate the original VAT system would not be sufficient to cope with the introduction of additional rates. Furthermore, during the first two years of operation it had been found necessary to devote more staff to enforcement work—that is, the chasing of late returns, making assessments and recovering unpaid tax. It was considered that a further 2,500 extra staff would be required, and by the end of March 1975 there were 10,500 persons involved in VAT (just over a third of the total Customs and Excise staff) controlling almost 1,250,000 traders and collecting £2,632 millions annually.

During the various examinations of the administration of the tax by the House of Commons Committee of Public Accounts certain misgivings were expressed, both about the delay in the collection of the tax and the amount of uncollected tax being written off. There is a natural tendency on the part of traders to delay the payment of tax for as long as possible, using the revenue as an interest-free short-term loan. In the French system of VAT there are provisions for fines in respect of overdue returns, but no such provisions exist in the British system, although in a slightly different context the Inland Revenue charge interest on overdue tax. Most of the arrears of tax written off are due from traders who have become formally insolvent, or whose whereabouts are unknown. The situation has greatly improved with the establishment of VAT control accounts, which give clear and accurate figures of the total tax liability and tax due at any given date, and with the introduction of speedier enforcement procedures to recover any unpaid tax.

In 1977 some changes were made in the VAT system: the limit of £5,000 for registration purposes was increased to £7,500 in October, and as a result some 9,000 traders were deregistered. (This limit was further extended in April 1978 to £10,000.) However, of the 70,000 eligible to deregister only 13,500 took the option to 'leave the club'—perhaps membership is not quite so onerous as some people maintain. A simplified VAT return was introduced, and greater encouragement was given to small businesses to simplify their VAT accounts by using cash book records. Perhaps the most revolutionary change was the granting of relief from VAT on bad debts. From the early days of the tax such relief had been strongly lobbied by the business world. Provision for bad debts had been allowed in purchase tax, but the control of the system had caused considerable extra work. The relief for VAT was introduced from 1 October 1978, and was applied in respect of debtors who had been formally become insolvent.

In the 1977 Finance Act it was indicated that the department would review the operation of VAT. It would consult various trade organizations and professional bodies to seek their views on the tax, and any suggestions they might have for improving the system. The review would be in two parts; the first devoted to matters of policy and the second on the administration of the tax. Its results were to be reported to Parliament.

The report was issued in December 1978, and it highlighted the various steps already taken to simplify the tax for small firms. Proposals to change from quarterly returns to an annual return based on accounts were considered. In discussing this matter with the various trade and other interested parties there was a marked lack of enthusiasm for such a change. It was generally felt that annual accounting would make the tax more complicated for small firms, and it was therefore decided not to pursue the proposal.

The report concerned itsefl with the department's administration of the tax. The cost of collection of VAT is high compared with that for other indirect taxes. In 1977–8 for each pound collected the cost was 2p, and the average cost of controlling each registered trader was £70. However, it must be realized that the presence of zero-rating distorts the costs: those traders must still be controlled without contributing any VAT. The department took a fresh look at its VAT training programme and fundamentally changed it to take account of the experience gained since the introduction of VAT.

During 1978 a very radical proposal was put forward that a major simplification of the tax could be achieved by eliminating VAT on transactions between registered traders, thus in effect substituting a retail sales tax for the existing system. The proposal was supported by the Consultative Committee of Accountancy Bodies in a detailed paper presented to the Commissioners. A working party was set up to examine the subject in depth. The proposal had certain attractions; it obviated the various payments and repayments which were costly to businesses, and it would show a resultant saving in administrative costs to the department. However, there were strong arguments against such a system. For instance, the retail stage was not so easy to recognize as supposed, and would place a large extra tax burden on retailers, with serious implications for the smaller trader. There were political objections to the scheme; a lower standard rate of tax would be needed, which would greatly affect the flexibility of the tax. Also such a revolutionary change in the system would have to be considered in respect to the country's obligations to the EEC. Although the working party agreed that it had been useful to examine any fresh views about VAT, they felt that the proposal did not provide a suitable basis for a change in the system of collecting VAT.

During the prolonged industrial action undertaken by the Civil Service unions from February to May 1979 the VAT computer at Southend was closed down. The normal processing of VAT repayment claims came to a halt, and there was considerable publicity in the media on the effect such a stoppage was having on small businesses. When computer operations restarted in May after a delay of some three and a half months there were about 400,000 repayment claims awaiting processing and payment. However, by the end of May the majority of these claims had been paid, with only a small number left outstanding. In the event no firms appeared to suffer greatly, and it seemed that once again the press had exaggerated the true effects.

With the election of a Conservative government in May 1979 it became fairly obvious that there would be some changes in VAT. The Tory election manifesto and campaign had promised changes in the taxation structure. In the event the Chancellor, Sir Geoffrey Howe, surprised virtually all the pundits by dispensing with the luxury rate of 12½ per cent and introducing a new single rate of VAT at 15 per cent—a rate intended to bring in an estimated extra £4,175 millions in a full year. The Chancellor gave his reasons for preferring to raise the additional revenue by VAT rather than alternative methods of indirect taxation. These reasons sum up the attractions of VAT as a sound revenue-raiser.

The Chancellor considered the tax to be broad-based, and that it even covered some of the alternative indirect taxes such as tobacco, spirits, petrol and beer. Also because of the wide zero-rating, many of the essentials—food, housing, public transport and medicine—would not be affected. It was estimated that VAT is only levied on about 50 per cent of consumer spending, and that with even a large increase in the VAT rate of 7 per cent, the new increase in the retail price index would only be about 3½ per cent. Perhaps one of the chief reasons, especially in these times of inflation, is that the VAT revenue (unlike other indirect taxes, which are specific—i.e., tied to volume and not value—automatically increases with inflation.

The newspaper headlines on the morning after the Budget suggested that there were only four shopping days 'to beat the VAT men'. Some of the large stores reported an increase of over 100 per cent in the sales of some articles— especially electrical goods, which were only being increased by 2½ per cent! Strangely, the large clothing stores reported only moderate increases in sales, considering that the saving on clothes would be an appreciable 7 per cent. The new single rate of VAT was not only a bonus for the retailers but it made the department's control somewhat easier with the disappearance of the two positive rates and the disappearance of the borderline cases between standard and luxury items.

One of the results of the increase in the VAT rate of 15 per cent has been to sharpen the difference between taxable and zero-rated goods and services. Since the Budget there has been an increase in the number of representations by various pressure groups and interested parties to obtain some form of VAT relief for their particular cause. Hardly a week passes without some correspondence and comment on the penal effects of the tax on a wide range of subjects, such as tourism and the hotel trade, bicycles, coin-operated launderettes, bloodstock breeding, charities, works of art and building repair work. The several campaigns launched by the theatrical profession to obtain zero-rating for the live theatre recall similar—and ultimately successful—exercises against entertainments duty. One of the latest campaigns is on behalf of the churches, and was reported in *The Times* under the headline 'VAT in the belfry troubles churchmen'. The Churches Main Committee is petitioning for some relief on the VAT paid on church repairs. There has always been, and I suspect there always will be, objections by any number of groups who feel that they have a particularly strong case for exemption or relief from taxation. As Edmund Burke said in 1774, 'To tax and to please, any more than to love and be wise, is not given to man.'

How does the United Kingdom's system of VAT compare with those in the rest of the European Economic Community? Since June 1979 we no longer have the lowest standard rate of tax; the rates vary from Denmark at 20½ per cent to Luxembourg at 10 per cent. Most countries have reduced rates of tax on food and other essential goods ranging from 1 to 14 per cent, but the United Kingdom and the Irish Republic are the only two to have zero-rates. Most countries impose higher rates for luxury goods, but none of the rates are as low as 15 per cent. There are also varying limits for registration, and once again the United Kingdom has the highest limit. Because virtually half the consumer spending in this country is not liable to VAT, the overall VAT bill in this country remains the lowest in Europe, while the United Kingdom's system of VAT is still considered one of the simplest forms of the tax in operation in the Community.

During the last three years considerable steps have taken to harmonize the principles on which VAT is applied throughout the Community. One of the most important instruments to achieve these aims is called the Sixth Directive. This Directive was implemented by the United Kingdom on 1 January 1978. It has thirty-eight articles, covering all aspects of the administration of VAT, and it does restrict the freedom of member states to alter greatly their system of VAT. For instance, although the United Kingdom is allowed to retain its zero-rated reliefs and special schemes for retailers it can make only marginal adjustments to the scope of the reliefs, subject to review by the EEC Council every five years. Moreover, the threshold limits for registration can only be increased to take account of inflation. VAT is now the major contributor to the Community's 'own resources' budget. Each member state contributes up to a maximum of 1 per cent from its total VAT yield. The United Kingdom's estimated contribution for VAT in 1980 will be £989 millions.

It is now barely seven years since the introduction of VAT in this country; in this short time it has undergone a number of changes, which have clearly demonstrated the flexibility of the tax. It is certainly no longer the simple tax envisaged by its proponents in the early 1970s, but neither is it the monster tax predicted by its opponents. Some years ago it was suggested by *The Times* that reactions to new taxes conform to a clear pattern—shock, opposition, understanding and finally acceptance. Judged on this scale, VAT would be halfway between understanding and acceptance: perhaps the most apt description would be tolerance. One thing is certain: it is now an essential part of the revenue of the country, and as such is ripe for development and refinement in the future.

CHAPTER TWELVE

The Department –
Present and Future

The Customs and Excise is one of the oldest government departments, and is justifiably proud of its long history and old traditions; it is therefore somewhat of a paradox to say that the structure, organization and work of the present-day department owes more to the events of the last ten years than much of its previous history. Compared with its evolution over the centuries, a decade is just a moment in time in the life of the department, but this decade has brought radical, sweeping and at times traumatic changes which have profoundly altered not only its own face but the working lives of all its staff.

In retrospect the events of the seventies appear crowded, giving the impression of a state of flux. This is in reality a false picture, but it is nevertheless an inevitable result of the number of fundamental changes introduced. The most crucial and far-reaching were brought about by decisions and influences outside the Civil Service, such as the introduction of value-added tax, entry into the Common Market and the containerization of goods. The other changes were occasioned either directly by the department or by influences within the Civil Service, and have ranged from the comprehensive reorganization of the department, relaxations in the control of revenue goods and incoming vessels, new import and export procedures, the introduction of new training methods and management techniques, a greater use of computers, to the final emergence of greater militancy in the various Civil Service unions. All these factors—some to a lesser degree than others—have played their part in moulding the department of today.

The most obvious change can be seen in the size of the department. In 1970 there was a total staff of 17,850, comprising three distinct services—Headquarters, Outdoor and Waterguard, each of sufficiently compact size to enable the majority of the officers of each service to know each other, and thus establish an esprit de corps. Today the total number of staff has grown to 27,420—an increase of over 50 per cent—while due to reorganization the three distinctly separate services have disappeared. There is now greater mobility throughout the department, but somehow much of the old camaraderie has gone. These changes have not gone unnoticed by members of the public: at the beginning of the decade the term 'Customs and Excise' was taken to mean the uniformed officers at the ports and airports, while ten years later it is now assumed by most of the public that all Customs and Excise staff are VAT officers.

To correct such notions without further ado: the functions of the department are to collect and account for the majority of indirect taxes, which besides value-added tax and car tax include the Excise duties on hydrocarbon oils, tobacco and alcoholic drinks, as well as the duties on betting and gaming. In addition it is responsible for all the Customs duties and levies on imported goods, most of which are now collected on behalf of the European Communities. The total revenue collected by the department in 1978-9 was £13,763 millions, which represented 35·4 per cent of the total taxation of the country; of this figure VAT accounted for £4,837 millions (35 per cent), hydrocarbon oils £2,469·4 millions (18 per cent), tobacco £2,449 millions (18 per cent), and alcoholic drinks £2,338·5 millions (17 per cent). The total (estimated) figure of revenue for 1979-80 is £18,250 millions or 39·7 per cent of the total revenue.

Besides these purely revenue activities, the department undertakes many other important duties on behalf of other government departments: for example, preventing the illicit import of narcotics and other dangerous substances; various import and export controls over prohibited or restricted goods, compiling overseas trade statistics and the monthly balance of payment figures; and other miscellaneous work under the Trade Descriptions and Mercantile Marine Acts.

The authority to carry out these functions is that of the Commissioners of Customs and Excise, who are not merely charged with the duty of collecting and accounting for the various revenues but also 'the management of all matters belonging and incidental to such collection'. They are appointed by the Queen collectively but by name through Letters Patent under the Great Seal in a form of words that has hardly changed since the days of Charles II. They have a direct responsibility to the Chancellor of the Exchequer and the other supporting Treasury ministers. The present Board is headed by a Chairman with two Deputy Chairmen, and comprises eight Commissioners, each in charge of a Directorate, each of which is concerned with specific functions and special interests. The Solicitor and the Accountant and Comptroller General act as legal and financial advisers respectively to the Board.

The Board's authority for the collection, accounting and management of the revenues and other activities is devolved by a series of formal delegations, and in some cases by way of commission to the various members of the organization which has been established to carry out these functions. Since its reorganization the department is divided into two distinct sections—the Headquarters and the Outfield.

The Headquarters administration is basically concerned with the formulation and interpretation of policy, as well as supplying technical and management support for the whole of the department. It falls into four broad categories—Customs, Excise, VAT and Establishments. The various directorates comprise a number of divisions each headed by an assistant secretary, whose equivalent post in the Outfield is collector. The two Customs directorates have responsibility for the physical control of all goods entering and leaving the country, either by land, sea, air or post, and the construction of the tariff, as well as all international aspects of the control of goods, especially in relation to the European Communities. The Excise section is concerned with the revenue duties on tobacco, spirits, beer, cider, matches and mechanical lighters and hydrocarbon oils, some of which date from the early days of the Excise, in addition to the more recent duties levied on betting and gaming. The two VAT directorates are self-explanatory, and are divided into administration and control. Administration deals with the operational machinery of the tax, changes in structure and liability problems; whereas the control directorate, which is centred on Southend, is concerned with all aspects of the control, recovery, assessment, payment, repayment and prosecution of the tax.

The rest of the Headquarters is involved with manpower planning, staff management and the provision of accommodation. There are also divisions which supply specialist management and computer services. The valuation division is concerned with all aspects of the value of goods (other than VAT), while the main function of the Statistical Office, also centred at Southend, is the production of the overseas trade figures. The Solicitor's office provides advice on legal matters and is responsible for prosecutions and civil litigation; whereas the Accountant and Comptroller General's office undertakes all the accounting and auditing functions, as well as preparing the estimates of the department. Finally, the Departmental Planning Unit deals with Budget planning, revenue statistics and forecasts and the general monitoring of indirect taxation in other countries.

The Outfield organization, which employs almost three-quarters of the staff within the department, is under the general management of a Commissioner. Unlike the Headquarters, the present Outfield arrangements retain more of the old traditions of the department. It comprises twenty-nine areas or collections, each headed by a collector, the oldest title to be retained in the department. Nowadays the collections cover a much larger area than they did previously. The collector is the Board's representative in the area in the fullest sense. The collections are divided into divisions, districts and stations, the districts being controlled by surveyors, another of the few old titles still extant.

Most of the staff employed in the collections are engaged in the practical work of collecting the revenue, and are in daily contact with the trading community or the travelling public. The work varies from dealing directly with importers, traders and passengers at ports and airports, visiting warehouses, oil-refineries, breweries, distilleries, wineries, cider factories and betting shops to the very wide range of visits and activities under VAT. The officers operate from some two thousand offices throughout the United Kingdom, which can range from large regional offices to isolated posts at distilleries or small ports. Most collections are concerned with all facets of the department's activities, and even the collections which are situated inland have become engaged in Customs work as the result of the increased number of inland clearance depots.

One of the more important aspects of the work of the department is undertaken by the investigation division, which concentrates on the detection of fraud and the prevention of smuggling, especially that of drugs. The main body of staff are centred in London, but there are several sub-offices situated throughout the country. In addition, each collection has its own investigation unit, which is under the control of the collector but works closely with the main division. The officers recruited to both the division and the collection units are specially selected from those showing a particular aptitude for such work. The division has grown rapidly in the last decade to cope with the increased workload as a result of VAT fraud and the very marked increase in drug-smuggling.

The figures for 1979 show that drugs estimated to be worth £38·5 millions were seized, and this figure represented 90 per cent of all drugs recovered in the United Kingdom. Despite such a successful year, when there were many news-worthy seizures which received wide press publicity, the division suffered a tragic blow when one of its officers was killed while on a drug operation in East London. The Chief Investigation Officer has commented, 'We are not thinking of arming our officers. We still think the best protection is that it is generally known that they are not armed and their reputation for integrity and fair dealing.'

The division is backed up by the recently increased cutter service. Again, this is manned from specially selected volunteers, and these new vessels are now making their presence felt around the coasts. In September 1979 the combined efforts of the cutter service, investigation officers and the Metropolitan Police resulted in the biggest ever drugs seizure made in this country, when £5½ millions of cannabis was seized in an operation code-named 'Cyril'. The smuggling vessel *Guiding Lights* was closely followed and finally arrested by the cutter service, the drugs were recovered by investigation officers after being landed and led to further seizures in London. The operation demonstrated superb teamwork, and gave even further satisfaction in that all the principals were arrested.

However spectacular the seizures made by the investigation officers, it must be remembered that at the end of the day the first line of defence is made up of the several thousand general duty officers, both in and out of uniform. Although these men are concerned ultimately with the whole range of Customs and Excise work, they also undertake preventive and investigation work as part of the ordinary duties. They are the backbone of the department, and it falls to them to collect the different taxes and duties and to administer the often unpopular laws. Such work requires patience, tact, persistence, self-confidence and of course integrity. It is largely due to these unsung heroes that the department's relations with the trading community and the travelling public are invariably amicable.

In view of the fact that the department had undergone a fundamental and traumatic reorganization which lasted for almost the first three years of the decade—being completed only in January 1974, although its repercussions lasted far longer—it would have been natural to expect a period of stability. Instead for the last five years or so there has been a series of reviews into certain areas of the department's work, which have resulted in some important changes.

Within months of the completion of the Headquarters reorganization a special management review team was set up, as part of a general Civil Service programme, to examine all aspects of personnel management, the planning and control of the department's resources and the organization of the Outfield, and generally to assess the impact of VAT on the department. The team reported in July 1975, and found that some improvement was required in the control of manpower, as well as a need to develop a management system. It felt that the structure of the collections was generally sound, but that there was further scope for increased delegation of work and control from Headquarters to the collectors. The team's general view—that the department had stood up well to the strains imposed upon it by the change and expansion experienced in the last four to five years—was to some extent a vindication of the large reorganization.

Perhaps the most far-reaching changes have been the development and application of automatic data processing in various areas of the department's work. Some of the earlier uses of computers have already been mentioned, and the London Airport scheme (LACES) has continued to operate most successfully, and is still attracting interest from abroad. In January 1979 the scheme was extended to Gatwick Airport with equal success. The project is due to come to an end in 1981, so for a number of years a working party has been examining the future of air-cargo processing into the eighties, a plan called ACP80 for short. The replacement for LACES is envisaged as allowing the interchange of information between the computers operated by the department, airlines, and the forwarding agents, as well as the provision of a computer bureau to provide cargo-processing facilities for commercial users who are without their own systems and the provision of export processing at present not available in the existing system.

Ever since the success of LACES—which heralded a new concept in the processing of Customs entries and the clearance of goods—it has only been a matter of time before some form of computer processing would be applied to goods arriving by land and sea. In 1973 a deferred payment system was introduced which allowed importers or agents to postpone payments of duty for an average period of thirty days. Duty payment was made by means of a bank Giro secured by guarantee, and this was the first time that any government department had made use of the direct debit system of payment. The arrangement was normally operated on a local basis, but since September 1978 a National Guarantee scheme has been introduced, enabling one guarantee to cover all import liabilities throughout the United Kingdom. A further improvement in import procedure was introduced in late 1977, when a new single-entry form was brought in replacing the existing twelve separate forms.

However, the biggest change in import procedure for over a hundred and fifty years has been the introduction of a new entry processing system, which is known as CPT from the Customs Project Team who developed the system. Traditionally Customs entries were processed in two distinct and separate stages. The first was undertaken in the Long Room in the Custom House, where various arithmetical and documentary checks were carried out. The entries were then passed to the landing stations at the ship-side, where the documents were further scrutinized and goods for physical examination were selected against the entries before their ultimate clearance.

The new CPT system merges the two separate functions, so that the clearance of the entries and of the goods is now one operation. The various checks are now carried out in entry-processing units situated in the various Custom Houses. The different checks in the EPUs include the selection of a proportion of entries for physical examination, examining the validity of the supporting documents and the extraction of statistical data. The system takes two forms—a computer-assisted version for the major ports which is connected to the main computer at Southend and a revised manual version which operates at the other ports. Manchester was the first to introduce the new manual system in November 1977, followed a month later by Bristol and Edinburgh. Local training of staff and shipping agents at the pilot ports prior to implementation helped the scheme to get off to a good start.

Before the computer-assisted system was introduced into any port, the manual version had been operating for some time. Once again Manchester was the first port to be computerized. This was in mid-1978, and it was followed by Dover, Harwich, Southampton, Hull, Liverpool and finally London Port, which came on the computer in summer 1979. The reaction of agents and importers to the new system has varied from port to port; Dover came in for some harsh criticism, but this was in the early days of development. As the system has become more reliable, and both the staff and the agents grew more accustomed to it, reaction has become more favourable.

There have been considerable concessions in the Customs examination of imported goods. A system has been introduced giving local import control, enabling cargo to be cleared at approved traders' premises. This local control will in the near future be extended to export goods. The facilities offered by inland clearance deports have recently been reviewed, and some minor changes made to enable them to operate more efficiently and economically. The review did not see the need for any increase in the number of depots, but rather a better utilization of those already existing, which seems to be the most likely pattern for the future.

A review team was formed way back in January 1974 to formulate ideas on the future patterns of preventive work: it became known as the Preventive Review. The team visited several EEC countries to examine their approach to such work, as well as undertaking a major programme of visits to various Headquarters divisions and the collections to gain the views of staff involved in the work. The actual review took over two years to complete, and the outcome of all this activity was contained in a two-volume report which made over a hundred recommendations.

It was suggested that the essential features of future preventive work should be selectivity, mobility, flexibility and simplicity. It was essential that the department's limited resources should be concentrated in the areas which presented the greatest risks; also, as the volume and nature of traffic was rapidly changing, a more mobile system of control was deemed necessary. To achieve such aims it was essential to use all available information to identify the areas of greatest risk, and furthermore not only to improve the flow of information but also to monitor the results of the various selective methods.

The changes to come out of this review were somewhat complementary to the changes in entry-processing. Mobile task forces were set up in the major ports, with other teams in selected localities. Integrated Customs stations were established for the control of all Customs work, including the entry-processing units and their related dockside controls. Collection co-ordination units have been introduced to receive, disseminate and record information on ships' movements and other revenue risks, and to liaise with the cutter service, investigation teams and other special units.

In March 1978 a new procedure was introduced for the boarding of all vessels from foreign ports. Previously all vessels including fishing boats were boarded by staff on arrival in the United Kingdom, and this had been so for many centuries. It was decided that in future the boarding of vessels on arrival would be carried out on a selective basis, and also that the remaining Customs responsibility for control of the health of crews should be passed to the local health authorities. One year later, just before the start of the busy season for yachts, some changes were made in the control of their movements to and from foreign countries. On outward journeys the owner is now compelled to notify the nearest Customs office of his intended departure and on arrival from foreign ports he is required to fly a yellow flag, notify the local Customs office and remain on board for at least two hours. This new procedure was introduced when the Customs cutter service was increased. There are now seven vessels patrolling the coasts—the biggest fleet since the early nineteenth century.

The developments within the European Economic Community are bringing it closer to a true Customs Union, which is the cornerstone of the concept of the Community. There is still much progress to be made in, for instance, the further development of the Community transit system of goods, to remove some of the non-tariff barriers preventing the complete free movement of goods. However, with the variety of indirect taxes in operation within the Community there will always be the necessity for some form of import control. Perhaps in the longer term the Customs Union will result in the uniform establishment of Customs laws in the member countries with the introduction of a Community Customs Code. Ultimately the future would seem to point to a paperless movement of goods within the enlarged Community.

Although Customs procedures have undergone radical changes, these have in no way affected the Excise, which still retains many of the department's traditional methods of control. However, while there have been certain relaxations in the visits to revenue traders such as brewers and distillers, these have not altered the basic method of control. In only one field has the situation drastically altered—that of tobacco. Before we joined the Community the revenue from this was derived mainly from a duty levied on the weight of tobacco used in manufacture. Since 1977 the Customs revenue duties have been converted to Excise duties, and in the case of cigarettes now partially include an ad-valorem duty (about 30 per cent) based on the retail selling price. It was this duty element which caused an anomaly in the last Budget, when the new VAT rate should have increased the price of cigarettes by 4p per packet. Because of the duty levied on the selling price, inclusive of VAT, the net increase was in the event 6p.

When one ponders the future of the Excise the presence of the European Community looms large. We have already seen the drastic effect it has had on the Customs. Although the harmonization of Excise duties in the Community was first proposed in 1972, it was discussed in some detail, but with little conclusion. Towards the end of 1978 the subject was resurrected and a framework directive was produced, although since then little progress or debate has ensued. One of the main stumbling blocks is the number of disparate duties in existence in the Community. They range from those on sugar, coffee, tea, salt, cocoa, playing-cards and entertaining to those on hunting and fishing. However, the main duties are similar to those in existence in the United Kingdom, such as beer, wines, spirits and hydrocarbon oils. All have lower rates than the equivalent duties in the United Kingdom, although they have slightly higher rates of VAT imposed upon them. Should some form of harmonization of Excise duties come, in structure if not in rates, it seems likely that this will happen in the next ten years.

For many years the presence of relatively high and punitive duties on tobacco, spirits and beer has been a feature of the taxation system of the country. Allied to the relatively high duties has been the department's close and somewhat restrictive controls based on physical checks during the production of the goods (although in the last few years such controls have been considerably relaxed). However, it seems likely that the greatest change in Excise procedure will be the introduction of ad-valorem payments to replace the present specific duties, enabling the department's control to be centred more on the trader's accounts and records.

Beer seems the most likely commodity for such a change. Most of the Common Market countries have a duty based on the values of the finished product on delivery from the brewery. For instance, in Germany the duty is levied at different rates on broad classes of beer, which range from small or simple beer to luxury or extra-strong beer. This system is reminiscent of the old beer duty in operation in this country before 1830. Such a change could be introduced into the United Kingdom, and it would have the added advantage of being more flexible in an inflationary economy; at the present time the specific Excise duties can only be 'inflation-indexed' by frequent changes in the rates of duty.

If the harmonization of Excise duties is to come about the next decade could see a general reduction in the rates of Excise duties in this country, with a possible corresponding increase in other duties or taxes or even the introduction of new duties, to replace the lost revenue. If the latter situation came about perhaps some of the existing Excise duties in the Community could be adopted, and of these the most likely candidates would appear to be coffee, tea and sugar; commodities which have in this country in the past been taxed quite heavily. Furthermore, the current problems in financing the Community budget have led to suggestions for alternative new Community taxes, the favourites at present being an energy tax or a duty on oils imported into the Community. However, whatever form any new taxes take, be they Excise or community-based, it seems likely that the department will be closely involved in their administration and collection.

The more radical changes within the department in the next ten years are likely to come from the wider use of computers. Work has already commenced on the new computer complex in the Southend area, which will house the replacement computers for the 1980s. Their primary role will be for VAT and the Overseas Trade Statistics. Nevertheless, the new system would seem to be capable of considerable development, and possible further uses may be the direct input of Customs entries with the computer systems of traders and importers, and perhaps ultimately with the systems of fellow-members of the Community. This would allow direct access to data at the point of export, and so achieve a simpler system of documentation at import.

The Central Policy Review Staff—more commonly known as the Think Tank—has expressed the view that the employment effects of computers in the Civil Service has at best only restrained the growth of clerical staff rather than reduced it. The development of micro-computers, and the coming revolution of the micro chip—which we are constantly assured is just around the corner—could have a far greater effect than computers because of the greater range of activities that can be performed. The consensus of opinion suggests that the impact of micro chips will be more rapid and significant in the office than elsewhere, and as such the Civil Service would seem to offer the greatest scope for change.

The introduction of such technology could greatly alter many departmental procedures. Micro-computers situated in local VAT offices would be capable of linking with the new computer in Southend, enabling local staff to interrogate the main computer, making accounting information more readily available to them. They would also enable the local staff to input their own data and information, as well as providing a centrally stored microfiche record to replace the present bulky traders' folders. Word-processors are currently being used by more businesses, both large and small, and their large-scale introduction into the Civil Service would achieve considerable savings in correspondence forms and storage.

The future growth or decline of the department ultimately depends on the taxation philosophy and policy of the elected government of the day. As we have already seen, the Customs department contracted during the nineteenth century in the wake of free trade, and the Excise suffered a similar fate, with the abolition of many old Excise duties. It was at this time that income taxes became a permanent feature of the taxation system of the country. However, it was not until the beginning of this century that the amount collected from direct taxation exceeded indirect taxation, and the difference became marked only at the outset of the Second World War with the introduction of PAYE, with over two million taxpapers being involved. The dramatic effect of this on the Inland Revenue can be seen in the growth of staff, from some 25,000 in 1939 to 85,000 in 1978. During this same period the Customs and Excise strength has grown from 17,000 to 28,500, and that increase has been largely due to VAT. During the last decade overall the proportion of revenue raised from income taxes has risen, while the real value of indirect taxes has fallen. The present Government has expressed the wish to redress the balance, and to this end has already reduced the rates of income tax, with a corresponding increase in VAT. Any further plans to extend taxation on expenditure must have a distinct bearing on the department's role in the future.

Perhaps it could be argued (certainly by many long-suffering taxpayers) that taxes are taxes, whether collected by the Inland Revenue or the Customs and Excise, so why the need for two separate departments? In April 1972, just before the advent of VAT, *The Economist* stated the case for an integrated 'Department of Taxes'. This was by no means a novel suggestion, for similar proposals had been considered previously: in fact, in the late nineteenth century such an amalgamation had been rejected on the grounds that no single person would be capable of heading such a large department! Certainly such a merger today would indeed create a 'super' department, with staff in excess of 100,000. This would in itself probably create more problems than it would solve.

After the wave of departmental mergers in the 1960s the current concept appears to be 'small is beautiful'. Some large departments have been described as cumbersome, and certainly their size can lead to problems in communication and co-operation between the various sections, as well as a tendency to greater bureaucracy. Their size, moreover, makes Ministerial control more difficult, and closer public accountability can be achieved with smaller and more compact departments. The division of responsibility and work between the two revenue departments has always been clear-cut: the types of taxes and indeed their method of collection vary greatly between the two departments, for contrary to public belief VAT has little correlation with income taxes, whether in scope or in method of control. In purely emotive terms, the suggestion that such an old and proud department as the Customs and Excise, rooted deep in history, could be merged into a faceless and amorphous 'Department of Taxes' would be anathema.

Few people would subscribe to the view expressed by an American judge—'I like to pay taxes, with them I buy civilisation'—but nevertheless, Britain has always had a very high standard of tax-paying integrity. Unfortunately, the last decade has seen a sad decline in this standard. Both revenue departments have had to face a marked increase in tax-evasion, even though this is more prevalent in the Inland Revenue sphere. The Chairman of that department has estimated recently that this so-called black economy amounts to £10,000,000,000 per annum, with a resultant tax loss of some £3,000,000,000, or about £60 per head of the population. It is a plain fact that one person's tax-avoision (a fashionable word to define the blurred area between legal avoidance and illegal evasion) becomes another person's tax liability.

Both departments have been compelled to devote more resources to enforcement procedures and fraud investigation, but still the incidence of evasion continues to grow. It is in the use of their powers in this field that both departments have suffered much public criticism. It must be remembered that they are after all merely administering the tax laws according to government policy, however unpopular, and with the knowledge that tax avoision causes deep resentment among the vast majority of tax-payers, who do pay their taxes whether they like it or not.

No account of the last ten years would be complete without mentioning the changes that have taken place in industrial relations within the Civil Service. Prior to the department's reorganization there were a number of separate staff associations representing the interests of separate grades. With the disappearance of the separate branches these associations merged in January 1972 to form a Customs and Excise group of the Society of Civil Servants, which represented all staff from assistant secretary down to executive officer.

The formation of the new group coincided with an increased militancy of Civil Service unions generally, which was directed in particular to the government's attitude to the Pay Research Unit report (formed to examine and report on the comparability of Civil Service pay with outside industry). During late 1972 and the early part of 1973, numerous pay protest meetings and rallies were held, and it was suggested that the government had lit a candle of revolt that would spread like wildfire. The revolt resulted in a one-day strike on 27 February 1973, when to quote one union official, 'The worm turned and bit the hand that doesn't feed it.' The day was unique in the annals of the Civil Service—it was the first all-out strike of civil servants.

Since that eventful day there has been a considerable increase in industrial action in the service over pay and conditions, together with an opposition to public expenditure cuts. There have been two more one-day strikes, in February and April 1979—again on account of a pay research report—but in addition various areas of the department's activities have been selected for either short or prolonged industrial action and work-to-rule. We have already noted the reaction and effect of the VAT computer stoppage at Southend, but it has been the action at the various ports and airports which has gained the most publicity, with suggestions of a 'paradise for smugglers' and 'a smuggler's haven', especially at London Airport. A cartoon published at the time of the strike shows a traveller pushing a trolley loaded with bottles, cigarettes, cameras and hi-fi equipment through the green channel, only to be stopped by a uniformed Customs officer saying—'Bless you no, sir, the strike was YESTERDAY.'

At the present moment the department, along with the rest of the Civil Service, is faced with manpower cuts as a result of the Government's objective to greatly reduce public expenditure. After the Government came to office in May 1979 it imposed a ban on recruiting for at least three months, which effectively reduced staff by some 20,000, or about 3 per cent. In this exercise the department was reduced by some 1,000. The Government's second step was a longer-term review of various activities, services and projects, which if reduced or curtailed could achieve major savings in the size and cost of the Civil Service. It announced the first of these cuts in December 1979, and they were all to be effected by 1982. The department's share of them amounted to some 465 posts (less than 2 per cent of the total staff). However, the Commissioners reported that during the year 1978-9 some difficulties were experienced in finding the manpower resources to meet all the demands on the department, and such difficulties are likely to increase in the light of the further cuts. This could lead to a reduction in some less essential tasks, with possible reviews of VAT, Excise and Customs controls, and the curtailment of trader's requests for new or enhanced facilities.

Criticism of governments, especially regarding their exaction of revenue, is part and parcel of public service life—the Civil Service always receives a bad press. However, a department is made up of people and not just procedures, and while commentators and historians write in sweeping terms of the financial policies of various governments they tend to forget that it is the staff of the revenue departments who are left to administer and collect the various taxes, however unpopular these may be. Throughout the centuries these men and women have received scant praise for their efforts, and have had little opportunity to express their views. It is this silent majority who through the ages—be they searchers, gaugers, landing waiters, boatmen, riding officers and latterly VAT men—have moulded the essential character of the Customs and Excise. We owe them all a debt of gratitude.

The long, eventful and colourful story of the Customs and Excise has been faithfully traced through some twelve hundred years of history. It has followed the vicissitudes of the two separate services, from their formation and development to their emergence as recognizable government departments in the nineteenth century, and finally to their amalgamation in the early years of this century. This chronicle has led inexorably to the department of today, which finds itself in a state of transition between the old established procedures of yesteryear and the new and largely untried methods of the brave new world. Can we stop looking back with nostalgia and instead use the long and distinguished past to divine the future? The department has always bravely accepted changes, and can look forward with courage to the challenge of a future bright with technological advances. It is this very ability that makes it a proud and great department. As Thomas Moore put it:

> For hope shall brighten days to come,
> And memory gild the past!

Bibliography

Main sources

Headquarters and Outport Records of H.M. Customs and Excise (CUSTOMS 28-102) at Public Record Office, Kew.

Collection of papers by Mr F. S. Parry, Deputy Chairman of H.M. Customs and Excise, at H.M. Customs and Excise Library, London.

Calendar of Treasury Books, Vols. I to XXXII, 1660-1718.
Calendar of Treasury Books and Papers, 7 Vols., 1714-1745.

Reports of Board of Customs, 1857-1908.
Reports of Board of Inland Revenue, 1857-1908.
Reports of Board of H.M. Customs and Excise, 1909-1979.

Secondary sources

Ashley, M. *Financial and Commercial Policy under the Cromwellian Protectorate*, London 1934 reprinted 1952.

Atton, H. and Holland, H. H. *The King's Customs* (2 Vols), London 1908 reprinted 1967.

Aylmer, G. E. *The King's Servants: the Civil Service of Charles I, 1652-42*, London 1961. *The State's Servants: the Civil Service of the English Republic, 1649-1660*, London 1973.

Carson, Edward. *The Ancient and Rightful Customs*, London 1972.

Chandaman, C. D. *The English Public Revenue, 1660-1688*, Oxford 1975.

Chesters, W. D. *Chronicles of the Customs Department*, Privately printed 1885.

Cole, W. A. *Trends in Eighteenth Century Smuggling : Economic History Review*, 2nd Series X (1958).

Crombie, Sir James. *Her Majesty's Customs and Excise*, London 1962.

Dietz, F. C. *English Public Revenue 1485-1641* (2 Vols), New York 1932 reprinted London 1964.

Dowell, S. *A History of Taxation and Taxes in England* (4 Vols), London 1884 reprinted London 1965.

East, R. *Choice Chips of Revenue Lore*, Portsmouth 1877.

Forster, D. Arnold. *At War with the Smugglers*, London 1936.

Hall, H. *A History of the Customs Revenue in England* (2 Vols), London 1885.

Hoon, Elizabeth A. *The Organisation of the English Customs Service, 1696-1786*, U.S.A. 1938.

Hughes, E. *Studies in Administration and Finance*, London 1934.

Johnstone, Dorothy. *A Tax shall be charged*, London 1975.

Kennedy, W. *English Taxation, 1640-1799*, London 1913 reprinted 1964.

Langford, Paul. *The Excise Crisis: Society and Politics in the age of Walpole*, Oxford 1975.

Mathias, P. *The Brewing Industry in England, 1700-1830*, Cambridge 1959.

McCoy, C. *Dictionary of Customs and Excise*, London 1938.

McGuire, E. B. *The British Tariff System*, London 1951.

Newton, A. P. *The Establishment of the Great Farm of the English Customs*. Transactions of the Royal Historical Society, Vol I, 1918.

Nicholls, F. F. *Honest Thieves*, London 1973.

Owens, John. *Plain Papers: a History of the Excise*, Linlithgow 1879.

Pacy, John. *The Reminiscences of a Gauger*, Newark 1873.

Phillipson, D. *Smuggling: a History 1700–1970*, London 1973.

Shore, Lt. Henry N. *Smuggling Days and Smuggling Ways*, London 1892 reprinted London 1972.

Smith, Adam. *The Wealth of Nations*, 6th Edition. Reprinted London 1950.

Smith, T. G. *A Customs History of Newport*, Gwent Local History, 46 and 47, (1979).

Teignmouth, Lord and Harper, Charles. *The Smugglers* (2 Vols), London 1923.

Watney, John. *Mother's Ruin: the Story of Gin*, London 1976.

Willan, T. S. *A Tudor Book of Rates*, Manchester 1962.

Williams, Neville. *Contraband Cargoes*, London 1959.

List of duties

Advertisements: Stamp duty imposed in 1712, repealed 1853. Excise duty on television advertisements, 1961–4

Almanacks: Stamp duty on almanacks and calendars introduced 1711, repealed 1834

Armorial bearings: Licence duty on crests, etc., from 1798 to 1945

Auctions: Excise duty from 1777 to 1845

Auctioneers: Licence duty from 1777 to 1949

Beer: Excise duty imposed in 1643, repealed in 1830, reintroduced in 1880

Betting: Introduced in 1926, repealed 1929. Pool betting from 1948 on; general betting and gaming duties from 1966 on

Bingo: Introduced in 1969

Books: Customs duty on imported books, 1660–1861

Bricks: Excise duty 1750–1850

Buttons: Customs safeguarding duty, 1928–33

Candles: Excise duty 1710–1832

Chicory: Excise duty 1860–1926

Cider: Excise duty introduced in 1643, repealed 1830, reintroduced 1916–23, reintroduced in 1976

Clocks: Stamp duty on British clocks imposed for one year, 1797

Clubs: Excise duty on registered clubs imposed from 1910 to 1959, replaced by licence duty (abolished 1967)

Coal: Customs duty on coastwise coal 1660–1831; on exported coal 1660–1850 and 1901–6

Cotton prints: Excise duty 1774–1831

Dice: Stamp duty 1711–1862

Dogs: Excise licence duty first imposed in 1796

Entertainments: Introduced in 1916, repealed 1960

Glass: Excise duty 1695–1845

Hackney carriages: Licence duty introduced 1662, eventually became motor-vehicle Excise licence

Hair-powder: Licence duty on users 1795–1869

Hats: Stamp duty 1784–1811

Hearths: Special duty imposed 1662–89

Hops: Excise duty 1711–1862

Hydrocarbon Oils: Excise duty introduced in 1928

Income Tax: Introduced 1799, repealed 1801, reimposed in 1803, it lapsed in 1816, but was reimposed in 1842

Inhabited House: Assessed tax imposed in 1696 on all dwelling-houses, repealed 1924

Key Industry: Customs duty of $33\frac{1}{3}$ per cent on special imports introduced in 1921, became incorporated in new tariff in 1960

Leather: Excise duty 1711–1831

Malt: Excise duty 1697–1880

Matches: Customs duty on imported matches from 1853; Excise duty on British matches from 1916

Mechanical Lighters: Excise duty imposed in 1916

Medicine: Stamp duty imposed on patent medicines introduced 1783, repealed 1941. Customs duty introduced 1916

Motor-cars: Purchase tax 1940–73, special car tax imposed 1973. Licence duty introduced 1888

Motor Spirit: Excise duty of 3d. per gallon in 1909, repealed in 1919, from 1928 part of hydrocarbon oils duty

Newspapers: Stamp duty introduced in 1712, repealed in 1855

Paper: Excise duty 1712–1861

Pawnbrokers: Licence duty 1785–1950

Pensions: Duty on pensions in public service, 1721–1859

Plate: Excise duty on plate 1756–77; licence duty on plate-dealers, 1758–1949

Playing-cards: Stamp duty and later Excise duty from 1711 to 1960

Post-horses: Assessed tax 1779, changed to Excise licence 1853, repealed 1869

Purchase Tax: Introduced 1940, repealed in 1973 on advent of VAT

Quarantine: Duty introduced 1800, repealed 1825

Racehorses: Assessed tax 1784, made Excise duty 1856, repealed 1874

Railway Passengers: Stamp duty 1832, converted to Excise duty 1842, repealed 1929

Registration: Tax on births, marriages and deaths and bachelors introduced 1695, lapsed 1706

Saccharin: Excise duty, 1901–62

Sails: Customs duty, 1713–1853

Salt: Excise duty introduced 1643, lapsed in 1660, reimposed 1694, repealed 1825

Soap: Excise duty 1643–60, reintroduced 1712, repealed 1853

Spirits: Excise duty introduced in 1660

Starch: Excise duty 1713–1853

Sugar: Customs duty, 1660–1874, reimposed 1901–62. Excise duty, 1837–74, reimposed 1915–62

Table Waters: Excise duty, 1916–24

Tea: Both Customs and Excise duties introduced 1660, Excise duty transferred to Customs 1834, repealed 1929, reimposed 1932, finally repealed 1964

Television: Introduced in 1957 at £1 per annum per licence, repealed 1964

Tobacco: Customs duty from 1602, converted to Excise duty in 1978

Vinegar: Excise duty introduced 1643, repealed 1844

Windows: Special tax introduced 1696, repealed 1851

Wines: Customs duty from 1303 onward. Excise duty 1786–1825. Excise duty on British wines (sweet) 1696–1834, reimposed in 1927

Wire: Excise duty 1712–1826

INDEX

For duties see also the general list on pages 224-225

CUSTOM HOUSE.